Writing to Persuade

Minilessons to Help Students Plan, Draft, and Revise, Grades 3–8

Karen Caine

HEINEMANN
Portsmouth, NH

Heinemann
361 Hanover Street
Portsmouth, NH 03801–3912
www.heinemann.com

Offices and agents throughout the world

The author and publisher wish to thank those who have generously given permission to reprint borrowed material:

"Sis! Boom! Bah! Humbug!" by Rick Reilly originally appeared in *Sports Illustrated*, October 12, 1999. Reprinted with permission from *Sports Illustrated*.

"Should Trans Fat Be Banned?" by Diane Glass and Shaunti Feldhahn originally appeared in *The Atlanta Journal-Constitution*, July 19, 2007. Reprinted by permission of the publisher.

"Should We Take Away the Voting Rights of 18-Year-Olds?" by Timothy Furnish originally appeared in *History News Network*, November 15, 2004. Reprinted with permission.

"Is America's Food Supply Safe?" by Dr. David Acheson, Assistant Commissioner for Food Protection, and Caroline Smith Dewaal, Food Safety Director for Science in the Public Interest. Published in *The New York Times Upfront*, October 1, 2007. Copyright © 2001 by Scholastic Inc. Reprinted with permission.

"Stop Illegal Immigration" originally appeared in *The New York Times Upfront*, September, 4, 2006. Reprinted by permission of Copley News Service.

"Petition About Circus Animal Cruelty" originally appeared on the PETA website: http://getactive.peta.org/campaign/stop_circus_cruelty_conv. Reprinted by permission of PETA. www.peta.org.

"Deal with a Kid's Designer Genes by Using a Clothing Allowance," by Steve Rosen originally appeared in Kids and Money at www.kansascity.com, September 30, 2007. Reprinted by permission of the *Kansas City Star*.

"A-1 Limousine Advertisement," courtesy of A-1 Limousine.

"Our Opinions: Home Depot Gets It: Consumers Rule" by Maureen Downey originally appeared in *The Atlanta Journal-Constitution*, March 15, 2007. Reprinted with permission from *The Atlanta Journal-Constitution*, Copyright © 2007. For more information about reprints by PARS International Corp. visit us online, at www.ajcreprints.com.

"Our Opinions: Schools Go Too Far to Play It Safe" by Maureen Downey originally appeared in *The Atlanta Journal-Constitution*, October, 20, 2006. Reprinted with permission from *The Atlanta Journal-Constitution*, Copyright © 2006.

"Our Opinions: Don't Sugarcoat Cupcake Menace" by Maureen Downey originally appeared in *The Atlanta Journal-Constitution*, June 21, 2006. Reprinted with permission from *The Atlanta Journal-Constitution*, Copyright © 2006.

Library of Congress Cataloging-in-Publication Data
Caine, Karen.
    Writing to persuade : minilessons to help students plan, draft, and revise, grades 3–8 / Karen Caine.
      p. cm.
    ISBN-13 978-0-325-01734-1
    ISBN-10 0-325-01734-4
    1. English language—Composition and exercises—Study and teaching (Elementary). 2. Persuasion (Rhetoric)—Study and teaching (Elementary). I. Title.
LB1576.C25 2008
372.62′3044—dc22   2008031504

Editor: Kate Montgomery
Production editor: Sonja S. Chapman
Cover design: Lisa Fowler
Author photograph: 2008 Kathleen Duxbury/Kathleenduxbury.com All rights reserved
Compositor: Publishers' Design & Production Services, Inc.
Manufacturing: Steve Bernier

Printed in the United States of America on acid-free paper
12   ML   4 5

Recently in my role as a literacy staff developer, I met with a group of bright and energetic young teachers. We hoped to plan an upcoming persuasive writing unit. Early in our conversation, we realized—with some distress—that we did not share a vision for the unit, nor did we agree on exactly what persuasive writing is. The air was filled with voices saying, "Yes, but what about . . . ?" One teacher saw the unit as "test prep." Another wanted editorial writing and still another imagined a book review study. One insisted we teach advertisements and jingles, while her teammate was convinced we'd better handle persuasive letter writing. I sighed. We had a great deal of work to do. If only we had had Karen Caine's book, *Writing to Persuade.*

Karen's much needed book guides us to deep, robust teaching of persuasive writing. She shows us that writing to persuade is indeed an umbrella covering various genres. As such, it is rich with possibilities for students to grow as writers and as thinkers. Teachers must not limit persuasive writing to one genre; in fact, with all it encompasses, Karen recommends at least two persuasive writing units per school year. Editorial, essays, letters . . . the varieties are as exciting as the possible topics.

Just as important, Karen shows us that persuasive writing enables young writers to grow by taking a stance and developing self-assurance, by stepping up to a topic and becoming expert enough to believe their thoughts are worthwhile and worth persuading others. The passion and honesty of persuasive writing leads to caring about audience, purpose, and outcome. It involves young writers in discovering specific and significant arguments, acknowledging opposition, and making informed and thorough cases for their opinions.

As I read Karen's book, I realized how often and with what fervor others work to "convince" me to do or change something. For example, in the past twenty-four hours, I've been exhorted by TV, radio, Internet ads, letters, newspaper writing, friends, or family members to consider scores of changes to my life, including some of the following: take vitamins, lose weight, buy a new car, donate my old car, save on car insurance, take public transportation, lose my wrinkles, eat fast food, adopt a pet, write to my legislators, rush to a store, get a tan, wear sunscreen, change to oil heat . . . and so on. While much of this is laughable (lose weight, ha!), it shows that persuasion surrounds us—seriously and persistently. Sometimes we seem to spend our days and energy fending it off. Yet wise and well-presented persuasion can be a great gift to readers. It convinces us to save our planet, feed hungry children, exercise our vote, get annual checkups, and so on. No wonder we must teach it wisely and well. Ultimately, persuasive writing inspires us to *revise* our lives. And revision is a way to think and to live. Teaching students to write persuasively is a blueprint for teaching them to speak for change and revision in their lives and the world.

Teachers, you will love this book. You will love Karen's minilessons. Each is thorough, clear, and adaptable. Karen shows us what we need to teach each lesson and how to teach it. She guides us through many issues teachers may face in teaching persuasive writing: formal versus informal language, audience, purpose, choosing a topic, elaborating, and so on. (And my all time favorite: Cut it Out: Deleting Unnecessary Words.)

Let me then, as Karen suggests, get straight to the point. I love this book for all it teaches us about persuasive writing and for how it strengthens our understanding of this expansive genre. Karen's book is filled with minilessons, student samples, resource pages, anecdotes from her own teaching, charts, and good, solid persuasive advice. Having read it, I am wiser about teaching—and writing—persuasion.

You will be, too.

—Janet Angelillo

To Cy, for all the times you said "I'm Proud of You" and
for the patience and kindness you show every day.

Patricia Maclachlan wrote, "What you know first sticks with you." And it's true. How grateful I am to have had Lucy Calkins as my first and most influential teacher. Her ideas profoundly changed (and continue to change) my teaching.

Thank you Randy Bomer who encouraged me to make purposeful and thoughtful decisions as a teacher and who always said that teachers have a responsibility to share their knowledge with one another.

Thank you Brenda Wallace and Isoke Nia who inspired me each and every day I watched you interact with children. You showed me how to teach students to love words, how to confer in writing, and how to hold students to high standards. You showed me by example what writing workshop could be at its best.

Thank you Erica Denman. You have meant so much to me these last thirteen years. You are a friend, a colleague, and teacher to me. I couldn't ask for a better person to think with.

Thank you Amy Ludwig Vanderwater. You are the reason this book is out in the world. Your advice, encouragement, and sense of humor helped me on many, many occasions.

Kathie Lasky, Rita Galett, Catherine Ramos, and Carolyn Goldfarb—you were the greatest teaching colleagues I could ask for. Gary Goldstein, Howie Schechter, and Shelly Cohen—you were leaders extraordinaire. To all of you I will always be grateful.

Thank you Ginny Arndt and Sabrina Manns for letting me use lessons from this book in your classrooms. Your flexibility, feedback, and insight were invaluable. And to Denise Grant, thank you for sharing your extensive knowledge of prompt writing with me.

Carl Anderson, thank you for your advice on writing a book—who better to get advice from? Janet Angelillo, thank you for writing the foreword for this book. Wow, what an honor. Kate Montgomery, thank you for your solid suggestions and unwavering enthusiasm. You let me explore and learn as I went. That was a gift to me. At the same time you made recommendations, helped me see things differently, and encouraged me to try new ideas. That was a gift, too. You have a knack for knowing just what to say and do. For that I couldn't be more grateful.

Thank you Dad for saying, "You really should write a book," over and over again until I did. And thanks Mom for your continued love and support and your exceptional proof-reading skills.

Alison, you always provided comedy entertainment each and every time we spoke on the phone. Immediately, I jumped from writing brain to hysterical laughter. I always started our conversations by saying that I couldn't talk and ended happy and ready to go back to work. Thanks, sister!

The pull-my-hair-out writing days were the times I was most grateful for you, my boys. Thank you Alex for the words of support that only you can give. I left our conversations wondering how a twelve-year-old got to be so wise.

Brian, thank you for bringing me snacks and rubbing my back. You asked often if I needed anything and then went and got whatever I needed. I am so grateful for your exceptional kindness.

Max, I remember the night I was reading a book and said it was fabulous. You looked up at me and said, "That's what people will be saying about your book, Mom." Your words echoed in my ear as I wrote. So, thank you.

Cy, this book is dedicated to you, but on this page, I must take a moment to say words I know I don't say often enough: Thank you.

How to Use this Book

Welcome to *Writing to Persuade: Minilessons to Help Students Plan, Draft, and Revise, Grades 3–8.*

This book can be used in different ways depending on your needs. Are you looking for a persuasive writing unit to be used as is? If so, read and follow the To Adopt directions on this page. Are you looking for some new lessons to supplement an existing framework or unit? If so, read and follow the To Adapt section. If you want to design your own unit, read through the To Create section. Enjoy!

To Adopt   *If you want a persuasive writing unit that is already designed:*

- Read the question-and-answer section (see following page).
- Read Chapter 1 and select a unit.
- Begin teaching!

To Adapt   *If you're looking to add some new lesson ideas to a persuasive unit you're already using (developed by your school or district, for example):*

- Read the question-and-answer section.
- Read the the first two pages of Chapter 1.
- Browse through the minilessons and select lessons that will enhance your persuasive writing unit.
- Begin teaching!

To Create   *If you're looking to create a unit from scratch:*

- Read the question-and-answer section.
- Read and discuss the first two pages of Chapter 1.
- Read, discuss, and write the answers to the questions on page 17, Unit VII.

- Create your own unit of study.
- Begin teaching!

Some Questions and Answers Before You Start

Why Teach Persuasive Writing?
Maybe you've chosen to study persuasive writing with your class because it's part of your curriculum. Maybe it's because of the standardized writing test that your students will take in the spring. Maybe it's because you just bought this book and are eager to try out a new study. All great reasons. The truth is, though, that even if none of these things were true, if you were not *required* to teach children how to write persuasively, you would.

Allow me to persuade you.

A good used-car salesman can convince us to buy a car he knows is a lemon, but the average person best convinces an audience when he believes what he is saying and has written the argument in such a way that the reader believes it too. In order to write well persuasively, the writer must have *an opinion* about the issue. The writer must also have *evidence* to support the argument. The old parent adage, "Because I said so," doesn't work here. A persuasive author must figure out how to show that what he is saying is true. And beyond opinion and evidence, the writing must have a convincing *voice*.

How to express an opinion, support it with evidence, and convey these thoughts using an intentional writing voice are skills urgently needed in writing instruction. This is why you should and do teach persuasive writing.

But let's think about the kind of learners we want our students to become. I don't mean what we want our students to know in terms of standards, but more broadly. In our ideal world, when our students walk out of our classrooms on the last day of school, what will they know how to do? How will they see themselves in relation to the world? Will they view themselves as thoughtful people who have opinions about the world? I hope so.

I'm thinking about Mandy, a fourth grader whom I taught in a public school in New York City. Mandy was doing well in school, so I was surprised when her mother wrote me a note saying Mandy didn't understand her homework. That afternoon, I spoke with Mandy and began to realize that she *understood* the homework but was *uneasy about putting her thoughts down on paper*.

When it was time to write, she asked me what I wanted her to write. When I asked her to find a topic of interest from the social studies reading, she wanted to know what I thought a good topic would be. She was consumed with pleasing me and getting the "right" answer. She had a difficult time figuring out what interested her—what *she* wanted to say in writing, in reading discussions, in her math log, in social studies.

During that school year, Mandy experienced small successes. Once she gave another student completely different advice from that offered by the rest of her group. She gave her opinion: *You need to cut your draft, not add to it.* She told why: *You repeat yourself too often.* And she gave evidence: *On pages two and three you say the same thing four times.* I wanted to jump up and down and tell her she was beginning to find her voice.

There are a lot of Mandys sitting in our classrooms. They approach learning passively. They are uncomfortable with open-ended assignments and constantly ask whether their work is "good." They sit quietly in class and are unaccustomed to thinking independently in school. These students are good at following directions but not as good at knowing and expressing what they believe.

In *Crafting a Life*,[1] Don Murray talks about why he writes personal essays. I believe that these reasons hold true for persuasive writing:

> To give myself voice. I am heard when I write; I vote in the human community, registering my opinions, what I stand for, what I fear, what I stand against, what I celebrate.
>
> To discover who I am. Writing the personal essay celebrates my difference, authenticates who I am, justifies my existence. (1996, 55)

Studying persuasive writing increases the chances that students will leave our classrooms and be more thoughtful about the world in which they live.

What Are the Different Types of Persuasive Writing?

There are many different kinds of persuasive writing that we come in contact with every day. Open any magazine or newspaper and you're likely to see editorials, op-eds (in this book the terms op-ed and editorial are used interchangeably—for information on the difference between these two kinds of writing see Unit III on page 8) advertisements, articles, advice columns, political cartoons . . . the list seems endless.

Some writing is noticeably persuasive; other writing is persuasive in a more subtle way. Recently, a friend of mine received a letter from an old friend of hers who wrote that she wanted to rekindle their friendship. Most of the letter was chatty and informational. Then bang! In the last paragraph she wrote that she was running for political office and asked her "old friend" to send a contribution to her campaign. (My friend found this approach sneaky and manipulative. She didn't contribute.)

To complicate the issue, some writing is purely informational, other writing is purely persuasive, and some seems to be a combination of the two. A few years ago, *Time* magazine ran a story on using the Bible to teach literature in public school. Even from the title it was clear where *Time* stood on the issue. Instead of calling the article, "The Trend Toward Teaching the Bible in Public School" or "The Reasons Some Teachers Use the Bible," the article was titled, "Why We Should Teach the Bible in Public School." As you might expect, the article cited the advantages of using the Bible but didn't discuss any of the disadvantages.

Reviews often fall into this informational/persuasive gray zone. Some reviews give a summary: "The princess falls in love with a man she believes to be a poor gardener. Then, in a case of mistaken identity, he is accused of stealing." Other reviews are sharply critical: "Another story of a spoiled princess and a case of mistaken identity! Give me a break. Don't bother. Save your money—don't even rent the DVD!"

What about infomercials? The first time I saw an infomercial I didn't know what it was. I thought I was watching a television program on fitness, when all of a sudden I saw the words *money-back guarantee* flash across the screen. Wake-up call! I turned the channel immediately. (I was informed. I was even entertained. A good consumer? That, I was not.) These advertisements are designed to look and sound informational and entertaining but are first and foremost persuasive. They employ more than one or two persuasive strategies,

---

[1]Murray, Donald M. 1996. *Crafting a Life in Essay, Story, Poem.* Portsmouth, NH: Boynton/Cook.

including the use of facts and statistics (although I use those terms lightly) and testimonials. Infomercials are notoriously deceptive, but many of them are very effective.

These days there are ads that sound like articles, charitable donation letters that sound like personal letters from a friend, talk shows with hidden agendas, talk shows with explicit agendas, writing filled with facts, and writing filled with propaganda. Confusing.

Personal essays—the kind you might hear on National Public Radio—are thoughtful, but are they persuasive? Sometimes and sort of. How's that for wishy-washy? This kind of writing tells what the author believes and usually has an identifiable thesis statement and examples to support the thesis. Simply put, personal essays fall short of persuasion because they are not primarily designed to convince the reader. Persuasive writing seems to say, *Please think this way.* Personal essays seem to say, *Think about this with me.*

Recently, I heard a personal essay that was part of NPR's This I Believe series. Robert Fulghum (the author of *All I Really Need to Know I Learned in Kindergarten* and many other books) wrote a piece called "Dancing All the Dances as Long as I Can." It was a heart-warming piece about getting older and continuing to challenge his body, mind, and spirit by learning how to dance the tango. "Unleashing the Power of Creativity" and "Living Life to Its Fullest" are two other titles of personal essays I have read lately. All inspiring. All well written. But not persuasive.

As teachers, we are left in a bit of a quandary. How do we decide what writing is persuasive and what's not? How do we explain to our students that some writing is informational, some is entertaining, some is persuasive, and some is any combination of the three?

Whether a text is designed to be persuasive is worth discussing with students. There is bound to be disagreement about some of the writing. Good! This is a great way to begin a study of persuasive writing. To determine what is persuasive, select one or two pieces of writing and have students ask and answer the following questions:

- What is the primary goal of the writer?
- What makes me think this?
- Is there another reason this writing was written?
- What makes me think this?

Of course, not all writing will warrant this type of discussion. Print advertisements and editorials are easily identified as persuasive. Some letters are obviously persuasive, as are most public service announcements. Some advice columns are persuasive, although the truth is I hardly ever feel persuaded by them. (Do people really adhere to this advice? *You should be honest with your former best friend and just come out and tell her you don't like her anymore.* No thanks, I'm not convinced.)

The chart that follows on page xvi shows some of the different kinds of persuasive writing and where they can be found. It can be used:

- As a jumping-off point to begin a professional conversation about persuasive writing with your colleagues.
- As a guide to help you collect persuasive writing to use with students.
- As a guide to help students gather published samples of persuasive writing to share with the class.
- To determine what kind of persuasive writing your class or grade will study.

How Does the Age and Writing Experience of My Students Affect What Kind of Persuasive Writing I Teach?

Age and writing experience are important considerations when determining the type of persuasive writing to study. This is because some types of persuasive writing are easier than others. Writing a personal persuasive letter is almost always easier than writing an editorial. Students as young as second grade are familiar with the structure of letters, because they've actually seen them. In addition, topics for personal persuasive letters are easy to find. What student doesn't want to convince another family member of one thing or another? (As I write this my older son is trying to convince one of his brothers to let him use his skateboard.) And letters can be short but still be well developed, whereas editorials require more elaboration.

Let me be clear. I'm not suggesting that persuasive letters are a better kind of persuasive writing to teach. Nor am I saying that op-ed pieces are too difficult. I do believe, however, that certain kinds of persuasive writing are more suited to certain grade levels and writing experience. So (with a little trepidation) I include a chart (on page xvii) on recommended grade levels for different kinds of persuasive writing studies. My hope is that this chart will lead to schoolwide discussion and then curriculum decisions.

At What Point in the Year Should I Teach Persuasive Writing?

On the one hand, the answer is *any time you can*. Better to teach children how to write persuasively than not. Ideally, though, you should begin a persuasive unit about one-third of the way through the year. Simply put, persuasive writing is difficult to write. The persuasive writer must find a topic, determine a stance on the issue, develop an argument, find reasons and examples to support the argument, consider other points of view, and on and on. This is hard work and likely to be labor intensive. Additionally, for students to write persuasively they have to trust one another and trust you. Creating this kind of classroom environment takes time. If persuasive writing is a first or second unit of study, students are more likely to select generic, safe (and overused) topics because they are worried about what the rest of the class will think. One fourth grader whispered this to his teacher, "I'm not really sure that I want to tell people what I think, because I know most kids won't agree." Your best bet is to begin a persuasive writing unit after students know one another and feel it's okay to share what they truly believe.

Not surprisingly, I would like to see more persuasive writing done in upper elementary and middle school. What about a study of editorials in January and a study of political cartoons in May? At a minimum, teachers should do one unit on persuasive writing and then revisit this kind of writing a few weeks before a writing test or assessment.

Do Writing Workshop and Persuasive Writing Work Together?

Yes! Students will learn to write persuasively if they have a chance to select their own topics, learn persuasive techniques a few at a time, write often, and receive both student and teacher feedback on their work. The best way to do this is to use a writing workshop approach to teaching writing.

Most days in the writing workshop proceed like this: The teacher begins with a short minilesson, the students spend the bulk of the writing period actually writing, and the period ends with a share session (whole class, small groups, or partners) in which students read some of what they have written or offer some advice to one another. There are of course

Some Types of Persuasive Writing

Type of Writing	Purpose of the Writing	Where You Are Likely to Find This Writing
Op-Ed	To provide and support an opinion, usually on a current events issue	Newspapers, magazines, television and radio broadcasts
Editorial (a professional letter to the public written by a member of the periodical's editorial staff)	To provide and support an opinion, usually on a current events issue	The back page of many newspapers or magazines (this section is sometimes called opinion)
Persuasive Letter (personal letter, business letter, cover letter, charitable letter, political letter)	To convince a decision maker to support a cause or position	Websites, spam, personal mail, direct mail
Letter to the Editor	To provide an opinion on an article and/or current events topic	Often appears on the inside cover of a newspaper or magazine
Political Cartoon (illustration or comic strip)	To convey a political or social message or view	Newspapers, magazines, political websites
Political Speech	To win support for a policy or position	Newspapers, books (*written*), television (*spoken*)
Petition	To make a formal request of some authoritative person or body	Court papers, websites
Public Service Announcement	To educate and convince the public to take a particular action or refrain from an action	Television, radio, magazines
Advertisement	To sell goods and/or services	Newspapers, magazines, television, radio, email, junk mail
Advice Column	To counsel, and recommend that the reader think or act in a particular manner	Newspapers, magazines, and websites

	3rd Grade	4th Grade	5th Grade	6th Grade	Beyond
Suggested Grade Levels for Persuasive Writing Studies					
Editorial/Op-Ed			☑	☑	☑
Persuasive Letter	☑	☑	☑	☑	☑
Letter to the Editor		☑	☑	☑	☑
Political Cartoon				☑	☑
Political Speech	☑	☑	☑	☑	☑
Public Service Announcement		☑	☑	☑	☑
Advertisement	☑	☑	☑	☑	☑
Advice Column		☑	☑	☑	☑
Petition		☑	☑	☑	☑

variations to this structure. The only thing that does not vary is that most of the time is spent writing. When I was new to writing workshop, using these structures and keeping a set schedule every day was extremely helpful.

While students are writing, the teacher confers with individual students or small groups of students. Teachers show students how to get ideas, write with clarity, elaborate, focus their writing—and so much more. Unlike minilessons, which are planned in advance, conferences do not usually have a set agenda. Below are suggestions about writing conferences.

1. Watch what students are doing before you meet with them. This may give you ideas about what to teach.
2. Read (or skim) the student's writing. Think about strengths and weaknesses.
3. Ask questions: *How is it going today? What kind of writing work are you doing right now?*
4. Try working from an area of strength: *Over here you have strong imagery; let's see how you did that and whether you can try it again.*
5. Try working with what you see as a weakness in the writing—a lack of focus, for example. Teach students how to help the reader follow what they're saying.

What Should I Keep in Mind When Teaching Persuasive Writing Lessons?
Keep persuasive writing minilessons short, and save the majority of the period for writing. In a forty-five-minute period, aim for a ten-minute minilesson followed by twenty-five to thirty minutes of writing followed by five or ten minutes spent sharing. Students will learn how to write persuasively with a little instruction and a lot of practice. It's difficult to keep lessons short. Here are a few suggestions:

- *Tell, don't ask!* Many of the questions a teacher asks during a lesson should become direct statements. It's more efficient to make a statement than ask a question. So instead of, *Who knows what part I decided to cut while I was revising?,* you could say, *Here is the part I cut and this is why.* Or, *Who remembers what we talked about yesterday?* can easily become, *Yesterday we worked on such-and-such.*
- *Teach one thing.* Try to avoid phrases like *and also, and just one more thing, also remember, another thing I want to tell you is!* We know this intuitively but sometimes we feel like we haven't taught enough. There is still more to say, so we are tempted to add another sentence and then another and just one more until we have talked about so many things that we have really taught nothing.
- *Use one or two quick examples to illustrate your point.* Don't reread a whole persuasive text in a minilesson, just the few sentences that illustrate the point you want to make. Show one or two short examples, not three or four.
- *Avoid combining two lessons in order to catch up or stay on schedule.* Combining two lessons usually means students don't retain the information in either because the lesson moved too quickly and there was too much information to process at one time.
- *Enjoy yourself.* Something happens to some of us (myself included!) when we teach writing that we know students will be tested on this year or next. We get serious. Nervous. Our tone changes. I try to use my poetry voice—the voice that is warm and inviting—even when I'm not teaching poetry.

Units

CHAPTER 1

Persuasive Writing Units

No matter what kind of persuasive writing you're teaching or which lessons you select, laying the groundwork before beginning will ensure that your unit goes more smoothly. Here are things to do to get your persuasive writing unit off to a great start.

Think About Environment   Create a classroom environment in which students respect one another and feel comfortable speaking honestly, asking for help, and sharing ideas.

To do: Read *anything* aloud to your students and give them time to talk to one another about what they heard. (Even three minutes is a start.) Talk to students about how you'd like to see them work together. Ask: *Who worked with another student today and how did that person help you with your work? Who took a risk today by trying something new in their writing? Did it pay off?* (Some risks do and others don't.)

Decide on Pacing   Decide on the length of your unit. The units in this chapter are fast paced—not breakneck, nobody-is-understanding-but-let's-move-along-anyway (been there, done that), but also not leisurely (never been there but would like to try it some day!).

To do: Pick a start date and an end date for your unit. Post these dates in your classroom. (This will keep you on track.)

Plan but Don't Overplan   Plan some of the lessons you'll do in your unit but save some free days to add lessons as needed.

To do: Read through the sample units in this chapter. Then browse through the minilessons in this book and note ones you want to try. This is also a good time to find an end-of-unit assessment tool (see the rubric on page 207) and decide how and when to publish and present student writing. For help with pacing your unit, see the chart titled Suggested Pacing Guide for a Persuasive Unit (page 17).

Title Your Unit   Talk with other teachers at your grade level about the focus and goals of the unit. Then title the unit. Don't fall back on "Persuasive Writing"; select one that narrows the topic and helps you focus on exactly what it is you will be teaching. Here are some examples:

Finding an Audience and Writing a Personal Persuasive Letter
Studying and Writing Editorials
Voice and Persuasive Writing
Structuring Persuasive Writing

To do: Discuss goals with your colleagues and decide on a title that will help you define and narrow your focus.

Enlist help
Ask, *Who can help me?* Possibilities are the school librarian, other teachers, the administration, parents with access to a newspaper or with a persuasive writing background, this book's appendix, websites, and so on.

To do: Make a list of people who may be able to help you and write down ways they can help.

Gather Sample Writing
Collect samples of published persuasive writing appropriate for your unit.

To do: Select and duplicate some of the sample writing in the Appendix. Look for some of your own samples too.

Ask Students to Bring in Samples of Persuasive Writing
Approximately two weeks before the unit begins, ask students to find and bring in samples of persuasive writing. Place this writing in hanging files or baskets and give students time to read it.

To do: Read and discuss some of the ideas presented in the persuasive writing samples. (See Chapter 2).

Find Out What Students Already Know
Informally assess what students know about persuasive writing.

To do: Talk to last year's teachers and find out if persuasive writing was studied in the grade before yours. If it was, find out specifically what kind of persuasive writing was taught. Ask students this question: *What do you know (or think you know) about persuasive writing?* If there is time, ask students to write a quick (ungraded!) persuasive paragraph. Skim these paragraphs to get rough idea of what students know how to do and what should be taught.

UNIT I: Introduction to Persuasive Letter Writing

A persuasive letter is written to convince the reader to think or act in a particular way. It can be formal or informal, depending on the subject of the letter and the writer's relationship to the recipient. A letter to your sister will undoubtedly have a different tone from a letter to your local congressman.

Grade Level
Second grade through the end of middle school

About This Unit   In this unit, students will write a persuasive letter. The focus of this letter-writing unit is on the process of writing—in other words, how to get ideas down on the page. There is one lesson on revision and one lesson on looking at writing techniques but the unit emphasizes how to find an idea, how to select a topic, and how to organize writing. (Persuasive techniques are mentioned but not covered in detail.) This study is especially appropriate for students who do not have extensive writing experience.

On the last day of the unit, students are asked to select another persuasive letter topic from the first day of the study and to draft this letter without the help of a minilesson or a writing conference. Use these letters as one way to determine what students have learned and are able to do independently. This study can be done in place of or in addition to a unit on friendly letters.

Special Considerations   Arrange for students to mail the letters they've written. As students get replies, have them share these responses with the class.

Although the majority of students will write letters that are serious, a few students may want to write humorous letters. (Although the minilesson on Using Humor to Entertain and Persuade—see page 71—is not included in this unit, you may want to use it with the whole class, with a small group of students, or in a writing conference.) Topics of persuasive humorous letters students have written include letters to a soccer coach explaining "why I should get more playing time even though I am the worst player on the team" and a letter to a principal about book fairs that begins like this: "Instead of banning books, I think we should ban book fairs."

Before Students Begin to Write . . .   Read, enjoy, and discuss sample persuasive letters with your class. Specifically:

- Discuss which letters are particularly persuasive and which ones are not.
- Make a list of what you notice about persuasive writing. (It has reasons and examples, and words that help convince the reader.)
- Notice the different ways persuasive letters begin. (With a butter-them-up paragraph, with a jump-in lead, with a question, etc.)

Day by Day Plans

Day 1   Finding an Audience: Whom Would You Like to Persuade? (p. 50)
Keep in mind: Have students take notes during share time because often one student's idea sparks another.

Day 2   Have students pick one idea from Day 1 and begin to write a persuasive letter.
Keep in mind: Students have not had time to develop their persuasive ideas yet so their letters are likely to sound like a piece of an idea—not a whole idea.

Day 3   Have students pick another idea from Day 1 and begin to write a different persuasive letter.
Keep in mind: You may also want to give students the option of taking their idea from yesterday and writing more about it instead of writing on a new topic.

Day 4   Selecting a Topic (p. 84)
Keep in mind: Some students will select topics that are informational and not persuasive. Help steer students toward persuasion.

Day 5   All Reasons Are Not Created Equal (p. 90)
Keep in mind: Some students may not have strong reasons as to why they believe as they do. Help students develop their reasons by asking them to answer the question: *Why is that true?* Some students will naturally develop examples and other students will have to be prompted to think of a "for instance" for their reasons.

Day 6   Some Might Think: How to Write Counterarguments (p. 96)

Day 7   Finding and Imitating Persuasive Writing Techniques (p. 58)

Day 8   Examining the Structure of Your Persuasive Writing (p. 108)
Keep in mind: Structure is difficult. Allow students time to develop a tentative letter structure but allow and encourage students to augment their structure as they draft tomorrow.

Day 9   Ready, Set . . . Draft! (p. 125)
Keep in mind: If you watch students draft you'll be able to understand their drafting process and what to say as you confer with them.

Take one or two days off from writing workshop. Take time to evaluate students' persuasive drafts and to determine class strengths and weaknesses. Determine what revision lessons you will teach.

Day 10   Call to Action (p. 149) *or* Elaboration 2: Expanding Your Own Writing (p. 137)
Keep in mind: Underdeveloped paragraphs are usually a problem with persuasive writing. You may want to do the first and the second Elaboration minilessons.

Day 11   Coaching the Reader by Using Punctuation (p. 154) *or* select another revision lesson and ask students to begin to edit during another point in the day or for homework.
Keep in mind: You may want to follow up and repeat or extend the lesson from Day 10.

Day 12   Ask students to do a final proofread by using Proofread Carefully (p. 167) and then ask them to recopy or retype their writing. (Do not ask students with severe handwriting difficulty to rewrite their work.)
Keep in mind: Older students can help younger students do a final edit and type their letters.

Day 13   Self-Assessment (p. 174)
Keep in mind: Students may want to email their letters in addition to sending a hard copy.

Day 14   Celebrate (and then mail letters).
Keep in mind: Students can read excerpts of their letters if they are very long.

Day 15   Have students select one of their letter ideas from the first few days of collecting ideas or choose a new topic altogether.
Keep in mind: Teachers will have to give students time to reread their lists from the first day of the unit and recall who else they wanted to write to.

Day 15½   Have students draft and revise a second persuasive letter. Remind students to use what they've just learned from writing the first letter to help them draft this letter. Tell students, *This letter will show me what you have learned from our persuasive writing unit so do your best work.*
Keep in mind: This is only one measure of students' understanding of persuasive letter writing. You may also want to use any of the following to help determine what students learned during the unit: class discussion, conferring notes, and observation.

Grade Level
Third grade through
the end of middle
school

UNIT II: Advanced Persuasive Letter Writing

A persuasive letter is written to convince the reader to think or act in a particular way. It can be formal or informal, depending on the subject of the letter and the relationship of the writer to the recipient. Some persuasive letters are essentially advertisements, others are requests for donations, and still others are personal letters.

About This Unit   This unit moves more quickly than Introduction to Persuasive Letter Writing. It's particularly suited to students who have had a good deal of writing experience.

Special Considerations   Students will write at least two letters. (The chart on page 53 lists different kinds of persuasive letters.) They can write both letters to the same person, or you can require that the second letter be written to someone who is more distant from the writer—a local school official or the head of school bus transportation for your county, for example. (Writing to someone they don't know personally is usually more difficult, so it's an added challenge.) You might also have students read a local newspaper and discuss local issues before they write their second letter.

Before Students Begin to Write . . .   Read sample persuasive letters with your class. Discuss these questions: What parts of this letter are particularly well written? What makes you think so?

Day by Day Plans

Day 1   Finding an Audience: Whom Would You Like to Persuade? (p. 50)
Keep in mind: Students can make a list of what bothers them in order to get ideas for persuasive letters.

Day 2   Have students pick one idea from Day 1, then use Writing Quickly and Continuously to Find First Thoughts (p. 74)
Keep in mind: Students can begin to free write by writing the target audience or the general idea at the top of the paper.

Day 3   Have students pick another idea from the list from Day 1. Then have students free write using this new idea. Use Writing Quickly and Continuously to Find First Thoughts (p. 74)
Keep in mind: If students want more time to write about their topic from yesterday, you may want to give them this option. (Other students will be more than happy to try out a new topic.)

Day 4   Select a topic lesson and then talk and create a chart similar to Resource 4–4 on page 91.
Keep in mind: Today's lesson is really two lessons. You should do this work when you have at least fifty minutes for writing. Also, encourage students to look back on their free writing from Day 2 or Day 3 and use that writing to help them with the chart.

Day 5 *I came. I saw. I conquered.* Short Declarative Sentences Persuade (p. 144)
Keep in mind: Younger students may already write short declarative sentences. If this is true of your students, select another lesson from the revision or developing ideas chapters. What about pinpointing some persuasive writing techniques from sample letters and trying these techniques?

Day 6 Leads That Capture the Reader's Interest (p. 123)
Keep in mind: Students often have very weak leads to their letters. Show students examples of strong leads from any type of persuasive writing.

Day 7 Ready, Set . . . Draft! (p. 125)
Keep in mind: For struggling writers consider making copies of one of their notebook entries. Use this entry as a draft.

Day 8 Cut It Out! Deleting Unnecessary Words (p. 141) or Reading Lead Sentence to Determine Balance and Clarity (p. 159)
Keep in mind: It may help students if they have a chance to work with a writing partner, read their writing aloud, and discuss their thoughts before writing.

Day 9 Coaching the Reader by Using Punctuation (p. 154)
Keep in mind: You may want to confer with groups of students who need this kind of instruction.

Day 10 Finding an Audience: Whom Would You Like to Persuade? (p. 50) Use Resource 3–7, Types of Persuasive Letters (p. 53)
Keep in mind: You may want to ask students to think more about today's lesson for homework. Sometimes quiet time to think helps an author think of more ideas.

Day 11 Have students pick one idea from Day 10, then use Writing Quickly and Continuously to Find First Thoughts (p. 74)
Keep in mind: There have been many days in this unit when students use free writing. Practice may not make perfect but it sure does make better. Don't worry about overusing free writing; if it works well, use it again and again.

Day 12 Students write a draft (no minilesson today—but many writing conferences).
Keep in mind: Students have drafted just a few days ago so it may not be necessary to do another lesson to lead students into drafting. As students draft, observe how they go about the process of putting words on the page.

Day 13 Self-Assignment Day
Keep in mind: Ask students to set individual wrting goals for today. Most students should reread their work or spend the writing period revising.

Day 14 Proofread Carefully (p. 167)
Keep in mind: Proofreading a letter that is going out into the world is very important. Let students know that their letters should be proofread to the best of their abilities.

Day 15 Celebrate (and mail letters).
Keep in mind: Ask students to select one of the two letters they would like to read to the class.

Grade Level
End of fourth grade
through middle school

UNIT III: Editorials

Editorials and op-ed pieces are published in newspapers and magazines and are often—but not always—about current events. The most important difference between an informational article and an editorial is that an editorial is written to share opinion (not just news, but the author's view of the news).

Technically, there is a difference between an editorial and an op-ed. An editorial is written by the editor of a newspaper or magazine and expresses the view of the writer and in some cases the staff of the magazine or newspaper. An op-ed piece, which gets its name because it used to be opposite the editorial page, also expresses the opinion of the author who is an outsider—unrelated to the newspaper. (For ease of reading, the term *editorial* will be used throughout this unit and this book).

About This Study   If your class is not familiar with persuasive writing or you are going to include class minilessons on research, your students will need more than three weeks to write an editorial. Don't let this scare you off—students learn an incredible amount about developing and supporting an argument in this unit.

Special Considerations   Elementary and middle school (and even some high school) students may be unfamiliar with editorials; therefore, before students begin to write, they should spend a minimum of four days reading editorials. Students will write much higher-quality editorials if they understand why editorials are written and what techniques authors use when writing editorials.

Research can be part of a unit on editorial writing. You may elect to teach whole-class minilessons on research or introduce research to the few students whose topic will benefit most from it. (For more information on research, read pages 81– 82. For minilessons on research see pages 60 and 63.)

Before Students Begin to Write . . .   Read and discuss editorials. Then read the same editorials again and point out what persuasive writing techniques the author used. When searching for editorials, look for topics that will be of high interest to your students—editorials that are well written, and editorials that are at the right reading level. Editorials that fit all of these qualifications are difficult to find. Therefore the Resources section has more sample editorials than any other kind of persuasive writing. To locate your own sample editorials:

1. Look at websites that specialize in persuasive writing (there's a list in the Appendix).
2. Google a current hot topic (airsoft guns, paintball, or Barry Bonds, for example).
3. Look in a national newspaper (or check its website). Editorials are often listed under *editorial*, *opinion*, *debate*, or *columnists*.
4. Look in magazines written for students (*Time for Kids*, for example).
5. Check your local paper.

Sometimes editorials are quick snippets of opinion with little or no proof or support. If you use writing like this, make sure you discuss both its strengths and challenges. What kinds of proof would make the editorial stronger?

Day by Day Plans

Day 1   Finding Persuasive Ideas: Rereading Written Responses (p. 42)
Keep in mind: Students can use the ideas in this lesson to get more than one idea for their own editorial writing.

Day 2   Things That Bother Me in the World (p. 44)
Keep in mind: You may have to show students the connection between some of their ideas and an editorial piece of writing. The topic can become an editorial if the idea can be made into a controversial issue and there can be an audience of many people. *I am angry when my mom takes away TV as a punishment* would work best as a persuasive letter, but *parents should not use TV as a punishment* might work as an editorial.

Day 3   Use a topic from yesterday's list and write more about it.
Keep in mind: Students sometimes have a list of topics, but they aren't sure how to get started with their writing. Show students ways to begin their writing: start with a reason that has the word *because*, start with a question, start with an image, and so on.

Day 4   Selecting a Topic (p. 84)
Keep in mind: As students look through their writing to find an idea to develop, they may realize that they don't have any ideas that they can or want to develop. If this happens with a few students, allow them to try out a few other topics on their lists. Tell them that they should be firm on a topic by the next writing period. They will have to do some catch-up work, like free writing on the subject, but you are allowing them just a bit more time to find a topic that excites them.

Day 5   Writing Quickly and Continuously to Find First Thoughts (p. 74) *or* Finding and Imitating Persuasive Writing Techniques (p. 58)
Keep in mind: You may want to do both of these lessons in one day especially if students have had experience free writing. First, ask your students to free write. This needs little or no lesson since students are familiar with this strategy. Then teach students a persuasive writing technique and ask them to experiment with this technique using one of the ideas from their free writing.

Day 6   Writing a Thesis Statement (p. 86)
Keep in mind: Writing a thesis is hard work. Confer as much as you can today and have students listen to other students' conferences so they get a better idea of what a strong thesis sounds like.

Day 7   Planning Persuasive Writing (p. 118)
Keep in mind: Confer with small groups of students. Show students how to put their ideas into a working organizational plan. Demonstrate with one student's writing and let the others watch. Ideas that you cannot group with others at this point can be placed on a sticky note. In a few days, when students draft, they can keep their sticky notes nearby and will see where these ideas fit in to their writing.

Day 8 Leads That Capture the Reader's Interest (p. 123)
Keep in mind: Don't skip this lesson. Working on different leads can really help an editorial. Since editorials tend to be longer than persuasive letters, it is particularly important that an editorial lead is a good one. If your students are new to writing workshop, you may want to bring their drafts home and read their leads. Do they lead them down a good road? If so, move on to the next lesson. If not, work with those students whose leads are weak and who you fear may be going down an unfocused or unclear path.

Day 9 Today students will experiment with writing techniques. Go back and reread the class' favorite op-ed or editorial pieces and discuss the writing techniques the author used. If you have time, ask students to try some of these techniques. Today is a *experimenting* day.
Keep in mind: Students like days when they feel they are just doing some "try it" writing exercises. This feels like a break from the more intense and serious work of sticking with one idea for a long time.

Day 10 Ready, Set . . . Draft! (p. 125)
Keep in mind: Now that students have leads that are likely to lead them down the right path and are also well written, give students enough time to write the rest of their drafts. (Spend time rereading students' drafts before beginning to teach revision.)

Day 11 Loaded Language: Positive, Neutral, and Negative Words (p. 94)
Keep in mind: At this point there may be one or two students who hate their drafts. If this happens ask these students if they would like to try writing another draft today and then ask them which draft they like better. Tell them that sometimes it is a relief to just start over. Give them this option and if they take it, help them get started writing a new draft.

Day 12 Smooth Transitions (p. 131) *or* Elaboration 1: Expanding Someone Else's Writing (p. 134)
Keep in mind: These lessons work well as a writing conferences, too.

Day 13 Copy Cat! Finding Great Writing and Doing It Again (p. 146)
Keep in mind: This is difficult for some students to do. Remind students to underline or circle two of their favorite parts and *then* figure out what they like about those parts. Help students determine what they like about that part of their writing.

Day 14 Proofread Carefully (p. 167)
Keep in mind: Some students may be ready to recopy or type their work. Let these students begin to do this work so that tomorrow is less stressful!

Day 15 Today students will put their writing in final form.
Keep in mind: Today students will be working on different things. Some students will be typing, some will be recopying, and others may be finished. If they are finished, they may write something else in their writer's notebooks, or ask students to begin to write about what they learned during your editorial unit.

Day 15 (again) Celebrate!
Keep in mind: Encourage all students to share at least a short excerpt of their editorial.

UNIT IV: Public Service Announcements

Public service announcements (PSAs) are helpful messages that are part of a public awareness campaign to inform, educate, and persuade the public about a specific health or safety issue. PSAs can be audio, video, or print. In this unit, students study and write public service announcements that appear in print. This kind of persuasive writing uses the following techniques:

Grade Level
Fourth grade and above—particularly good for middle school students

- scare tactics
- statistics and facts
- storytelling
- testimonials
- visual imagery
- a call to action

About This Study   In this study, students select a health or safety concern and create a public service announcement about it. They learn about gearing particular language to the target audience and writing a call to action. In addition, they study persuasive images and work on creating images that sway the audience.

Scheduling the Unit   Find out whether your school sponsors PSA programs or contests (during Red Ribbon Week, for example—a week highlighting the dangers of drugs), and teach the unit before students are offered the opportunity to contribute to these events.

Before Students Begin to Write . . .   Begin a study of PSAs by reading and discussing this type of writing. With a partner or in small groups, ask students to decide which announcements are very effective, somewhat effective, and relatively ineffective.

You may use the sample PSAs in the Resources section. These are all print PSAs and have been selected because they have persuasive techniques that students can easily identify and then try in their own writing.

You can find other sample PSAs on the Web by Googling *public service announcements* (narrow the search by adding the words *print*, *radio*, or *television*) or *Ad Council* (the largest producer of PSAs in the United States). Look for examples that your students will find interesting, are well written, and deal with an appropriate topic.

Some oldies but goodies are: This Is Your Brain on Drugs; Take Pride in America campaign promoting volunteerism; and the Things That Break Your Heart ads about dealing with and preventing diabetes. Asking students to locate sample PSAs is not a good idea because the subject matter is sometimes inappropriate. Don't avoid this study on these grounds; just gather your own PSAs.

Day by Day Plans

Day 1   Effective or Ineffective Persuasive Writing? You Decide (p. 34)
Keep in mind: Students will want time to discuss the content of the PSA before they analyze the writing, the image, and the overall presentation. This lesson works best if students are reading PSAs for the second time and have already reacted and responded as readers. (See lessons in Chapter 2.)

Day 2 Things That Bother Me in the World (p. 44). Students list their own health and safety concerns.

Keep in mind: Allow students time to think about their own health and safety concerns, even if some of these ideas do not lend themselves to a PSA.

Day 3 Call to Action (p. 149)

Keep in mind: Each student should experiment with different ways to call the audience to action—with a question, a statement, in the image, with a slogan, and so on.

Day 4 Studying How Images Work with Words (p. 111)

Keep in mind: You may want to begin the writing period by asking students the following question: *How does the image help the text? Would the PSA be less effective if it were only words? How?* (Help students be specific about what they notice about the images.) Then, do a short lesson on two or three of the things students noticed. Ask students to keep these things in mind while they create their own images today.

Day 5 *The Idea Is a Good One* or *I'm Hip to That: Formal Versus Informal Language* (p. 106) *or* Learning More About Your Topic 1: What Kind of Research Can You Do? (p. 60)

Keep in mind: Students may want to use some of their research findings in their PSA.

Day 6 Celebrate! Students share their PSAs with each other. (This celebration works well when students are in groups of four or five.) Reread their health and safety concerns list and begin to work on another PSA.

Keep in mind: The celebration will only take a few minutes so you may want to do a lesson first and save the celebration for the end of the writing period.

Day 7 Learning More About Your Topic 2: Internet Research (p. 63)

Keep in mind: It is easier to read information from paper rather than a screen. If possible, have students print their research and highlight important facts and information. This is a chance for students to learn more about their subject and to incorporate a fact or statistic from their research into their PSA.

Day 8 Using Precise Words and Phrases (p. 92)

Keep in mind: Students continue writing their PSAs and focus on selecting precise words. For an extra challenge, ask students to think of synonyms for some of their words—or to experiment saying what they want to say in many different ways. Then discuss what language is most effective.

Day 9 Studying How Images Work with Words (p. 111). Use the questions in the follow-up section of the lesson from Day 4 to help students understand that images can support words in many different ways.

Keep in mind: The more the students study the images, the more intentional they will be about creating their own images. Help students think about these questions: *What kind of mood does the picture create? How do mood and persuasion go together?*

Day 10 Celebrate: Students share their PSAs with each other.

Keep in mind: Display you students' PSAs.

UNIT V: Political Cartoons

Political cartoons (also called editorial cartoons) are written to make a statement, take a stand, give an opinion, or make fun of a political event or person. To understand the cartoon, the reader has to be familiar with the event or person referred to. Political cartoons use the following techniques:

- humor
- exaggeration
- symbolism
- labeling
- analogy
- irony

About This Study   In this unit, students study and create political cartoons. Students publish at least three cartoons in a three-week period. This quick publishing and celebrating is very appealing to students and teachers alike.

Special Considerations   Before beginning this unit, make sure students read and discuss current events. Student magazines like *Time for Kids*, *Junior Scholastic*, and *New York Times Upfront* (appropriate for middle school) are a great resource to help students find out about current news. CNN Student News (a daily ten-minute newscast) is another excellent resource.

Because images and words work together in political cartoons it's beneficial if an art teacher joins you in presenting this unit. (Use your powers of persuasion!)

Before Students Begin to Write . . .   As a class, study current events; read political cartoons in books, magazines, or newspapers; and discuss the meaning of the cartoons. Also study the techniques of political cartoonists (previously listed).

To find political cartoons on the Internet, search the words *political cartoons* or *editorial cartoons*.

Challenge   Create a political cartoon along with your students!

Day by Day Plans

Day 1   Read political cartoons and decide if they are effective or ineffective. What makes them effective or ineffective?
Keep in mind: The more students read and try to interpret political cartoons, the easier it will be for them to create their own.

Day 2   Discuss controversial news stories students know and care about. List these ideas. As you list topics with students, you may say things like, *Some people believe this about this politician or news story. Other people think this . . .*
Keep in mind: If students have seen political cartoons and have some knowledge of the current happenings in the world, you may want them to make a political cartoon today. As they work take notes and ask questions about what students are doing. This will give you a good sense about what students already know about political cartoons.

Day 3   Learning More About Your Topic 2: Internet Research (p. 63)

Keep in mind: The more students know about a topic, the better they can address the topic and form a point of view based on facts. Give students time to research current event topics of interest.

Day 4   Writing a Thesis Statement (p. 86). If time allows have students sketch ideas for a political cartoon.

Keep in mind: By writing a thesis statement students will understand that political cartoons are not only about the news, but are the cartoonist's *opinion* about a news story or political figure.

Day 5   Have students look at images and symbolism. Show students that everything that is drawn in a cartoon has a purpose. Use the immigration cartoon (see Appendix p. 237) to show students why Uncle Sam is drawn (he is a symbol of the United States), why each sign is drawn, and why Uncle Sam is on a fence of barbed wire.

Keep in mind: Students should be clear about what they are trying to show in their cartoon and should have a reason for everything they include.

Day 6   *I came. I saw. I conquered.* Short Declarative Sentences Persuade (p. 144)

Keep in mind: Use Resource 6–6, Example of a Short Declarative Writing. Have students experiment with different captions and words for their cartoon. If students finish a cartoon, let them begin another.

Day 7   Today begin with a political cartoon celebration. Let students share their political cartoons in a small group.

Keep in mind: Students can start on another political cartoon. Or they can write or sketch:

- Funny (ironic) things about life today. (For example, kids saying *I'm bored* but having a million different kinds of electronic gadgets. Kids not knowing what an encyclopedia is but knowing how to find any kind of information on the Internet, etc.)
- People (parents, local politicians, etc.) who say one thing but do another.
- Funny differences between parents and kids.

Day 8   Students write one last political cartoon.

Keep in mind: You may want to give students the option of working alone or with a writing partner.

Day 9   Set up a political cartoon museum in which students display their work and other students comment on what they like about each cartoon.

Keep in mind: Each student can have a comment sheet to place near his or her work so other students can write their reactions on each student's comment sheet. Show students how to write specific comments. Instead of "your cartoon is good" write "a very funny image" and so on.

UNIT VI: A Follow-Up Persuasive Writing Study

Grade Level
Grade 5 through middle school

This unit is designed as a follow-up unit for students who have already studied persuasive writing. In this unit, students are given three or four samples of the same type of persuasive writing they will study (select writings from the Appendix) and time to read and study these samples. Students work in groups or with partners for the first third of each writing period and then spend the bulk of the writing time, writing. There are no traditional mini-lessons. Instead students use essential questions to guide their learning discussions with each other.

While students are reading and discussing, confer with one group at a time. Teach students how to stick to one topic, reread their persuasive packet of writing, and how to build on each other's ideas. While students are writing you may want to confer with them individually.

About This Study   The study can be done in two ways.

1. All students study a new kind of persuasive writing together. (For example, the whole class can study advertisements and each student can write his or her own advertisement.)
2. Small groups of students study and write different kinds of persuasive writing. (For example, some students study and write advertisements, other groups study and write PSAs, other groups study and write political cartoons, and so on.) If you select this option, ask students who are studying the same kind of persuasive writing to sit near one another and discuss what they have learned.

Special Considerations   In order to hold students accountable for doing an appropriate amount of work, ask them to write a one-sentence goal at the beginning of each lesson. At the share time, ask students to check in with their writing partners and let their partners know if they met their goal for the day.

Before Students Begin to Write . . .   Remind students to use the resources they have gathered from the last persuasive study including: published persuasive writing, student writing samples, charts, and of course—each another!

Day by Day Plans

Day 1   What can we learn from reading this kind of persuasive writing? What techniques do these authors use?
Keep in mind: Before this lesson give students samples of persuasive writing. Using the information they acquired from the last persuasive study, help students to identify effective persuasive techniques like use of statistics and hypothetical situations.

Day 2   How will we get ideas for this kind of persuasive writing?
Keep in mind: As you confer, help students be specific and build on each other's ideas. If

one student says for example that he is going to look at what he has already written, tell the other students to ask him to say exactly what he will do. Where will he look and how will he look for this writing?

Day 3   How will we develop our own persuasive ideas?
Keep in mind: Remind students to think about ways they developed their persuasive writing in the last study.

Day 4   How will we write a strong persuasive draft?
Keep in mind: Students will start drafting today so make it as long a writing period as possible.

Day 5   How will we know what revision work we should do?
Keep in mind: This is the hardest thing for students to do. Remind students that they should reread their writing (not skim) and determine the strengths and weaknesses of the piece. Then have them revise their work. Ask students to edit their work for homework.

Day 6   Presentations and Celebrations.

UNIT VII: Create Your Own Unit of Study

Suggested Pacing Guide for a Persuasive Unit	
Lesson	*Number of Lessons*
Collecting	2–4
Selecting	1–2
Developing	1–4
Planning	1–2
Drafting	1–3
Revising	2–4
Editing	1–4
Assessment	1–2
Celebration	1–2

Create Your Own Persuasive Writing Unit:

1. Read through the units on the previous pages, review your state writing standards, and browse through the minilessons in this book. Working with your colleagues, discuss and write the answers to the prompts below.

2. Create a day-by-day lesson chart (like the ones in the other units) and fill in your lesson ideas. Use the pacing guide to help with planning.

3. At the end of the unit, discuss and write the answers to the reflection questions below.

Design Your Unit to Include:

About This Study

Special Considerations

Before Beginning This Study

Day-by-Day Plans (lessons we must do because they are urgent or because we can't wait to do them)

After Your Persuasive Writing Unit Ask:

- How did the unit go?
- What would I do differently next time?
- What other comments do I have about this unit?

Minilessons for Reading Persuasive Writing

Wait a minute, isn't this a book about teaching persuasive writing? What's reading doing in here? Actually, the decision to include a chapter on reading persuasive writing was an easy one. Reading persuasive texts before writing persuasively almost always yields better student writing.

When Reading Persuasive Writing . . .

. . . by published authors (and sometimes student authors), have students:

1. Discuss what they have read.
2. Pinpoint specific persuasive writing techniques the author uses.

Give Students Time to Read and Respond

Begin by reading persuasive writing for the pleasure of it! Let students agree or disagree with what is being said. Give them a chance to respond to what they read—not by answering a set of predetermined questions, but by reacting to the reading. Strong persuasive reading conversations are not focused on detached and disconnected thoughts: *Here's what I want to say. Here's another thing I want to say. Now what do you think?* They are conversations in which students listen to one another and build on each other's thoughts. The talk should be similar to the talk in an adult book club: *You talk. Hmmm. (I think about what you said.) I add something to what you said. Someone else says, "That's true but what about . . ."*

Many of you work with students who have a hard time expressing themselves—second language learners, children who have difficulty with word retrieval, or children who have specific learning disabilities. These issues make it even more difficult to teach students how to read and talk about what they've read. So start small, maybe just five minutes a day. Summarize the author's opinion about the issue and then ask students to talk about why they agree or disagree. Wherever your students are on the conversational continuum, teach them how to be better readers, thinkers, and talkers about persuasive text.

Students who do not face learning challenges are also often not adept at talking about what they've read. These students tend to summarize *not* analyze the text. Again, work with these students by *teaching* them how to respond thoughtfully to the text and to one another's ideas. Teach students to take one idea and discuss it even if they don't agree and even if they don't have a solution to the problem they are discussing.

As we give students time to read and respond to persuasive writing, something else happens: They begin to get excited about their own persuasive pieces. This excitement is almost as important as the minilessons themselves. We want students to think: *Hey, I've got opinions too. Let me tell you what I think. I've got something to say.*

Reading persuasive writing will help students begin to formulate ideas for their own persuasive topics. Recently, in a fourth-grade class where students were studying editorial cartoons, a student made this comment: "I totally disagree with the cartoonist, and if I were creating an editorial cartoon I would say that global warming is the number one issue that America ought to be concerned with." Weeks later, she was writing about that very topic!

Reread and Study Persuasive Writing

After reading and discussing persuasive writing, teach students how to reread and find the persuasive techniques the author uses. The more students study writing techniques and discuss how and why the author used rhetorical questions, for example, the better their writing becomes.

This point was illustrated for me when a friend asked me for help writing a business plan. I racked my brain for information about business plans and came up blank. I was stumped and then embarrassed to be stumped. I had *no idea* how to write a business plan because I had never written or read one. I didn't know the purpose, the audience, the sound, or the look of this kind of writing. When I decided to come clean and admit that I didn't know about business plans, I heard the disappointment in my friend's voice. I knew she was thinking, *Isn't she supposed to know about writing?*

I had to do something.

Over the next several weeks, we searched the Internet and read business plans. We found a few that we thought were well written—that stood out from the rest. We also talked to people who had written business plans. We needed to know:

Who is the audience?
What makes this kind of writing well written?
What makes this writing effective?
How is this writing organized?
What kind of language is used?
What's the ideal length?

We learned a lot in a short time—enough so she could start writing.

Imagine the kind of writing our students could do if we took the time to read and study writing *first*. Imagine if we spent a week (or two) studying persuasive writing before asking our students to write it. Writing would not only be easier, but the quality of the writing would surely be better. In addition, we would be demonstrating *how* to learn about writing in a way that students could use over and over again, with and without our guidance. We would be showing students that reading is something writers do when they want to be better writers.

Guiding students in reading and studying the kind of writing they will do is not just a nice add-on to the writing curriculum—it *is* the writing curriculum!

Predictable Problems and Possible Solutions
While Reading Persuasive Writing

Problem	Solution
You feel you cannot spend time reading persuasive writing since doing so is not part of the curriculum.	Study your state's reading standards. Determine which standards can be addressed while reading and discussing persuasive writing. Here are just a few examples: • Identifies and analyzes main ideas and supporting details. • Makes insightful and well-developed connections. • Relates new information to prior information.
Students do not seem to understand what a particular piece of persuasive writing is about.	If the reading is too difficult, try a different text. If the reading is at a good level, but students need background information to understand it, give students the information they need. Say, *One thing that is important to know is. . . .* Read the text several times. First, read it aloud, then ask students to read it independently, and then read it aloud again.
Your students do not know enough about a particular persuasive writing topic to be able to explain the reasons for their opinions.	Find persuasive writing about a subject familiar to your class. Look in student magazines like *Junior Scholastic* or *Time for Kids*. Have the students do quick research on the topic and then jot down notes in order to prepare for a class conversation.
Your students make general statements but do not refer specifically to the text.	Teach students how to locate and refer to evidence in the text that supports what they are saying. Assign one person the role of asking this question: *Can you prove that statement?*
There is too much repetition in student conversation.	Teach students how to ask these questions: *What ideas can we add?* *What questions didn't the article answer?* *What's another way to look at this?* *What things didn't the author mention?*

An Open Exploration of Persuasive Writing

Goals

To *build excitement at the start of the unit*

To *assess what students already know about persuasive writing*

To *assess how students attempt to study writing*

To *assess what strategies students use to build on one another's ideas*

Students are given different kinds of persuasive texts to read and study. (They aren't told that the writing is persuasive.) Some students may identify the writing as persuasive right away; many will not. By watching what your students do and listening to what they say to one another, you'll learn how they approach reading in general and what they know about persuasive writing. **Time:** Thirty-five minutes

Preparation

Collect about twenty-five examples of persuasive writing: a combination of travel brochures, advice columns, advertisements, and op-ed pieces. (For more suggestions on where to find different types of persuasive writing, see the Appendix).

Divide the students into groups of four.

Read Resource 2–1, Excerpt from a Persuasive Writing Conversation.

Minilesson

When I was in first grade my teacher put a bucket filled with rods on each table. There were long rods and short rods, red rods, and orange rods. There were short little beige rods, too. She told us to study and play with the rods. I learned how many beige rods it took to equal one orange rod, and I learned how to stack the rods on top of each other so that the longest one was on the bottom. I discovered patterns and talked with my friends about what I was learning.

In a few minutes you'll have a chance to explore some writing in this same way. This is an open exploration so I won't tell you how to study this writing. Today there will be no questions to answer except the questions you ask yourselves and each other. I do, however, want to make a suggestion about how to begin. When you first meet in your group, spend some time, probably about ten minutes, reading each kind of writing. All of you may not finish reading all of the writing, but you will at least have some ideas of what each text is about and how it is written.

I'm curious to see what you'll learn and what you'll talk about. Who knows (well, I do but I am not saying!), maybe we will write like this some day.

Hand out the writing and watch and listen as students explore. Write down some of what they say and read some of what they say during share time.

Share

Say, *Here are some interesting things I heard you say. This group noticed that . . . a few different groups said that . . . one group said one thing and then another group said the exact opposite for example . . .*

Ask, *What kind of writing do you think this is? What did you notice? What did you wonder about? What questions do you have?*

Possible Problems and Suggested Solutions

Students have no idea what kind of writing they have in front of them. Do the lesson again and give students more time to explore. Guide the exploration by asking, *Why do you think these pieces were written? What is the purpose? Who is the audience?*

Students identify the writing as informational. This is not that far off base, since much persuasive writing does give information. Tell students the writing does provide information but has another purpose, too.

Students switch topics too quickly during their small-group discussions. Show how to wait a few seconds after someone talks so everyone can process what was said. Show students how to respond to the last comment made instead of saying something unrelated.

Follow-Up

Look at the same persuasive texts again on another day. Ask students to focus on one thing they notice and see if it is true for all the texts. (For example, if students say a particular text contains questions, is this true for all the pieces?)

Look at different examples of the same kind of persuasive writing (all advertisements or all editorials, for example). What are their similarities and differences?

Ask students to think of a question they have about this kind of writing and write the question on a sticky note. Place the sticky notes in a central location in the classroom and let students read one another's questions. Refer to these questions throughout your unit.

Resource 2–1 *Excerpt from a Persuasive Writing Conversation*

Stuart: This one has information about visiting Florida, and this one has information about buying this candy bar.

Andrew: Yeah, I agree. This says that you should go to Reynolds Plantation, and it even has pictures to show you what it looks like.

Stuart: I know someone who's been there and it doesn't really look like that.

What the Teacher Notices Only two students are talking. The exchanges are quick, interrupted. Students are looking for a "quick fix." There is not enough exploring going on. Still, the teacher is impressed that Stuart started the conversation, since he usually waits for someone else to do so. Also, a few weeks earlier the class had read a number of examples of informational text, so informational writing is not just a random guess.

Teacher: Okay, let's see if we can slow down this conversation and stick to one idea for a while. I'm going to teach you something. Are you ready? One way to explore this writing is not only to tell what you see but also to ask a question about the writing or tell the group something you wonder about the writing. You know, something you don't know the answer to—for example, why are certain parts of the writing included?

Kyle: Okay, so what I think is that—I mean, what I want to know is why it says you should come to Reynolds Plantation? Why do they want us to come there? I mean, I know *why* they want us to come there, so that they can make money, but it seems like they are just trying to say how great it is.

The teacher sits with the group for two more minutes. She reminds the boys to leave some "wait time" after each child speaks. This helps the students build on what the person before has said. Kyle leads the group in talking about the purpose for the writing. The word *persuasive* is never mentioned but the concept of persuasion is alluded to.

Literal Understanding of Persuasive Text

When students read fiction, we sometimes ask them to retell what they've read so we can gauge their understanding of the text. Similarly, when students read a persuasive text, we want to be certain they understand the main point. (Sometime they can fool us because they seem as if they understand, but upon closer inspection, we realize they don't.) In this lesson, students learn some guiding questions to use as they read and then retell what they've read. **Time:** Fifty minutes

Goal

To help students use guiding questions in order to retell what they have read

Preparation

Choose a persuasive text your students have read recently and have them reread it.
Copy another persuasive text your students have read recently.
Look at Resource 2–2, Examples of Retelling Persuasive Text, to help you see the difference between a weak retelling and a strong retelling.
Copy Resource 2–3, Guiding Questions for Retelling a Persuasive Text.

Minilesson

Before we jump into our reading conversation, let's take a few minutes to learn about a strategy that will help you retell and summarize what you have read. From now on, we'll begin discussions by retelling. This will remind us of what we've read, and it will help the members of the group decide whether they understood the article or have questions about what they read.

We can keep certain questions in our minds as we read persuasive articles. If we try to answer these questions as we read or right afterward, we'll have a better understanding of what we read. Here they are. [Read Resource 2–2, Guiding Questions for Retelling a Persuasive Text, aloud.]

Now, I'm going to summarize an article we read the other day. First, I'm going to reread the article, keeping these four questions in mind. This will help me focus my reading. Then I'll use these questions to help me retell what I read.

Read the selected text and then demonstrate how to summarize the text by asking yourself the guiding questions aloud and answering them completely and succinctly.

Now I'd like you to summarize a persuasive article.

Hand out copies of an article your students have already read and ask them to reread it. (A short article is best.) Then ask them to summarize it using prompts like, *This persuasive text is mostly about . . .* and *The main issue here is. . . .*

Share

Don't ask students to share today. This minilesson is long, and students will have already reached their sit-and-listen limit.

Possible Problems and Suggested Solutions

Students do not understand the issue in the text. Reread the text or part of the text and have students identify key words that help determine the main idea. When choosing text to use in the future, ask yourself:

- Is this piece an appropriate length for my readers?
- Does it contain key words or concepts some children may not know? (If it does, give an overview of the text before students read it: *The piece we are about to read is about_____. The author makes the point that _____. He gives several reasons he believes this to be true. For example, . . .*)
- Can I find another piece of writing that is a better match for my students?

Follow-Up

Ask students to retell what they have read at the beginning of whole-class, small-group, or partnership work. Listen carefully and help them fill in any gaps or misunderstandings. (Some students may also benefit from highlighting or circling key words.)

Retell a harder or easier text.

Retell another persuasive text using the guiding questions but tell the students that you will purposely do a bad job. Ask students to tell how to improve your retelling.

Resource 2–2 *Examples of Retelling Persuasive Text*

Brandon's Retelling of "Science: It's Just Not Fair" by Dave Barry

Well this guy, the author, says that he likes science fairs but that some kids don't like science fairs because they have to go out in the middle of the night to get what they need and it puts too much pressure on them so they don't like them. That is the main point. He says that his wife did a funny science project.

The teacher notices: Brandon doesn't say that the article is mainly about how students wait until the last minute to prepare for these science fairs and how it is difficult for the parents to support students in doing this work. He doesn't seem to know that it is humorous either.

The teacher thinks: This may not be a great article to use, because Barry's humor and the way he switches subjects so quickly may be confusing. Then again, it might be a great piece to study, because many students appreciate wit and want to write humorous pieces. I'm just not sure yet. I will read it aloud tomorrow and see whether students understand it better.

Clark's Retelling of "Science: It's Just Not Fair" by Dave Barry

This writing is hysterical! Okay, so the main point is that science fair projects are really a pain in the neck (which can be true). And then there is the part where the kid only remembers the night before that he even has a project.

I think the main point is for us to think about whether these science fair projects are really worth it or not. Or it could be that there really isn't a main point, just that he wrote it to make you laugh. I am not sure if there is an issue here. That part I don't know.

The teacher notices: Clark understand the purpose of this article. He understands that the writing is humorous and that the author, using humor, asks the reader to question the idea of the at-home science fair project.

The teacher thinks: I will listen carefully to see if students understood the writing the way Clark did. Also, I wonder if students would like time to write an entertaining yet persuasive piece of writing. My teaching would be to show them how to write about a subject they know well and how to use details to create strong and humorous images.

Guiding Questions for Retelling a Persuasive Text

What is this writing mostly about?

What is the issue or main point?

How do you know?

What reasons, examples, arguments, and images does the author use to make her or his point?

Improving Comprehension 1: Read, Jot, Talk, Write

What's more important than giving students time to read and talk about what they've read? Almost nothing! In this lesson, students reread a persuasive text and take notes to prepare for a reading conversation. (These notes are not an end product, like a book report or research paper, but rather a tool to help students generate topics for discussion.)

Higher-level comprehension skills like analysis, synthesis, and evaluation become stronger each time they're used. The more opportunity students have to ask and answer their own questions about persuasive texts, the more thoughtful they will become as readers. **Time:** Sixty minutes

Preparation

Copy a persuasive text students have already read but not yet discussed. (If possible, shrink the text so that there are larger margins on the page, because students will write directly on the copy.)

Look at Resource 2–4, Example of Margin Notes/Questions.

Minilesson

Today, we are going to reread [name of article] *and prepare for a reading conversation that we will begin today and continue tomorrow. How should we prepare for a reading conversation?*

One of the things we know about good reading conversations is that all the participants have read the text and have things they want to talk about. Topics will arise that you haven't thought of before, but you should come to a reading conversation with ideas you want to discuss. One way to help you do this is to reread the article and take notes right on the paper about what strikes you. What might strike you? Here are some possibilities:

A part that makes you wonder.
A part you really agree or disagree with.
A part that weakens the argument.
A part that feels left out.
A part that you think is well written.

Watch me as I reread this article and write notes in the margin.

Demonstrate with a paragraph or two. Then read the next few sentences or paragraph. Have students tell their writing partners what strikes them and what they would write in the margin. Then have a few students share their ideas.

Now go back to your seats and spend ten or fifteen minutes rereading this text and preparing for a conversation about it. In a little while, we will have a conversation using our notes and we'll see how it goes.

If your class has not had experience with reading conversations, have a whole-class discussion. If students are already familiar with reading conversations, have them work in groups of four.

Share

Have students share one or two ways they prepared to talk about what they read.

Share parts of the conversations you overheard as you were listening and meeting with different groups: *This group brought up an interesting point,* or, *Sarah changed the entire conversation when she said. . . .*

Possible Problems and Suggested Solutions

Students jot down questions that do not yield much conversation. Explicitly teach students the difference between questions that have a predetermined answer (*What example did the author use?*) or can be answered *yes* or *no*, and questions that can have more than one answer. (This skill will also come in handy when students are asked to write interview questions.)

Students don't know what to write down. Give them more practice. Use student work to illustrate what strong note taking looks like.

Students interrupt each other and generally don't use good conversation etiquette. Explicitly teach students to make eye contact and listen to one another talk. Also, teach students how to pause after each person speaks in order to think about what the speaker just said. This will allow time for students to connect their thoughts to the previous thoughts.

A few students dominate the conversation; nobody else can break into the discussion. Teach students how to involve other students in the conversation by inviting everyone's contributions and by also asking open-ended questions.

Follow-Up

Present the Improving Comprehension 2 minilesson. Write down what students do well in this conversation and what they need to work on. Use these notes to plan your subsequent minilessons.

IS this article about Kids or parents? Seems like parents are too obsessive. (Bring this up with the group).

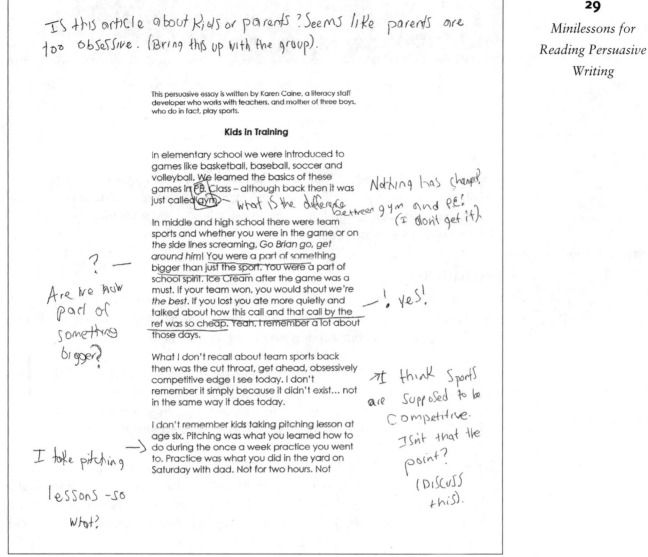

This persuasive essay is written by Karen Caine, a literacy staff developer who works with teachers, and mother of three boys, who do in fact, play sports.

Kids in Training

In elementary school we were introduced to games like basketball, baseball, soccer and volleyball. We learned the basics of these games In P.E. Class – although back then it was just called gym.

Nothing has changed. What is the difference between gym and P.E.? (I don't get it)

In middle and high school there were team sports and whether you were in the game or on the side lines screaming, *Go Brian go, get around him!* You were a part of something bigger than just the sport. You were a part of school spirit. Ice Cream after the game was a must. If your team won, you would shout *we're the best.* If you lost you ate more quietly and talked about how this call and that call by the ref was so cheap. Yeah, I remember a lot about those days.

*? —
Are we now part of something bigger?*

—! Yes!

What I don't recall about team sports back then was the cut throat, get ahead, obsessively competitive edge I see today. I don't remember it simply because it didn't exist… not in the same way it does today.

→ I think Sports are Supposed to be Competitive. Isn't that the point? (DISCUSS this).

I don't remember kids taking pitching lesson at age six. Pitching was what you learned how to do during the once a week practice you went to. Practice was what you did in the yard on Saturday with dad. Not for two hours. Not

I take pitching lessons – so what?

Resource 2–4 *Example of Margin Notes/Questions*

Improving Comprehension 2:
Read, Jot, Talk, Write

It's time to talk! This lesson focuses on improving student-to-student conversation by teaching students language they can use to stick to one topic and to delve more deeply into the topics that arise.* **Time:** Sixty-five minutes

Preparation

Read Resource 2–5, Language That Can Enhance a Conversation, and select the areas you would most like your class to work on. You can work from an area of strength and build on something students do well or teach students how to do something they have not been doing but you wish they would.

Minilesson

Yesterday, we prepared for and started a conversation about a persuasive article. Here are some things I noticed you did well yesterday during your reading conversations: [name strengths]. *Today we'll continue our conversations and try to dig a little deeper.*

Using Resource 2–5 as a guide, point out the things you want students to say in their conversations today. Ask, *Why do you think we might say these things in conversation?* Explain that these phrases will help them stay on one topic longer and build on an idea instead of jumping from topic to topic. Say, *Okay, let's start talking!*

Share   As students finish their conversations, ask them to free write (as much as they can as quickly as they can) about what they talked about. Suggest that they use any of the following questions to help them: What are your thoughts about this issue? What did someone say in the conversation that made you change your mind? At what point did someone say something that you had not thought of before?

Possible Problems and Suggested Solutions

Students' conversations are short and superficial. Explicitly teach students the difference between questions that have a predetermined answer (*What example did the author use?*) or can be answered *yes* or *no*, and questions that can have more than one answer. (This skill will also come in handy when students are asked to write interview questions.)

Students interrupt each other and generally don't use good conversation etiquette. Explicitly teach students to make eye contact and listen to one another talk. Also teach them how to add on to another student's ideas.

A few students dominate the conversation; nobody else can break into the discussion. Teach students how to involve other students in the conversation by inviting everyone's contributions and by also asking open-ended questions.

Follow-Up   Have students share their written responses with a partner and write down any new ideas they may want to pursue in their own persuasive writing.

The idea for this lesson is based on ideas from Lucy Calkins.

Language That Can Enhance a Conversation

Saying where you stand on the issue:

I believe . . .

I agree [disagree] with what [the author] said because . . .

What is most important here is . . .

Let's not forget that . . .

Adding information/looking at the topic from a different perspective:

What ideas can we add?

One question the article didn't answer is . . .

On one hand . . . , but on the other hand . . .

Another way to look this is . . .

One thing the author didn't mention was . . .

In my experience . . .

Comparing and contrasting ideas:

How does . . . compare with . . . ?

How is . . . related to . . . ?

This is similar to . . .

Clarifying/being specific:

Can you give an example of that?

Do you mean that . . . ?

Are you saying . . . ?

Proving the point:

The evidence we have for that is . . .

It's true because . . .

Exploring new ways to handle the issue/reframing the issue:

What solutions do you have for . . . ?

Isn't the real issue here . . . ?

What if instead of . . . ?

The Power of Persuasion 1: Forming and Expressing an Opinion

Students always have opinions and love to share them! In this lessons students do just that.

Time: Twenty to thirty minutes

Preparation

Post the reaction categories (see Resource 2–6 below) on chart paper, the blackboard, or a bulletin board.

Choose an editorial to share with your class and make copies for each student.

Minilesson

As we read persuasive writing, we react to it. Sometimes we think, No way! This author has it all wrong! *Other times we think,* Yes, this is totally true. *Then of course there is the in-between reaction:* Well, this author does have a good point here, but I'm not sure about this other point. *In a few minutes we will read an editorial and we'll decide how we feel about what the author wrote.*

Before we begin reading, let's investigate the possible categories of reactions. After we read, we will place our reactions in the category that most closely expresses our view about what we read.

Go over the reaction categories and descriptions. Then have students read a persuasive text that is likely to create strong feelings (see "Sis! Boom! Bah! Humbug!" in the Appendix, for example). Give students a chance to decide how strongly they agree or disagree.

Tell students to write their name on a sticky note and place the sticky note underneath the category on the blackboard that matches their reaction.

Discuss the article after telling the students that they may find themselves changing their minds as the discussion proceeds. Someone may bring up a point they haven't thought of or give new information or make a convincing argument.

Share   Some students tell why they thought their initial reaction belonged in a particular category and talk about whether they changed their reaction during the discussion.

Possible Problems

Usually none!

Follow-Up

Do this lesson again using another persuasive text.

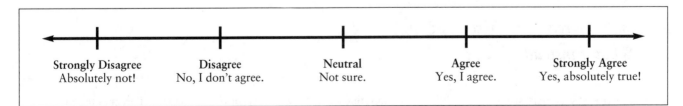

Strongly Disagree	Disagree	Neutral	Agree	Strongly Agree
Absolutely not!	No, I don't agree.	Not sure.	Yes, I agree.	Yes, absolutely true!

Resource 2–6 *Reaction Categories*

The Power of Persuasion 2: Remember What I Said Yesterday? Cancel That!

This lesson proves that a good reading conversation can really cause people to change their opinion. **Time:** Twenty to thirty-five minutes

Preparation

Make sure the reaction categories (see Resource 2–6) are still displayed.
Perhaps ask students to reread (as homework) the persuasive article used in the previous minilesson.

Minilesson

Today we will have a class discussion about the article that we read yesterday. It is very likely that after the discussion you will have changed your opinion somewhat. That's all I'll say for now, except let's be open to what other people say and see if we begin to question what we thought yesterday.

Have a class discussion about the persuasive text on which you based The Power of Persuasion 1 minilesson.

Share

Ask, *Did any of you change your mind a little bit or maybe even a lot? What specifically made you see the issue or topic differently?*
Tell students to place a new sticky note (in another color if possible) on the Reaction Categories chart (see Resource 2–6). What do most students believe now?

Possible Problems

Usually none.

Follow-Up

Do this lesson again with another persuasive text; this time, ask students to assess how well written they think the text is and place a sticky note with their name on it under the corresponding category on the board. Hold a class discussion about why the text is or is not well written.

Goal

To have students think through and form opinions about the persuasive article they read in the previous lesson

Effective or Ineffective Persuasive Writing? You Decide

This lesson asks students to try to determine what writing is persuasive and what is not. There are three options:

1. If your class has already identified a persuasive text that most students think is ineffective, study it and decide what doesn't work. Ask, *How would you change the writing in order to make it more convincing?*
2. If your class has already identified a persuasive text that most students think is effective, study it and decide what works. Ask, *What part(s) of the text are most persuasive and why?*
3. If you have not yet discussed whether particular texts are effective or ineffective, ask students to read a new piece of persuasive writing (junk mail works best) and discuss whether it is effective. (The lesson is scripted for this option.)

Time: Forty minutes

Preparation

Select option 1, 2, or 3 and then photocopy an appropriate piece of writing.
Copy Resource 2–7, Analyzing Persuasive Writing.
Gather some examples of advertisements or other kinds of persuasive writing.
Divide students into groups of four students if you haven't already. (Or rearrange previously assigned groups.)

Minilesson

Today, in our small groups, we'll read and analyze particular pieces of persuasive writing and decide what makes the writing fairly persuasive, not very persuasive, or somewhat persuasive. Here is the tricky part: You'll have to try to figure out what works in the writing—what makes it persuasive—or what doesn't work—what makes it ineffective. Be specific!

Let's look at this advertisement I received in the mail the other day [or whatever kind of persuasive writing you've chosen to use in this lesson]. *Let me read it to you.* [Read it.] *Is it persuasive?* Quickly elicit a few responses. Emphasize opposing perspectives: *Some people might think this writing is persuasive because* [list reasons]. *Other people might think it is not persuasive because* [list reasons].

You may see evidence of some of the things we have talked about in terms of persuasion, but just because these things are present does not mean that the writing is persuasive. For example, the writing may have examples, but they may not be good examples.

Begin reading. Read carefully. Then discuss with your group what works well and what doesn't. Remember that you may not agree with all of the members of your writing group. That's okay.

When only ten minutes remain, hand out a copy of Resource 2–7, Analyzing Persuasive Writing. Give students a few minutes to write down their thoughts (remember, the point of the lesson is analysis, not filling out a worksheet).

Share

During a subsequent writing period, ask students to read other students' analysis forms.

Possible Problem and Suggested Solution

Students are uncomfortable disagreeing with one another about what works and what doesn't. Encourage discussion of the different opinions and reassure students that *different* does not mean *wrong*. Point out that people with differing opinions can have a great discussion.

Follow-Up

Have students quickly jot down one thing they learned or were reminded of about persuasive writing.

Analyzing Persuasive Writing

Name: _____

Title of Article: _____

Author of Article: _____

What works well?

_____

_____

_____

_____

What does not work well?

_____

_____

_____

_____

The bottom line is . . . (how persuasive? how well written?)

_____

_____

_____

_____

CHAPTER 3

Minilessons for Collecting Ideas for Persuasive Writing

When Collecting Ideas for Persuasive Writing . . .

1. Begin to write persuasively, trying out many different persuasive ideas. Since beginning thoughts don't always flow in a neat and linear order, writing in this phase is often disorganized, underdeveloped, or choppy. This writing may sound like stream-of-consciousness writing—for the simple reason that it is.

2. Use these beginning thoughts to determine possible persuasive writing topics. Sometimes students know right away that they're not interested in particular topics or they don't have enough to say on a particular subject. Sometimes students need to write many times about one of their ideas before they know whether the topic interests them.

3. Reread what they've written, write more about one of their topics, tie two thoughts together, and sometimes group and organize ideas that seem to go together.

The goal is to come up with several persuasive topics so that when it's time to select one to develop, draft, revise, edit, and publish, students have more than one to choose from.

Assigning Persuasive Topics

For some reason, even if we usually begin a new writing unit by helping students find self-selected topics, when it comes to teaching persuasive writing, we often begin by assigning a topic. Maybe we feel less comfortable teaching persuasive writing than we do teaching other kinds of writing like memoir or fiction. Or maybe we feel rushed because the standardized writing test is only a few weeks away. Whatever the reason, before beginning to discuss how to collect ideas, I feel compelled to say a few words about assigned versus student-selected persuasive writing topics.

True, when we assign a topic (or offer a choice of two or three), we avoid hearing those six dreaded words that make us want to scream: *I don't know what to write!* We give students topics and they're off. Great! The writing moves along quickly . . . until the inevitable happens. Since students are not invested in the topic and often know little about it, it is more difficult for them to develop their ideas and harder for them to find examples to support their argument. It is harder to write convincingly—with conviction and voice—about someone else's topic. Connor, a quiet third grader who loves to write, said it best after he was assigned to write about what the school colors should be "I don't usually notice or care about colors so much. In my writing I like to write about stuff I understand."

On standardized writing tests that require persuasive writing students *will* have to know how to take someone else's topic and "make it their own" (thank you, Simon Cowell). It is, therefore, our job to teach them how to interpret a prompt and respond appropriately and convincingly (see Analyzing the Writing Prompt, in Chapter 9). But writing to a prompt is best taught *after* students have already had the opportunity to argue for or against a topic they've selected themselves.

In my own classroom, I've been in the position of having only two weeks to teach persuasive writing before a standardized test. I felt the pressure. (I also felt regret: Why hadn't I done a unit on this earlier in the year?) I had to rush through my teaching. It didn't go well. In subsequent years, I gave students time to generate their own persuasive ideas and explore these topics before drafting. Not surprisingly, the quality of the writing was much better.

If at all possible, I strongly recommend that you give students time to identify a persuasive topic that matters to them. If it's too late for this school year, plan for it next year!

Our Role in Helping Students Collect Ideas

Collecting ideas for persuasive writing means we not only have to give students time to find topics that matter to them but also have to *teach them how to go about finding these topics*. In other words, it's great when students are able to collect persuasive topics without our help, but most of the time, students need instruction on how to find their topics.

Start by thinking back to what students have already done to select their own topics in other writing studies. How can they use some of the same strategies to search for persuasive topics? You might even begin a persuasive writing study by asking, *What are some collecting strategies you have used in the past that you think you could use to find persuasive topics?* Figure 3–1 shows how to extend or alter strategies for collecting ideas that have been introduced earlier in the year.

Some teachers hang a tried-and-true strategies chart in the classroom—anywhere from three to eight strategies accompanied by one-sentence explanations—as a reminder and scaffold for students who have difficulty generating their own persuasive topics. Others prefer to help students create individual lists of getting-started strategies that the students then tape into their notebook and refer to when needed.

What is the strategy?	How have students used this strategy to collect ideas in past studies?	How could students use this strategy to collect ideas for persuasive writing?
Noticing	Looked at the world and wrote down what they observed.	Look at the world and write what they see. Then ask, "Could or should some of what I see be different? What is just and what is unjust? Or what do I notice about this product or situation that I could use to persuade the reader?"
Sketching	Quickly drew an object, a place, or a person.	Quickly draw something that annoys them. Move back and forth between sketching and writing down words.
Writing down what someone says	Used overheard conversation to create a character.	Write down something a news reporter says that strikes them. Or take a quote that seems to inspire strong feelings and write about it.

Figure 3–1 *Using Strategies from Past Studies to Collect Persuasive Topics*

Using New Collecting Strategies

During your persuasive writing unit, you will also use new strategies to collect topic ideas. Remember, sometimes when new strategies are first introduced, they don't work all that well—usually because students need more than one try with the strategy before they feel comfortable using it. If you suspect that another try might help or think that students did not have enough time with the strategy, fantastic! At this point you have your plan for the following day and the minilesson is guaranteed to be mini, since all you'll do is quickly review it. Your students will have more time to write and you'll have more time to confer.

Collecting Persuasive Topics Versus Making a List of Topics

When students begin to collect persuasive topics, they are not writing entire papers with a beginning, middle, and end. This is because they're not sure what they want to say about the topic yet. But collecting persuasive topic ideas does involve more than making a list of topics like this:

1. There should be a stoplight at my corner.
2. I think that school should start later in the day.
3. Recess should not be taken away.
4. Boys need to be given more attention in school.

This is a fast list of ideas. Although collecting persuasive writing involves listing ideas, it doesn't end there. When collecting ideas students are also asked to think and write about *what they have to say* with regard to the topic not simply list the topic.

Where Do Students Keep Their Ideas for Persuasive Writing?

Some teachers ask students to gather their ideas in a composition book (rather than a spiral notebook, the pages of which can be ripped out), which they call a writer's notebook. Other teachers prefer to have students use a binder of looseleaf paper so that ideas, notes from minilessons, and final published work can easily be grouped together. There is no right or wrong system. Where students write when they collect their ideas is up to the individual teacher. In this book I use the term *writer's notebook,* which can refer to a composition book, a spiral notebook, a binder, whatever. What matters most is that students feel free to write what they truly believe.

Getting a Strong Start

It is likely that up until this point the majority of entries in a writer's notebook have been narratives, often *personal narratives* or fictional accounts. These entries frequently start with the words *I remember* or *One day* or *Last year.* Ideas for persuasive writing usually begin quite differently. Although there may be instances of chronology, the writing in general is not linked to the passing of time. For some students, especially younger students accustomed to writing stories, this kind of writing is a big change. Therefore, it's helpful to introduce language students can use to help them begin a persuasive writer's notebook entry:

I think that . . .
It is important that . . .
Some people think . . . I agree/disagree because . . .
One thing that is true is that . . .
There are two sides to . . . On the one hand . . , but on the other hand . . .
The main thing the author is trying to say is . . . I feel that . . .

Enough talk. Let's jump in!

Predictable Problems and Possible Solutions
While Collecting Ideas for Persuasive Writing

Problem	Solution
Certain students have not yet found a topic of interest.	Let students talk with other students about possible topics. One idea often sparks another. Have students read a local newspaper or public service statements or political cartoons. Encourage students to try humor. Read a published piece of humorous persuasive writing or one written by a student the same age as your students. (For example, see the article "Is This Really a Discount?" in the Appendix.)
The topic is not debatable or controversial. It's too easy to argue: *We should clean up the reservoirs.*	Show students how to refocus the topic so that it is arguable: *The most effective way to clean up the reservoir is. . . . Cleaning up the reservoir never seems like a top priority, but it should be.*
The writing has opinion but no facts or evidence.	Ask, *Why do you believe what you have written is true and how do you know? Where can you find evidence to support your ideas?*
Some students are writing informational text with no element of persuasion.	Say, *I see that you are giving the reader information.* [Point out an example.] *I wonder though, what you want the reader to think about this. What do you want to convince the reader to think or do?*
Some students are not writing. They are staring off into space and "thinking."	Remind students that notebook entries should not sound finished. Show them examples from your own writer's notebook. Give these students a running start by asking them to spend a few minutes at home the night before jotting some quick ideas on an index card.
The study is losing stamina. Students are not as interested as they were.	Move on to choosing and developing an idea.

Finding Persuasive Ideas: Rereading Written Responses

Goal

To teach students how to reread their responses to persuasive writing by others in order to generate ideas for their own persuasive writing

Last week students read persuasive writing and were probably required to either (1) take notes to get ready for a conversation about what they read, or (2) respond in writing to what they read. In this lesson, students reread their notes or written responses to help them get ideas for their own persuasive pieces. **Time:** Fifty minutes

Preparation

Copy Resource 3–1, Response to an Article About Year-Round Schooling.

Minilesson

Remember the reading responses you wrote [notes you took] last week? Today you'll ask yourself these three questions as you reread: (1) What did I say that I could write more about? (2) What did I say that I really, really think is true? (3) What did I say that makes me think about another idea?

Let's try it. Here's a response that I wrote after reading an editorial on why year-round schooling is a good idea. I'll read the response and pause after each paragraph to think aloud about what I wrote. [Read the first paragraph.]

What I wrote makes me think that I could write about any of the following things: Time out of school does not mean kids aren't learning—what do kids learn when they are not in school? In this day and age, parents have to help kids spend their free time wisely. Whose fault is it that this generation of students is bored unless they're playing electronic games?

I feel excited by the third idea because it's something I have strong opinions about since I have kids. This might be what I write about, but let me read on. [Read on]

I'm not sure about the idea of forgetting the learning over the summer. If you really learn something, you will not entirely forget it over the summer. In writing, you might get rusty and you may have difficulty getting started, but forget? Maybe the problem is that kids aren't really learning as much as we think they are . . . hmmm . . . that could be a persuasive topic, too.

Allow time for students to reread their notes and find one that suggests a persuasive topic. Ask them to think aloud with a partner about what they wrote. They can start with these phrases: *This makes me think that . . . so I might write. . . .* Ask two students to share a few sentences from their response and to say what they might write. Then say, *Okay, so remember when you write today, begin by rereading.* Reread the questions to ask when rereading responses.

Share

Have students share samples of what they have written.

Possible Problems

Unpredictable.

Follow-Up

Do it again!

Response to an Article About Year-Round Schooling

Just because kids have time off from school does not mean that they will spend the bulk of their time watching TV and playing video games. Lots of kids do great things with all the time they have over the summer, like study abroad, learn how to play an instrument, read for pleasure, and spend time playing sports outdoors. Time without school doesn't mean time without learning.

If students are not really learning academic skills, they will "forget" them over the summer, but if kids really understand what is going on in school, they really won't forget that much. (Do I really believe this?)

It may be true that students who are struggling in a subject would benefit from continual school. I never thought about this in this way before, but if you are on the verge of learning something, summer break may not be a good thing. And I suppose that I have to admit that many students do forget their math facts over the long summer break.

The school year always feels so rushed, too. The weekends don't seem enough of a break for the students. There is not enough down time or even rest for students, and the higher the grade, the worse it is. Maybe shorter vacations would help this situation.

Do more frequent vacations mean more homework? Many teachers give homework over vacation, and if there are more vacations, will there be more long-term projects assigned? If so, the idea of frequent vacations and rest will be a nonissue anyway.

Why do we give students so many long-term/vacation assignments as they get older?

Things That Bother Me in the World

List making is a strategy that rarely fails. It's great for a writer at any level, and it often yields quick results.

Different types of lists can be geared toward particular kinds of persuasive writing. For example, for public service announcements students can list concerns that threaten the health and safety of people who live near them (fire? illegal drugs? kids being left home alone and not following safety rules? cigarette smoking?). For political cartoons students can list recent events in the news. **Time:** Forty-five minutes

Preparation

Create your own list of Things That Bother Me in the World to use with the class or copy Resource 3–2 to use as an example.

Minilesson

Today we will begin to search for topics for our persuasive pieces. We'll make a list in order to help us collect lots of different ideas. This may be a different kind of list from lists of topics you have made before now. We're not going to write down a list of topics or titles for persuasive writing.

Here's what we are going to do. When we make our lists today, we'll list things that bother or annoy us in the world. Some of the things on our list may lead us to persuasive writing topics.

I tried this strategy last night. I began by asking myself this question, which was a lot of fun to answer: What bothers or annoys me? In order to answer this question I looked out the window and just observed, I thought about my day yesterday, and I pictured something I remembered. And you know what? I was surprised by how many ideas I was able to put on my list.

I'll read my list and also talk about the reasons some of these things bother me. I'm going to try to be as specific as possible when I talk, so that I begin to think about what I have to say about each one of these ideas. By specific I mean that I will tell you exactly what bothers me and why these things bother me too. [Talk through the list, thinking aloud as you go.]

Today you'll begin to write and work with your Things That Bother Me in the World list. You may already have ideas to put on your list, but in case you haven't, I placed a few idea starters on chart paper to help jog your thinking. [Read list categories.]

The idea that _____.
People who _____.
When _____ happens.

Whatever you do, don't just stick to these categories! They are just places to start if you need help getting started, but I would like to see many of your own ideas on your list.

Talk to your partner and see if you can each come up with one thing that you could put on you list. Start by trying to remember something that annoyed you.

Chart two student responses. Allow these students to begin to talk about why they selected that topic.

Today, spend some time creating a list.

Share

Students share their ideas from their lists and tell how they thought of these ideas.

Possible Problem and Suggested Solution

Students find topics that are too general and vague, like war or money or people who aren't nice. If this happens teach a minilesson on questions partners can ask each other in order to get more specific ideas: *But why exactly does that bother you? Can you give me an example of what you mean?*

Follow-Up

Help students think of more persuasive ideas by considering people, places, or ideas that bother them.

Have students sketch things that bother them. Even older students love to sketch, and drawing helps students think.

Things that bother me

1. orange juice w/ pulp.
2. Having no time for a social life because of homework.
3. No time to read books I want to read.
4. Holocaust deniers.
5. War in the middle east.
6. kids feeling stupid because they are not in the gifted program.
7. teens being prejudged for obnoxious people.

6th grader

Things that tick me off

8th grader

1) After school some kids go home immediately where other kids have to wait for their bus.
2) Teachers won't let us have cell phones in class when they are on them through the period dicussing what they should have for dinner.
3) If we forget things at home we are not allowed to call.
4) Teachers punish us for speaking our mind or forgetting something.
5) we have assigned seats at lunch.
6) I can't go to certain web sites in case of cyber bullying.
7) Parents think if I go anywhere alone I will get into trouble.
8) I can't do homework in other classrooms, even if I am already done with busy work.
9) Teachers nag us on how our clothes look and expect every skirt to go to the knees or pants to be at our belly button.

Resource 3–2 *Things That Bother Me in the World (Samples)*

Hunting for Persuasive Topics: Wandering and Wondering

Whether it's an advertisement or an editorial, good persuasive writing is often the result of our looking and listening carefully and then commenting on what we think about what we see. In this lesson, students observe and then wonder about what they've seen.

If students are writing an advertisement for a product, ask them to bring in the product and spend time just observing the product. The more students know about the product, the more they are likely to come up with a big idea for selling it. **Time:** Sixty minutes (This long lesson can easily be separated into two lessons.)

Preparation

Look over Resource 3–3, the filled-in Wander and Wonder chart, or create your own.
Copy Resource 3–4, the blank Wander and Wonder chart. (If possible, provide clipboards.)

Minilesson

Today during writing time we're going on a field trip! Well, not exactly, but we will leave the classroom. Let me explain.

In other kinds of writing we have studied, we've noticed that many writers tend to be great observers. Writers may observe people or places or objects—anything and everything! [Give examples of writers the class has studied who are adept at observation—perhaps Cynthia Rylant (*When the Relatives Came*) or Ralph Fletcher (*Twilight Comes Twice*).] *But what about authors who write persuasively—are they observers too? I would guess that they are.* [If time allows, ask students to look back at the persuasive texts they've read and find evidence that persuasive writers are also careful observers.]

I went on my own field trip the other day and here's what I wrote. [Read the chart and discuss it.] *Here are some things I said to myself as I was walking. These questions are on your Wander and Wonder chart. Let's spend a few minutes reading these questions.* [Read the questions. If there appear to be too many questions, ask students to circle one or two questions that you think will be most helpful and focus only on these questions.]

[Hand out a blank Wander and Wonder chart to each student.] *Okay, now we're going to take a walk outside. Walk slowly and take notes on your copy of the chart.* [Allow time for students to walk, pause, and write. Encourage them to use quick words and phrases rather than complete sentences.]

Share   Ask volunteers to read an observation and corresponding idea from their chart.

Possible Problems
None.

Follow-Up
Ask students to choose one of the ideas on their chart and begin to write about it.
Ask students to try this activity at home with adult supervision.
Read the picture book *The Other Way to Listen* by Byrd Baylor. Show students how the author is a keen observer and listener.

Outside of School		
I spotted (or I heard)	*This made me wonder/ think*	*This made me think that things could be different if . . . (Or things should stay the same because . . .)*
A teenager driving	How old is he?	Kids were not allowed to drive at sixteen The driving test was much harder
Children walking to school	They look really tired.	School didn't start so early Kids got more sleep
Our neighbor mowing his lawn at 7:00 A.M. on Saturday morning	Shouldn't there be a law against this?	There was a town ordinance prohibiting homeowners from starting outdoor equipment motors before nine in the morning

In School		
I spotted (or I heard)	*This made me wonder/ think*	*This made me think that things could be different if . . . (Or things should stay the same because . . .)*
Students rehearsing for the talent show	Kids feel so badly when they don't get in.	Maybe the talent show should be just for fourth, fifth, and sixth graders. Then there would be fewer children trying out so fewer would be cut. That way less students would be upset.
Students in the library	Could the library be open before school starts one day a week so we could check out books more often?	If we had more access to books—especially books that are interesting to us.
The second graders doing their economy project	How come we don't do more projects like this?	We could do more projects that involve money since money is a big part of what we learn about in math this year.

Resource 3–3 *Wander and Wonder Charts (Samples)*

Wander and Wonder Chart

1. What do I see that could or should be different here?

2. What do I see that is unfair or unjust?

3. What do I see that I think is good and should stay just the way it is?

4. What do I not see but I would like to see?

I spotted (or I heard)	This made me wonder/ think	This made me think that things could be different if . . .

Goal

To prompt students to generate a list of people they would like to write to

One way to find a persuasive topic is to start by thinking about an audience. This lesson focuses on helping students think about which family members or close friends they would like to persuade.

You can augment this lesson by asking students to write to companies and organizations instead of family members. If you do the lesson this way, use the materials suggested under option 2. **Time:** Forty minutes

Preparation
Option 1:
Make a copy of Resource 3–5, Persuasion in Everyday Life.
Copy Resource 3–6, Audience Chart.

Option 2:
Make one copy of Resource 3–7, Types of Persuasive Letters chart.
Copy Resource 3–8, Types of Persuasive Letters.

Minilesson

If you were going to write a letter to someone—anyone you like—to try to convince that person of something, who would you write to and what would you say? It may be easiest to think about the members of your family. Have you tried to convince a parent or sibling of anything lately? [If you have a real-life example, share a quick story of trying to convince family members or close friends to think or act in a certain way.]

Let's look at a list called Persuasion in Everyday Life. This is a list of some things that third-, fourth-, and fifth-grade students tried to convince their parents to do. The ideas on this list may help jog your memories. As I read the list, write down your ideas. [Read the list.]

[Have students take a minute or two to talk to a partner whom they would like to persuade. If you are asking students to write to companies and organizations, show the Types of Persuasive Letters chart and discuss.] *Turn to a partner and share one or two of the most important ideas on your list. Tell your partner why these letters are important to write. What are you hoping to convince this person?*

Instead of jumping in to writing a letter, let's spend the next few minutes of writing time thinking of people to convince. In a few minutes we'll pick one of the people on our list that we most want to write to and we'll begin to write. Work hard!

Share
Have some students share their ideas and the beginning of their letters with the class.

Possible Problem and Suggested Solution
Students do not have strong answers in the third column of the chart. (In other words, they do not know how they would convince the reader to see the issue from their point of view.) As students develop their ideas, they will naturally grapple with this question. Fig-

uring out how to convince the reader is the essence of good persuasive writing and an ongoing process. So the fact that students may not be able to answer this question at this point in the study shouldn't be of major concern.

Follow-Up

If small groups of students complete their lists quickly, work these students to brainstorm and rehearse different ways of beginning their letters or ask students to stop after a few minutes of creating their lists and sneak in another quick minilesson on ways to begin a letter. Letters can begin with a question, a friendly hello, or a direct request. (For more ideas about how to begin a persuasive letter, see the minilesson on leads, page 123.)

Have students write an answer to this question: *How does your reader feel about this issue or topic at this point?*

Do this lesson again but this time, ask students to think of an audience that is more distant like a company, organization, or politician.

- My brother not to hog the computer.
- My teacher to let us play outside because all we did in P.E. that day was a Pacer test.
- My dad to do the dishes for me after I mowed the lawn for one and a half hours.
- My mom to let me have outside time before I started my homework.
- My mom to let me sleep over at a friend's house. (Mission accomplished!)
- My dad to buy a toy called a flip stick. We saw the advertisement on TV. (It obviously didn't work because I don't have it and don't plan to get it!)
- My sister to give me some of her Valentine's Day candy. I reminded her that the week before she gave me a sour gummy worm. (It worked.)
- My mom to buy me a cell phone. I have tried eleven times and it still hasn't worked. (Any advice?)
- Christian to clean out his desk in school because his stuff was falling into my desk. (It didn't work.)

Resource 3–5 *Persuasion in Everyday Life*

To *whom would I like to write?*	*What do I want to try to convince that person or company of?*	*How would I convince my audience to see this issue my way? What would I say?*

Types of Persuasive Letters	Audience	Purpose
Personal	Parent Friend Acquaintance	To ask the person to help you, do you a favor, or reconsider an action
Letter to the Editor	An editor of a newspaper, magazine, or newsletter	To give your opinion about a previous story
Advertisement	Consumer	To sell a product or service
Request	School principal Store manager Politician	To ask the person to do something
Recommendation	School administrator Manager of a company Award committee	To urge the person to hire or consider hiring a particular person for a job To propose that a particular person or group of people receive an award

Resource 3–7 *Types of Persuasive Letters*

Types of Persuasive Letters

Name _____

Types of Persuasive Letters	Audience	Purpose
Personal		
Letter to the Editor		
Advertisement		
Request		
Recommendation		

Uncovering Persuasive Topics

In this lesson, students are asked to reread notebook entries from past writing studies and to find hidden persuasive topics. (The lesson requires that students have many old entries with self-selected topics. If most of the entries in students' notebooks are from assigned topics, skip this lesson and select another.)

Allow time for students to find connections between what they have previously written (often as a narrative) and a persuasive writing topic.

To make this minilesson shorter, *either* have two students show the topics they've found by rereading their notebooks *or* show the Potential Persuasive Topics in a Writer's Notebook chart—but don't do both.

This lesson is well suited for students in fifth grade and above. **Time:** Fifty minutes

Preparation

A day or two before the lesson, confer with two students and help them reread their writing and find hidden persuasive topics. (You are essentially doing this actual lesson as a writing conference with two students and then asking those two students to help you teach the minilesson on the following day.) Show the selected students how to take their topics and turn them into persuasive topics. It may help to copy and then read Resource 3–9 with the students so they get an idea of how topics can be looked at from a persuasive angle.

Minilesson

A few days ago, [name of student] and [name of student] and I had a writing conference in which we went through their notebooks slowly and reread—not skimmed but carefully reread—old entries. We wanted to see if we could find hidden persuasive topics. These topics were a bit tricky to find. They had to read slowly and ask themselves this question: What is hiding in here that may be a topic for persuasive writing? At first they didn't see much, but then they began to realize that there was more in their notebooks than they realized. I wonder if the same is true for the rest of you. In just a few minutes, we'll find out. First though, I'll let [name of students] tell you about what they did and what specific things they found. [Help these students talk about what they found in their notebooks and how what they found could lead to persuasive writing.]

Before we go back into our notebooks and begin rereading, let's spend a few minutes looking at a chart that shows what other students have found in terms of persuasive topics from rereading their notebooks. [Show the chart.] *Now go through your notebook and see what you can find.*

Ask students to reread their writing silently for eight to ten minutes and place a sticky note on pages that may contain persuasive topics. Confer with students to help them find potential persuasive topics or just walk around and write down some ideas about what students have found. If there is time, chart two or three examples of what students found.

When you go off to write today, see what other hidden topics you can find. When you have hit on something that you would like to begin to write about, just begin!

Share

Have students share surprising things they found in their notebooks that may be able to become a persuasive topics.

Possible Problem and Suggested Solution

Only a few students are able to find persuasive topics. Sometimes this happens because students do not have enough past writing in their notebooks. If this is true, move on and try a new lesson. Sometimes this happens because students can't find connections between what they have written and a persuasive idea. If this happens, give students time to try this work again, but this time have them work in partnerships and think aloud. Or, do this work of digging for persuasive topics with some students in writing conferences.

Follow-Up

Ask students to write about potential persuasive topics even if they are not certain about what they want to say or if the topics are persuasive.

Potential Persuasive Topics in a Writer's Notebook

Writing in the Notebook	*Possible Persuasive Topics*
I can't believe that there is no P.E. class today but instead we have to write! Why is P.E. always cancelled lately? It's ridiculous and unfair. [sixth grader]	The importance of physical education in school, especially for middle school students. Why is P.E. an optional class? [Type: editorial, letter, petition, PSA]
Whenever my alarm goes off I just want to throw it across the room. I just can't, I mean I am not capable of getting up that early in the morning. [fifth grader]	School starts too early in the morning. A later start time might alleviate some of the bus transportation problems our school has. [Type: editorial, letter, petition]
. . . and then I have to do my homework, which is a lot more than last year. [sixth grader]	What is the value of homework? Have educators gone too far? [Type: editorial, letter, petition]
I watched the Democratic presidential candidates debate last night. None of them seem to know what they're doing. [eighth grader]	So many possibilities here! [Type: editorial, letter, political cartoon]
Spending the whole year studying Georgia history is stupid. [eighth grader]	Is Georgia history really the best curriculum? [Type: editorial, letter, political cartoon]
When my parents got divorced, things really changed. [third grader]	Divorce through the eyes of a fourth grader. [Type: Letter to either or both parents]
Year-round schooling is really different. [fifth grader]	The pros or cons of year-round schooling. [Type: editorial, letter, political cartoon]
I hate working as a group in math. [third grader]	The disadvantages of collaborative groups. [Type: editorial, letter]

Finding and Imitating Persuasive Writing Techniques

In this lesson, students are introduced to a published author's writing techniques (also called *author's craft* or *style*) and then imitate these techniques in their own writing. Make sure that students understand that the goal is not for everyone to sound like Rick Reilly or Maureen Downey or any other particular author. The goal is for students to broaden their repertoire of ways to say things. **Time:** Sixty minutes.

Preparation

Look at Persuasive Writing Techniques Linked with Examples in the Appendix on page 202. Select a technique (such as rhetorical imagery, exaggeration, or headings/subheadings) and read the appropriate persuasive writing sample that uses that technique. (See the Appendix for samples.)

Minilesson

Whenever I want to learn how to do something new, I look at someone who does that thing well and I try to learn from him or her. [Give examples like learning to ski, playing a sport, sewing, or writing music.] *The first year I taught, I really admired Mrs. Galett, the teacher in the classroom across the hall. I wanted to learn all I could from her, so I asked her if she would keep her door open when she taught. I learned so much! One of the things I admired was the way she spoke to her students. When she spoke, everyone dropped what they were doing and listened intently.*

I remember the way she asked her students to get ready to go to recess and lunch. I'd tell my class, It's time for lunch, so remember to take your jackets and line up. *But she said;* It's cold, cold, cold out there today! The wind is fierce in January, so bundle up every part of your body! You know those great hats and gloves your parents bought you? This is the day to wear them! *Essentially we were saying the same thing, but we said it so differently. And it's no surprise that many of my students didn't bother to take their jackets, but all of her students took their jackets every day! I just loved how she said things. I listened carefully to the words she chose, when she paused, what she said first, and what she said next. In a way, she was* my *teacher!*

So far, while we've been collecting ideas about what we might write about, we've focused on just getting our thoughts on paper. But today we'll spend some time focusing more on the way we want to say things. We'll look at some of the persuasive writing we've already read and talk about what we like about the way the author chose to say something. Then we'll try using some of the same techniques this author used.

[Discuss one of the techniques you have pinpointed. Then try this technique together as a class.] *Let's quickly try this technique with one of Molly's topics. At this point one of the ideas that Molly has is. . . .*

Today, as you write, see if you can find a place to try out this persuasive technique with your own writing. [Give students the option of trying these techniques with a topic they have already written about or a subject they would like to write about but haven't yet.]

Share

Have students share examples of their attempts to use the persuasive technique.

Possible Problems and Suggested Solutions

The writing sounds awkward and not at all like the published author. This is okay and to be expected. Practice makes perfect; try again with another technique on another day.

Some students notice that some techniques in persuasive writing are also used in other kinds of writing. All problems should be like this! These students are beginning to realize that although certain kinds of writing tend to rely more heavily on certain writing techniques, many techniques are not exclusive to a single genre. This is an important thing to learn.

Follow-Up

Have students study a persuasive writing text that you have selected because you think it is particularly well crafted. Spend two to five days studying just one piece of writing and trying out the various persuasive techniques students notice. Suggested pieces to study are (see Appendix):

"Kids in Training"
"Sis! Boom! Bah! Humbug!"
Chris Wondra's Letter to His Students

Learning More About Your Topic 1: What Kind of Research Can You Do?

In this lesson students learn various ways to research their topics. **Time:** Forty minutes

Goal

To help students apply what they know about research to determine what kind of research they could do to find pertinent information on their topic

Preparation

Create a class chart that lists research strategies as shown in Resource 3–10.
Copy Resource 3–11, Kinds of Research Our Class Could Do.

Minilesson

It is common for persuasive writers to do research to learn more about their topic. Let's think for a minute about different kinds of persuasive writing and what kinds of research the author might have used. [Talk about the kinds of research appropriate for each kind of writing on the Types of Persuasive Letters chart (page 53).]

Today, we're going to think about what kind of research you could do in order to learn more about your topic. Let's say I was writing a persuasive advertisement for the Bellford Hotel in Vermont. There isn't really such a hotel. I just made it up! But let's imagine it. What kind of research would I want to do before writing my persuasive ad and what would I want to know?

I'd want to know if this hotel is an inexpensive, no-frills place that wants to attract a money-conscious traveler or a fancy, expensive place that offers a choice of three restaurants and a big outdoor pool. Where would I go to research the answers to these questions? [Take quick responses.] *I would also want to know where the hotel is located. Is it near a city and great shopping or is it on the top of a scenic mountain where one can see beautiful sunsets?*

Now let's switch gears. Let's say I was writing an editorial against hunting. In order to make a good case about why hunting is wrong, I would say something like, Many people believe that hunting is okay because. . . , but the truth is that. . . . *But in order to write this, I would have to know what hunters believe about hunting. Where could I get this information? You guessed it! Research. I could interview a hunter or survey a group of hunters and find out why they hunt and why they think that it is okay to hunt.*

Here's one last example. Alex, a third grader in Decatur, Georgia, was writing a letter to Larry King to convince him to stop interrupting his guests. Larry King is a late night talk show host on TV. He is very popular but is known for asking a question and then interrupting his guests as they try to answer. Alex only had one example of Mr. King interrupting someone and knew he needed more. What kind of research do you think he did in order to get more examples? He watched TV! Really! He researched by watching The Larry King *show. In this kind of research he was looking for specific examples, specific times that Larry King interrupted his guests.*

These three examples demonstrate very different kinds of research. Let's think briefly about the kinds of research you could do. Look at these research strategies. [Hand out a photocopied list or call students' attention to the strategies you listed.]

Take one of the topics a student has written about and brainstorm with the class the kind of research that student might use to learn more. Write the students' ideas on the chart in Resource 3–11, Kinds of Research Our Class Could Do.

Today before you start writing, think about what kind of research you could do to learn more about your topic. Talk about it with your writing partner and see if you can come up with more than one kind of research.

Share

Have some students share research ideas for their topics. Record their answers on the Kinds of Research Our Class Could Do chart. Encourage students to be as specific as they can. If they say they could do an interview, ask them who they would interview and how they would find this person.

Possible Problem and Suggested Solution

Students' research suggestions don't fit well with their topics. For instance, a student writing to persuade students to flush the toilet after they use it (I can't make this stuff up!) wants to research people who invented toilets. This kind of research is related to her topic but is not likely to help her writing. Ask students how they think the kind of research they have selected is likely to help their persuasive writing. Help students think through what it is they are hoping to learn or understand from their research and be honest with students about what kind of research you think will work best and why you think this way.

Follow-Up

This lesson does not distinguish between primary and secondary research—but feel free to teach this or use this terminology if students have already been exposed to these concepts. Remember to give students time to research and discuss what they have learned.

- Conducting interviews

- Giving surveys and questionnaires

- Checking Internet websites

- Consulting books, magazines, and newspapers

- Observing a process or activity and taking notes

- Having a phone conversation with an expert

Resource 3–10 *Some Research Strategies*

Kinds of Research Our Class Could Do

Topic	*Kind of Research*

Learning More About Your Topic 2: Internet Research

In this lesson students use the Internet to research their persuasive topics. This lesson works best with students who have moderately strong typing skills and who have had experience with the Internet.

If possible, enlist older student buddies to help your students do this research. Student helpers should be at least three years older than the students they are helping. High school students are ideal. **Time:** Fifty minutes

Goal

To have students use the Internet to research a persuasive writing topic

Preparation

Read through the lesson and decide what topic you will use to demonstrate locating information on the Internet.
Copy Resource 3–12, Questions to Ask Yourself When Doing Internet Research.

Minilesson

In order to write a strong persuasive piece, you should find out as much as you can about your topic. Finding out about your topic will help you figure out what you want to say and even whether you have enough to say about the topic in the first place. So the point of Internet research is not so that you can include every fact or piece of information that you find. Remember that we are not writing a traditional research paper in which we want to give the reader as much information as possible. We are writing a persuasive argument in which we may or may not include some of the information we learn today. The goal today is to learn more about your subject and consider what information, if any, will help you persuade your audience.

Internet research is tricky. Obviously, the great thing about the Internet is that you can get information quickly. Most people like the Internet for just that reason. But there are some difficulties in doing Internet research, too. Let's talk about what they are and what to do if you have any of these problems.

1. *Sometimes the information isn't relevant. That means it is not related to your topic. So ask yourself,* Is this information going to help me learn more about a possible persuasive topic? *If the answer is no, keep searching and probably look for a new website.*

2. *Information on the Internet is often written for adults or people with a specialized background in certain subjects, so it can be very difficult to read. If you run into this problem, ask your teacher, parent, or other adult to help you. While researching in school, I'll help you read some of the information and we'll decide together if you should use it.*

3. *This last problem is something that many adults don't even consider. Some of the information on the Internet is inaccurate. It's not correct! If you come across some information you think might not be right, we can try to check it with other websites and other sources.*

Now let's see if we can do some Internet research. [If you can, use a topic that one of your students may write about and discuss key words and websites that might have information on this topic. Alternatively, you can use the topic of healthy dinners, as in the example that follows. If you have a computer with Internet access in your classroom, demonstrate an Internet search and think aloud with your students.]

The other day I did some Internet research because my family is getting tired of the same old foods for dinner—baked chicken, pasta with vegetables, and more baked chicken! I wanted to find other dinner ideas so I sat down at the computer and asked myself these questions. You will ask yourself the same questions, so listen carefully. The first question is:

1. Do I know any Internet websites that might have what I am looking for?

This is a logical place to start. You may already be familiar with some websites that will help you locate information on your subject. I realized that I did know the names of two websites that might be helpful, so I tried them.
The second question is:

2. What words can I put into Google or another search engine that will help me search for information on my subject?

I thought and thought. What words do you think I should have looked under? Talk to your writing partner about what words you think I could look under. [Get responses.] *Here are the words I used for my search:*

Dinner menu
Dinners for kids
New dinner ideas

The third question is:

3. How can I change my key words to narrow the information that comes back?

Dinner menus *brought back many dinners that had too much cheese or took way too long to prepare. So I changed my search to* quick and healthy dinner ideas. *This gave me the information I wanted.*
Talk to your partner about how you might start your Internet search to find out more about your topic. Focus on question 2. [Repeat the question].
For the first few minutes today, I would like you to work with a partner or by yourself to think about and then write down the key words you could put into a search engine to locate information about your topic.

Share
Have students share the key words they came up with in order to search for information.

Possible Problems and Suggested Solutions

Most students cannot come up with words for the search engine. Give them more examples or have them try to think of helpful search words in groups.

Students have found information but cannot read it. Instead of conferring this week, spend time reading some of the information to the students.

Students have particularly difficult topics to research online. For example, one student wants to write to the mayor to ask him to put a stoplight at a dangerous intersection and another student is writing to her ballet teacher to ask her to consider putting the weaker student dancers closer to the mirror so that they can see themselves as they dance. Discuss other research methods like interviews, surveys, and questionnaires.

Follow-Up

Allow time for students to print, read, and highlight important information.

Let a student describe how she found useful information. For example, *I wasn't sure what websites to go to, so I started by putting these words into Google. That search didn't help me so then I. . . .* Ask students how listening to this student could help them with their research.

Questions to Ask Yourself When Doing Internet Research

1. Do I know any Internet websites that might have what I am looking for?

2. What words can I put into Google or some other search engine that will help me search for information on my subject?

   Key words related to the topic

   Research about/on [topic]

   A question about the topic

3. How can I change my key words to narrow the information that comes back?

Search Engines Especially for Kids

Askforkids.com   Thinkquest.org/library

Yahooligans.com   Google.com.Top.Kids

Kidsclick.org   Google.com.Top.Teens

Learning About Your Topic 3: Writing Strong Survey and Interview Questions

This lesson works particularly well if students have already had exposure to surveys and interviews. If most students have not had this experience, you may want to try this lesson in a student conference or with a small group of students before presenting it to the class.
Time: Forty minutes

Preparation

Copy Resource 3–13, Helpful Hints on Writing Survey and Interview Questions.
Copy Resource 3–14, Hockey Survey.

Minilesson

Some of you will find it helpful to conduct an interview or pass out a questionnaire as part of your research. [Define the words *interview* and *questionnaire* if needed.] *Today we'll talk about how to write good interview and survey questions. As we sometimes do, let's think about weak questions first—you know, questions that don't give us much information.*

Here's a question that I call the you-agree-with-me-right? question. Don't you think that the lunch menu should be changed? *This is a leading question. Here's another:* When you go to the movies, doesn't it bother you when people talk too much? *You'll want to stay away from these leading questions because you'll never know if people really agreed with you or if they politely agreed because they didn't think they had a choice.*

Here is another kind of question you'll want to stay away from. I call it the slip-in-more-than-one-question-at-a-time question: Do you like the food in the school cafeteria and would you like to have chicken? *This question is really two questions.*

A third kind of question that isn't very effective is the it-took-me-longer-to-ask-than-it-took-you-to-answer question. For example: Many people have favorite sports and favorite colors and lots of favorite things. What is your favorite color? *This question is long and contains information that is unimportant. Try to word your questions as directly and specifically as you can.*

Let's spend a few minutes looking at helpful hints on writing interview and survey questions. [Hand out Resource 3–13 and discuss.]

Now let's imagine that we want to survey students in the school to see if they think homework helps them learn the material they're taught in school. Talk to your writing partner and see if you can come up with a strong survey question on this topic. [Have a few students share. This is really difficult, so don't expect students to have great questions. The point is to show students how difficult and time consuming it is to write good questions.]

Today, spend a few minutes thinking about and making a short list of whom you might interview or survey to get information related to your persuasive writing topic. Some of you have topics that easily lend themselves to surveys and interviews. Others of you may have a harder time coming up with people to interview or ideas for a survey. But spend a few minutes thinking about these kinds of research in regard to your topic. [Select a student's persuasive topic and talk about what kind of survey or interview could be written for this topic.] *Remember that you should not interview or survey anyone without first getting my or your parents' or teacher's permission.*

Try working with a partner as your write your list.

Give students five to ten minutes to work together and to think of ways to incorporate surveys or interviews into their research. Then review with them what makes a good survey or interview question. Impress upon them that this is not an exact science but that some questions are more likely to lead to stronger answers with more usable information. Because some students will not find surveys or interviews relevant to their topics it is particularly important that students have a choice today about how they will use their writing. Some students will use the minilesson while others will do other kinds of research or even do more writing on their persuasive topics.

Share

If you've given some students the go-ahead to write a survey or interview, ask them to share their questions.

Possible Problem and Suggested Solution

Students would like to interview someone about their topic but are not sure how to find someone. Brainstorm as a class how to find someone to interview.

Follow-Up

If students spent a long time generating their lists and you did not get to talk about what makes a strong interview or survey, do a lesson on writing interview and survey questions during your next writing time.

Teach students how to imbed results of their research into their persuasive writing. Less is more here—one or two pieces of information is sufficient. Perhaps show students how to begin a paragraph with a fact or a statistic. (See the minilesson on leads, page 123).

Analyze and evaluate the hockey survey (Resource 3–14). What questions are particularly well written?

Helpful Hints on Writing Survey and Interview Questions

Survey Questions

1. Write easy-to-follow directions at the top of the page.

2. If possible, test the survey on two or three people before you distribute it. Make any necessary changes.

3. Keep it brief (three to five questions will usually give enough information).

4. Ask short, easy-to-understand questions.

5. Avoid leading questions.

Interview Questions

1. Write questions that get the interviewee to give lots of information.

2. Avoid leading questions.

3. Make this your last question: *Is there anything else on the subject that I haven't asked you about that you think is important to say?*

Hockey Survey
(for girls only)

Please return to Ms. Casey's room

Please circle the appropriate answers and take a moment to write comments.

Do you play hockey on a team? Why or why not?

_____

_____

If you don't play hockey on a team, why not?

_____

_____

Do you think that if you did play hockey on a team, you would enjoy it? Why or why not?

_____

_____

Would you say that hockey was encouraged, discouraged, or even discussed in your house when you were growing up?

_____

_____

Does anyone in your immediate family play hockey?   Yes   No

Thank you for your time.

Using Humor to Entertain and Persuade

This lesson is an invitation for students to try their hands at writing with humor. The lesson will not fit neatly into your current persuasive writing unit. In fact, it's likely to lead to chaos and possibly some awful writing. Are you ready to try it? Good!

The jury is still out on whether humor is an effective persuasive device. While some people think that humor persuades, others say that although humor may put readers in a better mood it doesn't help to convince the reader. Ask your students what they think.

One way to think about humor is as a kind of voice in writing. One of the things we can show children is to move out of their comfort zone and try a new voice. This lesson works particularly well with middle school students but has been done successfully with younger children, too. **Time:** Sixty minutes

Preparation

Before the lesson, have students read a humorous article like Dave Barry's essay "Science: It's Just Not Fair" and highlight parts they think are funny. (You can get this essay by searching the Internet. Dave Barry also has an article about frogs that works quite well.)
Have students read over and have in front of them a list of persuasive ideas. If you have done the Things That Bother Me in The World minilesson (page 44) make sure students have this list accessible.
Copy Resource 3–15, What's Funny?

Minilesson

Most of you have been writing about serious topics. [Name some.] *Persuasive writing is often, but not always, serious.* [If students are familiar with political cartoons, tell them that the humor in political cartoons is usually intended to be persuasive.]

Today we're going to switch gears and attempt to write with humor. Some of you may think that humor and persuasion don't go together, and of course they don't always make an effective combination. But one thing that is really interesting to me, and I hope to you too, is that funny and persuasive sometimes do go together. Just like any other technique in writing, a great way to learn how to do it is to first study a good example of that kind of writing and then practice it on your own.

We have all read and laughed at Dave Barry's science fair article. Before we talk about our own writing, let's spend a few minutes looking at and studying it together. I know the first time we read it, it made many of you smile and even laugh—so let's dig in to the text and try to figure out why.

Ask students to read sentences and words they find funny and talk about why. You may want to use the What's Funny? chart for this discussion (see Resource 3–15). Point out the persuasive techniques of exaggeration, comparison, and surprise.

Today we are going to think about persuasive topics we can write about with humor. This is difficult to do. Try it for the first ten minutes. If your writing seems to be going well, keep going! If not, you may want to stick with humor a bit longer and see what develops or you

may want to write something more serious. The point of this lesson is for you to think about humor today, tomorrow, or at some other time when you are writing and to be aware that this is a technique you can try.

To get started, reread your list of topics (or what you have written in your writer's notebook) and spend a few minutes thinking about how to approach that same topic with humor. [Have a few students share their ideas for topics.] *Go to work.*

Share

Ask volunteers to read funny lines from their own writing.

Lead a discussion about the process of writing something funny. What was difficult?

Possible Problem and Suggested Solution

Some students tried to write with humor but didn't succeed. This is perfectly understandable; after all, they didn't have much practice. The point of the lesson is exposure, not mastery.

Follow-Up

Pinpoint other funny parts in the Dave Barry article and try again.

Read humorous writing with your students—both persuasive and not persuasive. Examples include: "Letters from a Nut" by Ted L. Nancy; any and all Dave Barry articles.

Allow students to have more time to write with humor.

What's Funny?

Sometimes these things can be funny.

Exaggeration

Surprise

Funny comparisons

When the writer wrote . . .		*We thought it was funny because . . .*

Writing Quickly and Continuously to Find First Thoughts

Sometimes, with the best of intentions, we expect students to have big and brilliant thoughts right away. In this lesson, we show students how to write quickly and continuously without worrying about the quality of their ideas. Many writers use this free-writing technique in various stages of the writing process. Here, students have the opportunity to free write in order to figure out what they have to say about a particular persuasive topic. Suggested amounts of time to spend free writing:

Second grade: two or three minutes
Third and fourth grade: four to six minutes
Fifth and sixth grade: seven to ten minutes
Seventh grade: ten to fifteen minutes
Eighth grade: ten to twenty minutes

Time: Thirty minutes

Preparation

Copy and read the Rules for Free Writing (Resource 3–16).

Minilesson

Right before I fall asleep at night my mind likes to wander. I think about all sorts of things, like what I did during the day and what I will do tomorrow. Sometimes just as I'm about to drift off, a thought pops into my head out of nowhere. I might think about an old friend whom I haven't spoken to in years or something that happened a long time ago. I don't plan on thinking these things. I don't say to myself, Now I'm going to think about a friend I haven't thought of in years!

Today we are going to try a strategy called free writing. *In some ways it's like my thoughts just before I fall asleep because when you free write you don't think first and then write, you write almost as fast as the thoughts come to you. (Of course, when writers free write, they are wide awake!)*

When I free write, I try to get my mind to work quickly enough so that I don't have a chance to say things like, That's no good, *or,* Is that the correct spelling of that word? *The best part about free writing is that sometimes you discover thoughts you didn't even know you had. Often when you free write, you surprise yourself with what you say.*

Watch me as I free write. I will keep my pen moving and just keep going. Let's see if I write something that surprises me. [Demonstrate and discuss.]

Now let's go over some rules of free writing. [Review the rules.]

Okay, it's your turn. Write a word or two at the top of your page in order to remind yourself of your topic. I will time you. See if you can keep your pencil moving for the whole time. It's hard. Just do your best. Ready, set, begin.

Share

Ask students, *What did you write that surprised you? How did it feel to free write like this?*

Possible Problems and Suggested Solutions

Students are embarrassed by the way their writing looks. It's messy or there are words spelled incorrectly and they find this troublesome. Reassure them that this writing will not be graded. Also assure them that in this case, messy writing shows evidence of thinking quickly, which is exactly what they were supposed to be doing.

Although you just taught a lesson on free writing, it seems as though nobody actually free wrote! Students wrote slowly and censored their words as they wrote. If this happens, try this lesson again. It may be difficult for some students who are overly conscious of spelling and "making it right" to get the hang of free writing. Try again.

Follow-Up

Once students have a persuasive topic, ask them to free write in order to develop their ideas.

---

1. Try to write for the whole time. If you need to stop, that's okay, but begin again as soon as you can.

2. Don't erase—spelling and handwriting don't count. Remember, this is not a final copy!

3. You don't have to reread what you've written as you are writing. Rereading takes time and we want to *write* as much as we can. This is one of the few times you don't have to reread your writing.

Resource 3–16 *Rules for Free Writing*

When Deception Meets Persuasion

Four out five students who participate in this lesson score higher on state math tests. (Now that's deception!) In this lesson, students learn about deceptive advertising. If your class is studying another kind of persuasive writing, help students see that deception occurs in all kinds of persuasive writing. **Time:** Sixty minutes

Preparation

Copy Resource 3–17, When Deception Meets Persuasion.

Copy Resource 3–18, Ways Persuasive Writing Can Be Deceptive.

Find information on deceptive advertising by using these key words on a search engine like Google: *FTC deceptive advertising* or *FTC vs.* (FTC stands for Federal Trade Commission).

As I write this, there are deceptive advertising cases against Hasbro, New Balance, Apple, Bumblebee Tuna, and Blockbuster, so if you put any of these company names into a search engine along with the words *deceptive advertising* you will find information on these cases.

Minilesson

Here is a copy of a print advertisement written by a seventh grader. There is something fishy—something not quite right—about this advertisement, and it has to do with the amount of money the customer will pay for this cell phone service. Look carefully. [Read the ad and help students identify the part that is deceptive.]

This writing is deceptive. Deceptive is an adjective that means something is meant to fool someone. [Write the word and the definition so students can see it.] *Persuasive writing can be deceptive in many ways. Let's look at just a few.* [Read the Resource titled Ways Persuasive Writing Can Be Deceptive.]

Unfortunately, there are many examples of deception in advertising and in other types of persuasive writing. In our own writing we will work hard to make a strong case, but we will also work to make sure that we are not deceptive. [Discuss current FTC cases or show students an example of deceptive advertising from the Internet.] *For your writing assignment today, I'd like you to create a deceptive advertisement.*

Share

Have students share their deceptive advertisements. In what ways are they deceptive?

Possible Problem and Suggested Solution

Students see every persuasive technique as deceptive. Review the definition of the word *deceptive* and discuss what is deceptive and what is persuasive. Sometimes there is a fine line between the two.

Follow-Up

Study court cases of deceptive advertising (use a search engine and enter the words *FTC sues*).

Create a bulletin board with the heading Deceptive or Not? Ask students to bring in advertisements that they suspect are deceptive and look at one every day at the beginning of writing workshop.

Discuss deception in other types of persuasive writing. For example, using misleading statistics in an editorial is deceptive. Al Gore has been accused of misleading the public about global warning by inflating statistics. Have your students discuss this. Is this deceptive?

While students research their persuasive topics, have them ask themselves, *Does any part of this research feel deceptive?* Have them share what they have found and ask the class to help determine whether the research is deceptive.

Go a step further! Show examples of propaganda (this concept is especially appropriate for a social studies class). Help students see that propaganda is the ultimate form of deception. What are the differences between these two words?

Resource 3–17

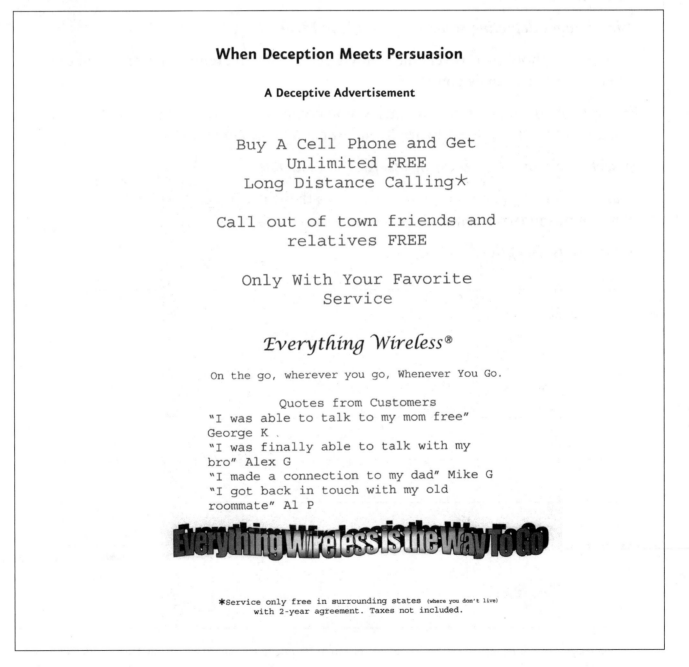

Ways Persuasive Writing Can Be Deceptive

Using words or phrases that make the reader think that something is true when it's not.

Example: An advertisement says by switching to a particular cell phone company you will get a free phone, when you actually have to purchase two phones to get the third one free.

Using images depicting something that is not true.

Example: A photo in a travel guide shows people playing tennis at a resort where there aren't any tennis courts.

Example: A toy action figure in a television commercial does things [like flying or making noise or standing by itself] that it cannot actually do.

Making a claim on the basis of insufficient evidence.

Example: A diet-pill manufacturer advertises that their product will help you lose ten pounds in two weeks.

What else is deceptive?

_____

_____

_____

_____

_____

_____

_____

Minilessons for Selecting and Developing Ideas for Persuasive Writing

When Selecting a Persuasive Topic . . .

. . . students reexamine their ideas for persuasive writing and ask themselves, *What topic really strikes a chord with me?*

When Developing a Persuasive Topic . . .

. . . students write more and more about their topic in order to figure out what they want to say. Students read through what they have written and often change their focus or narrow their topics. Students develop their ideas by:

1. Reading about and researching their topic ideas.
2. Writing a working thesis or position statement and creating an argument.
3. Beginning to figure out what evidence to use to support their argument.
4. Thinking more about their audience and how that audience will respond to particular examples and reasons.

Developing a persuasive text is best done through research, writing, and of course, discussion.

Helping Students Select and Develop Persuasive Topics

It is our job to help students select *good* ideas about which they are *passionate*. (They don't want to write about a topic that leaves them cold, and truthfully, we don't want to read the results if they do.) Almost as important as passion is knowledge of the subject. Students may research their topics to learn more, but they will be more likely to write well if they already know something about the topic and don't need to rely on research.

Whether students know about the issue is difficult to assess. Anyone who has ever met a teenager knows that knowing a subject and having strong opinions about it are not the same. This is also somewhat true for younger children. Raising the driving age? It's bad. Why? My older brother said so. The United States should pull out of the war in Iraq! Why? My parents think so. The United States needs to stay the course in Iraq. Why? I heard it on the radio. You get the idea. If students don't know about the topic, they will have a hard time elaborating. When this happens, their writing is vague and underdeveloped. It's hard to get students to write more when they simply don't know any more. In their effort to elaborate, they repeat themselves.

So here's a good rule for us to teach students when it comes to selecting a topic for persuasive writing: *Write about a subject if they know more than a little something about it. This is not the time to learn about a subject of interest.* We have to teach this to students explicitly if we want them to be able to elaborate on their ideas. As we help them select a topic, we should ask ourselves, *Do I think this will be a topic that I can help this student write about?* You don't have to know about the topic, but you need evidence that they do.

The topic students pick will need to be developed. However, to speak of *developing* persuasive writing is perhaps misleading. The word makes us think students are enlarging and expanding their topics. In fact, they are often doing the opposite—narrowing their topic or taking a stance on it.

Teaching students to narrow their ideas is the hardest part of teaching persuasive writing. It will take more than one minilesson to show students *how* to make their topics smaller. Thinking, writing, and researching before beginning a draft will often mean the difference between a vague persuasive paper and a clear, fresh persuasive piece that has something real to say. "Recycling is good" may be an acceptable way to *begin* a persuasive piece on recycling, but it's not a good thesis statement for a finished editorial. If students are taught how to develop initial ideas about recycling, they may end up with any one of the following stronger articles such as:

The Right Ways to Get the Average Household to Recycle
Stiff Fines Are Needed for Those Who Don't Recycle
Recycling Has to Be Made Easier or We Just Won't Do It!
The Key to Living Greener Is Reusing

You Can't Change Your Mind Now!

It is bound to happen.

It happened to me in my third year of teaching. Emily came in to class one morning and announced that she had changed her mind. She had always been against single-sex education but as she read about it, she began to think that single-gender classes were a good idea. How was I to respond? She had written so much against single-sex education already. She had great reasons why it was a bad idea and educationally unsound. "Hmm," was all I could muster.

So I did what any self-respecting (and desperate) teacher would do. I tried to convince her that her *first* position on the subject was the right position. I told her she had already done all the work on that position and she couldn't change her mind now. "Don't you want me to write what I really believe?" she asked me. *Not really,* I thought, *I just want you to be finished!* Although I was thrilled that she had done enough research, writing, and reflection to change her mind, I wasn't sure how to handle this change of position. And we were just about to start drafting!

In the end, Emily persuaded me to let her change her position on her topic. She worked hard on her writing and was ready to draft with the rest of the class. She wrote an editorial that was pro single-sex education for elementary students. As you might expect, she did a particularly good job considering and dismissing the counterargument. If a scenario like this comes up in your classroom, I suggest you:

1. Ask these students to write two shorter persuasive pieces instead of one longer piece. Have them take different points of view for each piece.
2. Ask students to use what they have written to help them write the other side of the argument.
3. Ask students to narrow their topic in order to be able to write a thesis statement that is somewhat aligned with their first belief. For example, if a student wrote that schools should eliminate homework, she could argue that there is too much homework in schools today and that it serves little educational purpose.

Remember that although the words *I changed my mind* may grate on our nerves, they do show evidence of thoughtful learners and isn't this what we strive for?

To Research or Not to Research, That Is the Question

Ask three teachers about the role of research in persuasive writing and you are likely to get three very different answers. Teacher 1 may say, *Research is essential. How can you write persuasively without knowing the facts about the subject?* Teacher 2 may say, *Research is important and helpful, but not essential.* Teacher 3 may say, *Research is a distraction. If students take the time to research, they won't be able to allot enough time or energy to writing.* Who is right? Everyone.

In the world outside of school, most persuasive writers think of research as one of the ways to build a strong argument. Research is the beginning, the middle, and the end to writing good ad copy. You have to know your audience and you have to know your product. You have to study your product and find out everything about it. Then and only then can you convince the audience to buy it.

In school, though, we have a limited amount of time and we can't always (or ever, for that matter) teach each subject for as long as we want. We know that the more teaching we try to squeeze into one unit, the less students learn.

Research is a valuable process and a great tool. Under certain conditions research adds to the study of persuasive writing. Under other conditions it can make studying persuasive writing more difficult. Perhaps the question is not whether to research but under what conditions research is useful. The following are some helpful rules of thumb.

Include research in your persuasive writing unit if:

- The unit is more than three weeks long, so students will have enough time to learn about the process of research and begin to conduct research with your support.
- The research part of the unit matches students' abilities as readers, writers, and recorders of information.
- Students understand the purpose of research and have done research before *or* they know how to paraphrase information.
- The process of research is valued over the product—in other words, there is no pressure to find a particular number of facts to stick into the persuasive article. (When a specific number of facts is required, the quality of the writing diminishes.)

Predictable Problems and Possible Solutions
When Selecting and Developing Persuasive Topics

Problem	Solution
Some students cannot articulate why they have selected their topic.	Try having them write the answer to this question: *Who do you think your audience might be and how do you hope they will react?*
Students can only find one reason or example to support their argument.	Ask the students to informally research additional examples or supporting evidence (see the research minilessons in Chapter 3). Also teach students to stretch a position or concept by using the word *imagine*.
Students' writing is underdeveloped: *The first reason is _____ and the second reason is _____.*	Ask students to take each reason and put it at the top of a new sheet of paper. Then teach them how to expand their ideas by giving examples and using imagery.
Some students have given general, generic answers: *I chose it because it is interesting to me . . .*	Help them give a more elaborate answer by asking questions such as, *Is there a reason this is important to you right now?*
One or two extremely disorganized writers tend to write about more than one idea at a time: *First this, then this, then back to this.*	Help these students organize their writing before they begin. Help them jot down key words so they will remember what they will write in each section. For example: *First, talking in the movies and why it's wrong. Then, why talkers talk during the movies. Finally, a call to action (or in this case, a plea for silence).*
Students' thesis statements are still weak.	This is usually true because the thesis statement is too vague or the topic is not controversial. Show the students other ways to write the thesis statement where a "reasonable person" could disagree.

Goal

To help students evaluate their persuasive ideas and determine which to continue working on

Most students will select only one topic to develop further, but there may be a handful who select two topics because they're not sure which one they want to pursue. Also, some students may select a topic related to but not the same as one they have previously explored. (For example, *a letter to my mom about buying healthier food* may become *we should make better decisions about what we eat as a family*.) **Time:** Forty minutes.

Preparation

Select a student to help you with this lesson and explain what the lesson is about. Then skim the student's notebook entries and quickly talk with the student about which entries she might like to work on and develop into a finished piece of writing. Follow the same procedure as you would in the lesson, giving each entry a yes, no, or maybe and telling why. Then replay this conversation for the class during the minilesson. (See Resource 4–1 for an example.)

Minilesson

You have been collecting persuasive ideas for some time now. Today you're going to think about what idea you will stick with and draft and develop into a finished piece of writing. Making this decision requires a lot of thought. This isn't a pin-the-tail-on-the-donkey decision where you close your eyes pick a topic at random. This is more like playing chess—spending time thinking and making very purposeful choices. Let me show you what I mean. For the next few minutes we'll watch and listen as [student's name] thinks aloud about what he has written and what idea is worth developing. What things does he consider when selecting his topic?

[Read the beginning of a number of the student's notebook entries and guide him as he talks about each one (*This is not a good one to develop because I don't really know much about the subject*, etc.).] *Here are some questions you might ask yourself as you choose your own topic:*

- *Am I excited to write about this topic?*
- *Do I have enough to say about this topic?*
- *What might I say? (This is a really important question and one that we don't usually ask ourselves when we write narrative, especially personal narrative.)*
- *Will this topic be easy or hard for me to write about? Or will it be somewhere in between?*

If more examples are needed because your students have not done this work before, read Resource 4–1, Excerpts from Kevin's Thinking About Possible Topics, to help you.

Share

Ask a few students to tell what topics they are developing and why.

Have a few students share what topics they will not use and why.

Encourage a few students to talk about what they might say about their topic.

Possible Problems and Suggested Solutions

Students are selecting topics that are too broad. Ask students to talk about how they might narrow their topic (but remember that narrowing will be a big part of what students do when they develop their ideas).

Students have great topics on their list of possibilities but select the not-so-great ones. This is so difficult—but if the deal is selecting their own topics, you have to let them do so. (In a few instances, you may have a hunch that a particular topic is a good one because the student has a fresh perspective. You might suggest that these few students develop more than one topic and see how each one goes.)

Follow-Up

Have students talk with one another about their possible topics.

On a chart or a bulletin board, list possible student topics. Give students time to read the list and see what other students are writing about. They may be able to offer advice on arguments related to a topic or have quick conversations with students with related topics about what they might write.

Resource 4–1 *Excerpts from Kevin's Thinking About Possible Topics*

"Nascar makes me mad. The race car drivers only care about their own fame and not at all about the environment."
Not a good topic, because I don't really know much about it and I don't care so much about it.

"Yesterday we missed recess with our substitute teacher and it made me mad."
It doesn't usually happen and it's not really a problem, so why write about it?

"Judy Blume is right about the Harry Potter books."
I am sick of this topic.

"There should be a light at the corner of Bell Road and Medlock Bridge Road."
This is a maybe, because I do have enough to say about it and I feel strongly about it.

Teacher: Well if you wrote about this topic, what would you say? How would that writing go?
I would say that my brother nearly got into an accident at that intersection because he was waiting and waiting for all of the cars to pass. We waited for so long and then we had to go so we went, and out of nowhere a car came speeding toward us. I would also say that nobody wants to take that road because it's so dangerous; they all go the other way, and nobody ever shops in that shopping center. I really think that this should be my topic, because it is the one I like the most.

Writing a Thesis Statement

Some kinds of persuasive writing have thesis statements while other types don't require a thesis. Persuasive letters, editorials, and any kind of argumentative essay (usually taught in middle school) always have a thesis. Advertisements, editorial cartoons, and public service announcements may or may not embody a thesis statement.

Do this lesson after students have had some time to develop their ideas. In this lesson, students experiment with writing a *tentative* or *working thesis*. A final thesis is the result of a lengthy thought process. It is likely that students will refine their thesis statements at least once (and sometimes more than once) as they research and plan their persuasive pieces.
Time: Fifty minutes

Preparation

Before the lesson, ask students to read "Kids in Training" in the Appendix.
Copy Resource 4–2, Helpful Hints for Writing Thesis Statements and Resource 4–3, Experimenting with Thesis Statements.

Minilesson

Skim and summarize the article, "Kids in Training," page 217. Consider, *What does this article argue?*

Today we are going to talk about what your persuasive writing will argue. When authors write persuasively, they often ask themselves, What am I for or against? *They then try to write a sentence or two that helps them figure out exactly what they are trying to say. This is different from other kinds of writing because the author is not asking,* What can I tell them all about? *as if he or she were writing a book that is all about cats or all about being an older brother. Instead authors of persuasive writing often ask themselves,* What do I want readers to know, believe, or understand?

Today you will work on writing thesis statements. These statements are one sentence and try to help you figure out exactly what you are arguing for or against. The author of "Kids in Training" wrote and rewrote her thesis statement many times before she figured out exactly what her essay was about. Let's look together at the resource page for this lesson and review some helpful hints when writing thesis statements. (Then in a few minutes, we'll see if we can figure out what the thesis statement might have been for the article, "Kids in Training".) [Hand out and review Helpful Hints for Writing Thesis Statements.] *Now watch me as I think about the thesis statement for the "Kids in Training" article.*

Competition in sports is bad. *No, that's not a good statement, because it's too general.*
Sports should be competitive. *That doesn't really say it because the author doesn't say that sports should or should not be competitive, just that they may be too competitive right now.*
Parents should stop being so pushy. *The word* parents *is good, because it's more specific than just saying* people *but it still doesn't have the right words. That statement doesn't have the word* competition *or the word* sports.

Using some or all of these words parents, sports, competition, *let's see if we can come up with a thesis statement for this article. Turn to your partner and try to work this out together. Try to use the word* should *in your statement like this:* Parents should *or* competition should . . .

Today you will experiment writing working or tentative thesis statements. As we keep thinking and writing, it is likely that your thesis statements will change. Start today by rereading what you have written about your topic and then try your hand at writing thesis statements. Don't just go with the first statement that comes into your head. Work on refining your thesis. Some of you may want to work in partnerships today and think aloud with your partner. Okay, go to it.

Share   Instead of a share time today, you may want to spend more time writing and conferring. Conferring with small groups works very well because students can listen in to what you are saying to other students and because the whole group can think together about one person's thesis.

Possible Problem and Suggested Solution

Thesis statements are weak! Do this lesson again.

Follow-Up

Do follow-up lessons to this lesson. In the next few lessons on thesis statements, show students how a strong thesis usually answers these questions: *How? Why?* and *So, what?*

Give students examples of strong thesis statements. Use a search engine and type in persuasive writing thesis statements. Then ask students why these statements are well written.

Use Resource 4–3, Experimenting with Thesis Statements, for follow-up lessons or share it with students as you confer.

Helpful Hints for Writing Thesis Statements

1. Does it focus on a single topic?

2. Does the topic have more than one reasonable answer?

3. Does it convey specific information instead of being general or vague?

4. Does it reveal your stance or opinion on the subject?

Which of the statements below have all four qualities listed above? Which are good examples of thesis statements? How can these thesis statements be rewritten to be stronger?

- Drugs are bad.

- Children today are badly behaved because their parents want to be their friends, not their parents.

- Recycling is very important.

- Elementary schools need to teach more.

Experimenting with Thesis Statements

A thesis statement is _____.

Sometimes when we begin to think about writing an editorial, we have a topic but not a thesis statement. Also, it's often helpful to experiment with more than one thesis statement for a chosen topic. Writing and selecting a thesis statement helps us narrow or figure out the slant of an editorial. As you can see below, the possible thesis statements for an editorial about homework really changes the slant of the piece. Talk or write about what information you would expect to find for each thesis statement. What statement would you use in order to help build your argument? Why?

Topic: homework

Possible thesis statements/questions:

The kind of homework given in school is not only useless but dangerous.

More homework is not better homework.

More and more homework in school makes no sense.

When is too much of a good thing no good?

Pouring over books is good, but at what cost?

Do the ends justify the means?

Homework is not a necessary part of education.

Kids have time to be kids *only* after the mounds of homework are done.

All Reasons Are Not Created Equal

Strong persuasive writing should have a strong argument and equally strong reasons that support the argument.

Sixty minutes is the ideal amount of time for this lesson. If this is not possible, this lesson can be divided into two sessions presented on consecutive days.

Preparation

Select a student to participate in a role play. Explain the scenario and show the student a copy of Resource 4–4 so she can get an idea of the kind of reasons she can use. Take a minute or two to practice the role play before doing it in front of the class. The student won't have to rehearse or learn any lines, just make sure that she understands her role and the point of the lesson.

Minilesson

In persuasive writing, we give the reader reasons why what we're saying is true. Good reasons can make our argument stronger. But some reasons are better than others. In other words, all reasons are not created equal. There are certainly bad reasons that just won't help you prove your point. For example, if you are arguing for less homework and you say that less homework is good because lots of other schools don't have as much homework. That is a weak reason. Usually as a persuasive author we'll be choosing between a good reason and a great one. What makes the difference?

You are designing an advertisement for a new car that you think is great. You have to give the consumer reasons why he or she should buy the car. You write that this car has more comfortable back seats. Is this a good reason? Turn and talk to your neighbor and decide. [Let one or two students share their ideas.]

That was a trick question. We don't really know if it's a good reason. Why? Because whether the reason is good or not depends on the audience—what they believe and what they value and want from, in this case, a car. If I believe that the back seats in my car are fine already, then this reason is not persuasive. When selecting reasons, let's ask ourselves this question: Of all of the reasons I could give, which ones are great? Which ones are likely to convince the reader to see it my way?

Today we are going to do a role play. I will be the mother and [student's name] will be my child. [Student's name] desperately wants macaroni and cheese for dinner. Our conversation is just beginning. Listen carefully to the reasons [student's name] gives to support her or his argument about wanting mac and cheese. Decide which reasons are not good, good, or very good.

Role play the scene. Stop occasionally and ask, *What reason did [student's name] just give to support her or his argument? How good was that reason?* Have a miniconversation (not more than a minute and a half!) about the quality of each reason.

Ask, *What else could [student's name] say?* Then have the child try what the other students suggest.

During the role play, create a chart like the one on the Resource page. (The specifics of the chart will differ depending on the ideas students contribute.)

When the role play is over ask, *What did you learn from the reasons in the role play that you can take back to your writing today?*

When you go back to your writing today knowing what you now know about reasons, you will want to look at the reasons you have already written and decide whether you think they are not so good, good, or very good. You will also want to think of new reasons and then decide how good the new reasons are. One way is to make a quick chart in your notebook like the one we created in class.

Share

Have students share their thinking about their reasons. What reasons are not good? Which ones seem good?

Possible Problem and Suggested Solution

Looking at their reasons, students (or you) realize they do not have a clear argument. Help them with their argument—it usually needs to be narrowed—and then ask them to go back and write reasons.

Follow-Up

Have a student take a bad reason and talk with a partner about why that reason is not a good one.

When revising a persuasive text students have seen before, project a transparency of the text and use two different-color highlighters to show what part of the text is argument and what part is reason and example. Talk about the balance of opinion and example in persuasive text. Ask students what they need to add to make their work more balanced.

My Mother [or Father] Should Make Macaroni and Cheese for Dinner	
Bad Reasons *(probably won't work for the reader)*	*Good Reasons* *(likely to work for the reader)*
I like it.	Cheese is good for me. It gives me calcium and protein.
It tastes good.	Milk is good for me. It makes my bones stronger.
I am a good listener and I should get what I want.	It's fast and easy to make; you'll have more free time.
	Dinner will take less time to prepare so we'll be able to spend more time together.

Resource 4–4

Using Precise Words and Phrases

This lesson looks at evaluative words and phrases. Students are prone to vagueness and to extremes. It's good or it's bad. It's right or it's wrong. In this lesson, students learn to ask themselves a specific question that will help them write more precisely. (What question? Read on and find out.) **Time:** Forty minutes

Preparation

Copy Resource 4–5, Examples of General Evaluative Words.

Minilesson

Listen to this conversation:

That movie was bad.
I know, I thought so too.
It made me so upset. I hated to watch it.
That's not why it was bad. The script was awful. It was really hard to believe.

Have you ever come out of a movie and thought it was bad? If I think a movie is bad and you think a movie is bad, do we agree that it is bad for the same reasons?

Certain words are not specific enough. In other words, they don't say what we want them to say. Let's think about that for a minute. If we say that a movie is bad, we could mean many different things. What are a few of them? [Take quick student suggestions.]

What if we say a particular candidate would make a good president? What do we mean by good? *Well, we could mean* honest, trustworthy, *or* hardworking. *We could mean that he speaks well or that he has started great programs that have helped the homeless in this country or that he has helped bring peace to the world.*

Often when we write persuasively we want to take general evaluative words like good *and* bad *out of the text and replace them with more specific information. To do that, ask yourself this question:* In what way? *When you say that a presidential candidate is good, ask yourself,* In what way? *When you say that a movie is bad, ask yourself,* In what way? *When you say that wind energy is good for the environment, ask yourself,* In what way?

As you write today, think about the words you're selecting and find places where you can use more precise language. If you find a place to write more precisely, do it. Then read the sentence both ways to see which wording is better. There may be times when the general word is better than the precise word; times when both the general and the precise word are appropriate; and as we just said, times when you'll want to use only the precise word. When we come back and share, let's talk about how you experimented with word choice and the decisions you made regarding evaluative words. Let's get to work.

If time allows, use Resource 4–5, Examples of General Evaluative Words and have students come up with alternative sentences using more precise words.

Share

Ask volunteers to share how they used more precise language in their writing.

Possible Problems

None.

Follow-Up

Give students time to work together in pairs and to rewrite the example sentences in more than one way. Encourage students to play with words; it will help students later on when they revise.

Good

He would make a good president.
It would be good if our family grew a vegetable garden.

Bad

Homework is a bad idea.
Curse words are bad.

Right

There is a right way to get people to believe what you say.

Wrong

The death penalty is wrong.

Resource 4–5 *Examples of General Evaluative Words*

Loaded Language:
Positive, Neutral, and Negative Words

In this lesson, students explore which words have negative or positive connotations. **Time:** Forty minutes

Preparation

Use the words in Resource 4–6 and any other words you have found in your persuasive pieces and create a chart titled Loaded Language.

Minilesson

The words we use to describe something can make a big difference in how readers view the topic. Persuasive writers know this, so they choose their words very carefully in order to influence how the reader feels, what they believe, and how they act.

Let me give you an example. I saw an advertisement the other day that said that if you enter into a two-year agreement with a particular cell phone company, you'll get a cell phone for only $12.99. Wow, that seemed like a good deal. (And maybe it is.)

But I started to think about the word agreement *and the idea of entering into a two-year agreement. The word* agreement *has a positive feel to it. After all, it's nice to agree. When I agree with someone, there is no problem between us. Agreeing is good. But in this case, the company used the word* agreement *as a synonym for the word* contract. *A contract is a legal document. I am leery of the word* contract. *When I hear the word* contract *I stop and think. I listen carefully. Do I want to have a contract?* I think to myself. *Can you see how different words create a different feeling in us? Let's look at some other words.* [Refer to Resource 4–6, Loaded Language. If students have done a great deal of writing, ask them to reread their work and talk about some of the word choices they made. If they haven't written much yet, skip this part of the lesson. The last thing you want to do is to waste time asking students to look for something that isn't in their writing!]

Today, while you are writing, think about the language you use. How can words create a positive, negative, or a neutral feeling in the reader? Try to use different words that help the reader feel positive or negative about the topic.

Share

Read your writing to your partner.

Possible Problems

Usually none.

Follow-Up

Ask students to look at advertisements and find words that elicit emotions.

Create a loaded-words chart that students can add to as they write. These words can be their own words or words they find as they read persuasive writing.

Invite a persuasive writer to speak to the class—an editorialist, a lawyer, a grant writer, a speechwriter, a book reviewer, a critic, a fundraiser, a publicist, a marketing manager, etc.

Ask parents to visit the class and discuss how persuasion and word choice play a part in their job. If parents are unable to visit in person, ask them to write a quick note about how they use words in their job; read it before the minilesson or turn the information in the note into a minilesson.

Preowned versus *used*

Limited edition

Deaths versus *casualties*

Agreement versus *contract*

Spend time versus *waste time*

Life insurance versus *death insurance*

Resource 4–6 *Loaded Language*

Some Might Think: How to Write Counterarguments

Before doing this lesson, ask students to spend time thinking and writing about "what someone who disagrees might say about their opinion." Teach them how to consider the counterargument.

This lesson shows students a way to write a counterarguments. Define a counterargument as *the other side* or the *I don't-agree-with-you-and-here's-why statement*. Persuasive writing often considers the counterargument and tells why it's wrong. For example, *Some of you might think that a stop sign at the corner of Peachtree and Bell Road is a good idea, but in actuality a stop sign would make this intersection more dangerous.*

How do writers determine whether they will present counterargument? Counterarguments should be presented when the reader is likely to find this point of view noticeably absent. In other words, if the reader can easily argue the other side, the author would do well to argue it, too. **Time:** Forty minutes

Preparation

Copy the article "Kids in Training" from the Appendix.
Copy Resource 4–7, Presenting a Counterargument.

Minilesson

In the (reading) discussions you have in class, you don't always agree with each other. In fact, there are times when your opinion is the exact opposite of someone else's in your group. [Give examples from your classroom.]

When writing persuasively, an author sometimes chooses to present the other side of the argument and tell why it's wrong. This is called the counterargument. It's as if the author is saying, now some people think this, but let me tell you why that is wrong. Sometimes authors write a sentence or two of counterargument, sometimes a paragraph or more.

If you were writing about why vending machines that sell junk food should be removed from all schools, you might say that access to more and more bad foods contributes to American kids becoming unhealthy. In order to write the counterargument you must consider what the other side might think. Someone who disagreed might think that junk food is not the problem, after all junk food has been around for a long time. The problem is that we do not do a good enough job teaching kids how to make good food choices. So, if you don't know it already, you should try and figure out the other side (or other sides, because there could be more than one) of the argument.

In order to present the counterargument, it helps to know three things:

1. *How to begin your counterargument.*
2. *How to write the counterargument in a way that leads the reader to realize that the other position is not as reasonable as yours.*
3. *Where in your writing to place your counterargument.*

Let's look at the "Kids in Training" article. [If the students have read the article prior to today's lesson, quickly summarize the article by saying, *Remember that this article is about . . .* and then show students where the counterargument appears.] *Notice how the author introduces the counterargument. She writes,* I can hear the critics now. *Counterarguments can begin in many different ways. We will look at that shortly.*

What does the author say that convinces the reader that the other argument is not a good one? [Read the last two paragraphs of the article aloud.]

In this article, the counterargument begins three-quarters of the way through the writing. The author has made her point and given examples and then toward the end she deals with the other side. It is common to find that counterarguments begin at least halfway through the persuasive writing or speech. Why is this case? Usually it's a matter of timing. Authors think it's important to share their ideas and make their case before they tell the reader why opposing ideas are faulty. Their case comes first simply because it's most important. Let's look at ways a counterargument can be introduced. [Hand out Resource 4–7, Presenting a Counterargument, and briefly discuss these ideas.]

Today, I would like you to write the other side of the argument for your issue. In your final piece of writing you may or may not include opposing viewpoints, but it is important to know what the opposing views are and how you would answer a question that begins like this, But what about. . . . ?

Turn and talk to your writing partner and tell him or her how you might present the counterargument for your topic. What would your first sentence be? You can select one of the sentences on the resource sheet or use your own way to begin. [Solicit one or two examples.]

Today, we'll work on counterargument. We'll try to write about the counterargument for at least one paragraph (or longer) even though in your actual writing you may not write about it for that long. Go for it.

Share

Ask students to read their counterargument to their writing partner and discuss where in the text they could place it.

Read *The Cat in the Hat* and discuss the fish's counterargument. How could he have made it stronger?

Possible Problem and Suggested Solution

Students write a counterargument that is stronger than their argument. Talk with the student about building the argument more strongly and perhaps leaving the counterargument out or even making the counterargument the argument.

Follow-Up

Read *The Cat in the Hat* aloud and discuss the fish's counterargument about playing in the house. The Cat is all for it and the fish is against it. What is the fish's counterargument and how could he have improved it?

Create a two-tiered chart. In one column, write the argument; on the other side, write counterargument. Summarize the points and counterpoints of the persuasive argument your class has read.

Reread other persuasive texts with counterarguments and talk about where they are placed.

Presenting a Counterargument

Authors often decide to include a counterargument to show the reader that they have considered the opposing view. Including a counterargument helps the reader say, "The author has considered both sides and has chosen this one."

Turn against your argument for only a short time and then turn back to your original argument.

How to introduce the counterargument:

It might seem that . . .

Some might think . . .

Of course . . .

But why . . .

But how about . . .

But what about . . .

How to tell why the counterargument is wrong:

But . . .

Yet . . .

However . . .

Still though . . .

Examples we have found of counterargument:

Rhetorical Questions: Statements in Disguise

In this lesson, students learn about rhetorical questions and how to use them. These questions can make the writing more interesting and vary its rhythm. **Time:** Forty minutes

Preparation

Copy Resource 4–8, Examples of Rhetorical Questions.

Minilesson

Usually when you're speaking to someone and you ask a question, it's because you want an answer. What time is it? Do you think the president is doing a good job? *and* What road should we take to drive to Aunt Betty's house? *are all questions we might ask in order to get information.*

In persuasive writing, we sometimes ask the reader questions but don't expect an answer! (You will see this technique in other kinds of writing, too.) One kind of question that does not require an answer is a rhetorical question. A rhetorical question requires no answer because the answer is obvious or expected.

Writers use rhetorical questions to address readers directly, when in fact, the writers are just making a point—in much the same way as they would if they were making a statement. Let's look at examples of rhetorical questions. [Read Resource 4–8.]

Take a few minutes to read over your notebook writing. See if you can find a statement that could be written as a rhetorical question. [Allow two or three minutes for students to look over their writing. Have a few students share their thoughts. As students try out their ideas, help them extend their thinking: *Yes, that might work as a rhetorical question at the beginning of a paragraph and then you could say. . . . That's a question, but not exactly a rhetorical question because. . . . What if you changed that question a little and said. . . .*]

As you write today, see if you can slip in a rhetorical question or two. Here's a hint: The easiest place to try this is the first or the last sentence of a paragraph. When we come back and share, some of you who have tried this technique will share and we'll see if the rhetorical question makes the writing more persuasive, less persuasive, or if just keeps it at the same level of persuasion. Good luck. Work hard!

Share

Ask students to read their rhetorical questions.

Possible Problems and Suggested Solutions

Students write rhetorical questions that make the writing sound awkward. This is okay. When students try out persuasive techniques as they develop their ideas, they aren't locked in to anything. This is not a finished draft.

Students write questions but they aren't rhetorical questions. This is to be expected. Let students share their questions and then try to label the kind of question. For example, *That was a great question but I might call that a surprise question or a what-do-you-think question,* etc.

Follow-Up

Ask students to look for rhetorical questions in advertisements. (This is a popular advertising technique.) Examples include:

- Do you want to be more beautiful?
- Would you like to go on a family vacation you'll always remember?

Thoughout the unit, have students identify rhetorical questions and rewrite or restate these questions as statements.

Examples of Rhetorical Questions

Wouldn't you like to know how to . . .

- Make a great first (or last) impression?
- Write a letter that gets results?
- Get people to cooperate with you?
- Win people over to your way of thinking?

If you said yes to any of those questions, then this might be the most important unit you've ever studied.

Looking for a New Year's celebration to remember? Come to Hamington Forest . . .

Don't we all want our children to be the best on the team?

How can we expect to enjoy the scenery when all we can see for miles are garbage dumpsters?

Can you believe how hot it is today?

Challenge:

Can you restate these rhetorical questions so they are statements?

May I Ask You a Question?

In this lesson, students read and write questions. **Time:** Fifty minutes

Preparation
Copy Resource 4–9 and "Tonight At . . . " in the Appendix. (Have students read this article prior to the lesson.)
Give out highlighters.

Minilesson

When we look at "Tonight At . . . " by Carol Herson, one of the first things we notice is her use of questions. She asks the reader many questions in her writing and she does it intentionally. Why do authors ask questions in their writing?

Some authors ask questions because they want to give the reader information *like this: Would you really buy a PC if you could get a Mac for a lower price, which has a lifetime warrantee, built-in webcam, and a free high-speed Internet cartridge?*

Sometimes writers ask hypothetical questions that start with the words what if *like this: What if you could get a computer cheaper than a PC? What if you could get a computer with a built-in webcam? What if that computer had a guaranteed lifetime warrantee? Now you can . . . Mac book.*

[Ask students to highlight the questions in "Tonight At . . . " and use Resource 4–9, May I Ask You a Question, to guide your discussion about why Carol wrote each question.]

Now let's quickly try asking these kinds of questions with your writing: Turn and talk with your partner about what question you could ask in order to give readers information on your topic. Turn and talk with your partner about what question you might ask in order to give your opinion about your topic.

Share
Ask students how it went. Was it harder or easier than they thought?

Possible Problems and Suggested Solutions
Students ask questions that do not make sense in the context of their writing. Remind students that the questions have to have a purpose. Ask them to circle the two questions they wrote that have a clear purpose in the writing.
Students ask rhetorical questions but the answers are predictable. Explain the meaning of the word *rhetorical* and tell the students that they are asking a rhetorical question, another device used in persuasion.

Follow-Up
Ask students to find examples of authors who ask questions in their writing.
Find examples of questions in other kinds of nonfiction writing.
Discuss which questions in Carol Herson's writing are most important. Why are these questions needed most? In other words, what do they do for her writing?

May I Ask You a Question?

There are all different kinds of questions in persuasive writing and they are used for different reasons. Some different kinds of questions are:

Rhetorical

Ridiculous/sarcastic

Deep thought

Advice

Hypothetical

Information

And more and more and more.

The following questions come from some of the persuasive writing found in the Appendix. What kinds of questions are these, and why did the author write these sentences as questions?

From "Should We Take Away the Voting Rights of 18-Year-Olds?" (page 213)

Are you kidding?

From "Sis! Boom! Bah! Humbug!" (page 215)

It's crazy, isn't it?

What's that spell? Frostbite.

From the Chris Wondra's Letter to His Students (page 241)

You know that feeling you get on the last day of school?

From Emily's Five-Paragraph Essay (page 225)

Are they willing to allow the "Pledge of Allegiance" in schools? Or are they willing to sacrifice children's rights to respect veterans, years of tradition and God in order to please a select few?

Storytelling in Persuasive Writing

In this lesson, students look at storytelling as a persuasive technique. **Time:** Fifty-five minutes

Preparation

Copy Blake's writing, "Boys are Invisible in School," from the Appendix.

Minilesson

Telling a story can be a really effective persuasive writing technique. Storytelling can help prove a point and can also change the reader's mood. Changing my mood may cause me to act or think differently.

If I become angry about how quickly people drive down my quiet little street, there is a good chance that I'll do something about it. I might write a persuasive letter to the county, talk to my neighbors about the problem, or start a petition to get speed bumps installed. One of the most effective ways to draw the reader to act is to change the reader's mood.

What if the writer started like this:

Last week, Nicholas was riding his bike down our quiet street in broad daylight, enjoying the day and completing his paper route. He never saw the red minivan whizzing down the street at a breakneck speed. He reached out to throw his last newspaper of the day when he was struck. He was thrown off of his bicycle and landed twenty feet away in the middle of the street. He was bleeding from his head.

Because of the angle at which he landed he was lucky and walked away from the accident with just seven stitches. It could have been much worse. Do we have to wait for much worse to come before we put speed bumps into our subdivisions?

Chris Wondra, an eighth-grade teacher in Wisconsin, knows about storytelling and persuasion. Remember his letter to his students about doing their best during their persuasive writing unit? Let's find the places where Mr. Wondra tells a story in order to convince his students to do their best work. [Read the letter and point out where the storytelling appears.]

Now the question is what kind of story could you tell that is related to your topic that would help persuade the reader? Find a place in your writing that you think a story might work. You don't have to be sure that it will work, you just have to think that it is a possibility. [Ask two students to share their ideas. Try, as a class, to think about how the story might begin.]

As you are writing today, be on the lookout for places where you could try telling a story.

Share

Ask, *Who tried to incorporate a story? How did it go? Will you read just that part of what you wrote today?*

Possible Problems and Suggested Solutions

Students write a two-sentence anecdote! This is okay and perfectly normal for a first attempt. Celebrate what students are able to do and move on.

The anecdote relates only marginally to the topic. Discuss what the story is supposed to show. See if the student can identify why it doesn't do what it should.

Follow-Up

Find more examples of anecdotes and storytelling in persuasive writing.

Point out that some stories are written in the present tense, and that they can even take place in the future (*how bad things will be if . . . , how good things will be when . . .*).

As you discover storytelling in the pieces you read, talk about *how* storytelling moves the reader to action. (Most of the time the writer uses a story to inspire readers or to scare them!)

Notice the length of the stories that are told. Some stories are many sentences, even paragraphs, while others are snippets of story.

Present this lesson again when students are revising their persuasive writing. Students will be better at it the second time, and the stories may strengthen their writing.

The Idea Is a Good One or I'm Hip to That: Formal Versus Informal Language

This is a good lesson for any kind of persuasive writing and for any age. **Time:** Sixty minutes

Preparation

Before you present this lesson, have students discuss both the purpose and the target audience for their writing. Ask them to be as specific as possible.

Copy Resources 4–10, Examples of Word Choices Based on Purpose and Audience.

Minilesson

Once when my children were little they were misbehaving in a restaurant. We were with some good friends and their kids. My boys were playing with the salt shaker and salt was spilling out of it. I looked up and said, Hey, guys, knock it off! *And they did.*

Another time we went out for dinner with my husband's boss. The kids were a little older but not much. They were playing with the sugar packets and talking too loudly. I made sure I had their attention, and then I said, Gentlemen, this is not the time or the place for this behavior. *They stopped at once.*

I was saying the same thing both times but in very different ways. Turn to your partner and talk about why you think I said, Knock it off! *the first time and,* Gentlemen, this is not the time or the place for this behavior, *the second time. [Ask a few students to share their ideas.] Yes, I think you've touched on it. There are two factors that help us answer this question and here they are: The first is* purpose *and the second is* audience. *My purpose happened to be the same both times: To get the boys to behave better. The first time, I was annoyed and felt comfortable showing it; the second time, it was imperative that I stop the misbehavior as quickly and as unobtrusively as possible.*

What about audience? The audience certainly influenced the way I worded what I said. With my friends, I could be casual and direct. I felt I needed to be more formal, distant, and less emotional in front of my husband's boss. I didn't want to sound too strict or angry.

Let's take a look at some other examples of intentional word choices based on purpose and audience. [Hand out Examples of Word Choices Based on Purpose and Audience and discuss one or two examples.]

As you write today, I want you to think not only about what you're saying but how you're saying it—formally, informally, or somewhere in between. When we share today, I would like some of you to read a sentence or two of your writing in which you made a decision about the way you said something. We will then imagine how else you could have written this. Okay, do great work!

Share   Have students share examples from their writing.

Possible Problem and Suggested Solution

Students overdo their informal writing. This is one of the most common (and therefore unavoidable) problems when teaching persuasive writing. But since students are still developing their ideas, too much informality is not a big deal. Show students that sentence length is often related to a formal or informal tone. Longer sentences are usually more formal, and shorter sentences are usually more informal.

Follow-Up

Copy examples from Resource 4–10 on to chart paper and have students add on as they encounter other instances. Students can pinpoint examples of particularly formal or informal
language and then imagine how this same sentence could have been said in another way.

Use dialogue as another example. As you read narrative writing to your students, or as they
read it independently, invite them to point out examples of the way characters speak that
is particularly formal or informal.

There's just one problem, it's not true.
However, a growing body of research shows this to be incorrect.

That will take guts.
It requires courage.

Oh, I know you. I can just hear you talking over lunch.
You no doubt discussed this with your colleagues or friends.

Don't get me wrong. I say, be the best parent you can be.
Please don't misunderstand me. I know that parents strive to be the best parents
they can be.

Who wants perfection?
Most kids prefer a mom who ignores the occasional mess to one who is always
cleaning up.

Resource 4–10 *Examples of Word Choices Based on Purpose and Audience*

Examining the Structure of Your Persuasive Writing

Goal

To examine a traditional essay structure and then have students think about their own persuasive writing and determine possible organization

In this lesson, students examine the five-paragraph essay (the most traditional structure for a school essay). They begin to look at the way a particular piece of writing is organized. This lesson should be done more than once with many different pieces of persuasive writing so that students begin to see a range of ways to organize their writing. **Time:** Between fifty and sixty minutes. I broke the "mini" lesson rule for this lesson. I recommend that you do this right after recess or P.E. when students are able to sit for a long period of time or break the lesson into two lessons on consecutive days.

Preparation

Copy and also enlarge or project "Emily's Five-Paragraph Essay" from the Appendix. The lesson will work best if students can actually see you writing on the text. If students have not read this essay before today, ask them to read it at the beginning of the writing period.

Minilesson

Soon, very soon, you will begin to draft your persuasive pieces. Before you begin drafting let's look at the structure—or organization—of an already published editorial. Today, we'll examine Emily Nabong's editorial about the Pledge of Allegiance.

Let's read the first paragraph and figure out why it's part of the article. What purpose does it serve? [Read the first paragraph aloud.] *This paragraph is the introduction. By starting with the words* Picture if you can, *the author shows us what it would be like if students were not allowed to recite the Pledge of Allegiance in school. Then she directly states her thesis.* [Read the second sentence in the paragraph that starts: *By terminating the Pledge . . .*] *in the last three sentences she gives us a taste of her reasons for not wanting the pledge terminated. The first paragraph shows one kind of introduction that answers the question: What is this piece of writing about and why was it written?*

The second paragraph gives us one reason why the pledge is important. The whole paragraph discusses that one reason. [Read the second paragraph aloud.]

The third paragraph gives us another reason why the pledge should continue to be recited in school. [Read the third paragraph aloud.]

Skim the next paragraph and tell a partner what work the fourth paragraph does.

The fifth paragraph does not give new information—it just restates what has been said already. This paragraph ends with a call to action. It gives the reader a task. It says, here is what I want you to do. [Read the last paragraph aloud.]

The author has written a five-paragraph essay, which is one way to organization a persuasive text.

There are many ways to organize persuasive writing. The author could have decided to add to her writing by discussing why it is particularly important to recite the pledge these days. If she did this, her five-paragraph essay might have been six paragraphs. She could have added more reasons why we should believe as she does or she could have also told us why some people don't think reciting the pledge in school is a good idea and told us why they are wrong!

Before we go off and write today, I would like you to reread some of what you have written and talk to a partner about one or two ways you could organize your writing. You could say things like: I might start by saying . . . and then I would say . . . this will lead into . . . or, there is one thing that I want to say but I am not sure where it fits in.

Give students time to reread and to talk with their writing partners about organization and then give them time to write. Students may want to free write using a sentence or idea they want to explore, generate a list of reasons and examples to include in their draft, or work on rewriting their thesis statements.

Share

Skip the share today. The minilesson was long, so spend the rest of the period writing.

Possible Problem and Suggested Solution

Some students are not writing. They seem to need my direction. Have an on-the-spot "get started" meeting (one or two quick suggestions) with the students who don't know what to do.

Follow-Up

Present this lesson again using another five-paragraph essay. Select one that you consider to be well written. You can find essays on the Internet by using the key words *five-paragraph essay examples* into a search engine.

Present the lesson again using an essay that is organized very differently. Suggested essays for this purpose are: "Boys Are Invisible in School" and the letter from Zahra to her mom and dad found in the Appendix.

Repetition, Repetition

Using a repeating phrase or sentence is a great way for students to structure their persuasive writing. Repetition can be the glue that holds the writing together and makes it cohesive. If students have read books with repetition and written poetry or narrative with a repeating word or phrase, draw on this past knowledge while teaching this lesson. **Time:** Forty minutes

Preparation

Copy Winston Churchill's speech in the Appendix (or alternatively, use the "I Have a Dream" speech by Martin Luther King Jr. (go to Americanrhetoric.com and click on the Top 100 Best Speeches link).

Minilesson

We have seen repetition in narrative writing and in poetry, but repetition in persuasive writing? Yup! Let's read a speech by Winston Churchill [or substitute the one by Martin Luther King Jr.], *who was one of the greatest persuasive speakers in history.* [Hand out copies of the speech and read it aloud.]

As you heard, the words we shall fight *are repeated many times in one part of the speech. Why would the author want to repeat these words? Churchill could have said,* We shall fight on the seas and the oceans and with growing confidence and growing strength in the air and on the beaches *but he chose instead to repeat* we shall fight *each time. Why?* [Solicit student responses.]

In this speech, repetition seems to be used for emphasis, as if to say, here is the most important part of what I'm saying. It also seems to add a poetic flavor to the writing. Some authors choose to repeat a phrase—a group of words—like Winston Churchill does. Some repeat a whole sentence. And some repeat just one word.

Let's quickly try this with our persuasive writing. We'll have someone read his or her writing to us and we'll see if we can find a word or sentence that might be repeated. We might not be able to find one, but let's try.

Call on one or two students to read their writing and see if students can think of a persuasive phrase or word to repeat. Then add your own ideas. Write these ideas down on chart paper.

As you write today, think about repetition as a persuasive device and experiment with it. Word hard!

Share

Ask students to share examples of repetition. Ask, *Which way do you like the writing better, with the repetition or without?*

Possible Problems

None.

Follow-Up

Find other examples of repetition in persuasive writing. Include examples where repetition works well and when it detracts from the writing.

Studying How Images Work with Words

Today's students are bombarded with all sorts of images each and every day. In this lesson students study visual images. The lesson can be used to study public service announcement (PSA) images or traditional print advertisement images. Students like this lesson because it gives them an opportunity to think more deeply about visual representation and to create their own image. **Time:** Thirty-five minutes

Preparation

Copy Resource 4–11, Studying Images in Persuasive Writing.
Copy some PSAs from the Appendix—or find your own examples.

Minilesson

Did you ever hear the expression, "A picture is worth a thousand words"? Images stick in people's minds—and in some instances may even be more important than words. Movie makers know this to be true, which is why they spend so much time trying to get the images just right. [Give an example of an appropriate recent movie that most of the class it likely to have seen. Talk about the images that your remember from the movie and why these images have stuck in your head.] *Advertisers know that images are really important. They know that the right image may influence people to buy the product and the wrong image will make the ad less effective.*

Today we will spend a few minutes looking at images in public service advertisements and then you will begin to experiment with creating your own image for your PSA.

Look at images from PSAs. Using one or two PSAs (from the resource section or ones you have found on your own) ask and answer the questions from Resource 4–11, Studying Images in Persuasive Writing. Thinking aloud in front of the students about the Peace Corps PSA (see Appendix) might go something like this:

First I want to think about how important this image is and how I know it's important. In this public service announcement the first thing that hits me is the size of the image. It's so small you can barely see it. It isn't done with detail either. It looks like a fast sketch, so I believe that the image here is not so important. I'm also not sure what the image does. It's a small picture of a wine or champagne glass but it looks more like a logo of some sort. The image in this case doesn't seem to add to the words.

Now with this public service announcement you can see right away that the image is important. It is a large photograph that takes up almost the entire page. What does the image do for this public service announcement? There are people in this image, which right away makes the message more personal. This photo also shows us something that the words don't tell us. It shows us that if we join the Peace Corps we will create relationships with people . . . you see if you look closely at the picture you can see how the Peace Corp volunteer has his arm around these two boys, which leads us to think . . . [Continue to think aloud for a few minutes and then hand out Resource 4–11 for this lesson.]

Today, as you experiment with images for your public service announcement, keep this resource page handy and look at it to help you as you create your image.

Those of you who easily get ideas for images in your head may begin by sketching different images and seeing which one you like best. But it's hard to pick out just one image, so refer to Resource 4–11 after you have created more than one image. Use the questions to help you determine what picture you like best.

If you are like me (and have trouble creating pictures in your head), you will probably want to start by reviewing the questions on the sheet, letting your mind wander and then sketching your image.

No matter what way you begin—let's do great image work!

Share

Some students will share their images and/or their process for how they went about creating the image. If there is time, have students ask their writing partners what works well in the image and use them to make suggestions for improvement.

Possible Problems

None.

Follow-Up

Continue to study images in persuasive writing. Use the following questions to help students learn more about images.

Does the image illustrate one of the words in the text?

Example:
Text: You drink you drive you lose
Image: Glass of wine or champagne

Does the image represent or symbolize something?

Example:
Text: This is your brain on drugs
Image: A picture of a fried egg

Does the image illustrate something that is not said in the actual words?

Example:
Text: Be the kind of person people look up to
Image: An older boy playing basketball with a younger one.

Studying Images in Persuasive Writing

Questions to ask about the way images work with words

How important is the image? How do I know this?

What does the image do?

Does the image work well with the text? How?

Minilessons for Planning and Drafting Persuasive Writing

A Day or Two Before Drafting . . .

. . . students create a tentative plan to help them keep their writing focused. Time spent organizing persuasive texts in advance often makes the difference between an all-over-the-place-what-is-this-author-saying draft and a more cohesive one.

When Drafting . . .

. . . students read through their persuasive ideas, write their thesis on the top of each drafting page, and read through the organizational work they've just done. Then, for one or two days, usually on paper separate from their writer's notebook, they write their draft based on their previous thinking and writing.

Just Before Drafting

In my first years of teaching, I rarely asked students to do any organizational work before they wrote their drafts; I believed that planning and organizing wouldn't allow spur-of-the-moment thinking or creativity. I also disliked planning sheets because students had a tendency to copy the words they had written on these sheets directly into their drafts. The writing became stilted and underdeveloped, like notes from a lecture, full of incomplete thoughts and weak transitions.

There was only one problem: Students' drafts were consistently weak. Their draft writing looked and sounded like three or four stream-of-consciousness notebook entries smushed together. Too many rewrites, minilessons, and writing conferences were needed to make the writing sound, well, like the writing I had imagined they would produce the first time around. Too many drafts lacked organization and focus. Something was amiss.

My first response was to structure students' writing for them: *In the first paragraph, state the problem. In the second paragraph, give the first reason you believe as you do. In paragraph three. . . .* Immediately I saw clear advantages to this approach. As expected, students' drafts were more organized and easier to read. Unfortunately, there were two big disadvantages as well.

First, this writing lacked voice. Students who had written with a strong sense of style while studying personal narrative and poetry, when given this follow-the-directions structure, produced writing that was so boring it was often difficult to finish reading: *The first point I want to make is. . . . In conclusion I would like to say again that. . . .* Yuk! This wasn't the kind of writing I wanted my students do.

An even bigger problem was that by providing the structure of the writing, I wasn't *teaching* students how to get better at organizing their writing. They knew that when it came time to write a draft, I would tell them how to organize it. I didn't want that kind of overreliance on me. I wanted students to learn how to organize their writing themselves. And I wanted the writers in my class to have a sense of ownership of their work.

So I began to teach students how to organize their writing and give them time to do it. Minilessons and writing conferences just before drafting prompted students to think, talk, and write about how their drafts might be organized. Whether students are asked to use a planning sheet or sticky notes or some (any) other kind of persuasive writing organizer isn't important. What is important is that students benefit tremendously from explicit teaching about organization.

Using a Persuasive Planning Sheet
Students often misunderstand the reason to use a planning sheet before drafting. Make sure students know that a planning sheet is one way to help organize their thinking before they begin to draft. Reiterate that a planning sheet is not an end unto itself but is a vehicle for organization. Keep the following in mind when helping students tentatively organize their ideas before they write a draft:

- Teach students how to think, talk, and write about the organization of their persuasive writing. (See the minilesson for Planning Persuasive Writing, page 118.)
- Ask students to review their thesis statements so that they stay focused on their issue as they write.
- Remind students that the plan they make is tentative and that they are not locked into it. If new ideas pop into their heads as they draft, allow and encourage them to go in a new direction.
- Teach students to jot down notes on their planning pages, not write in complete sentences. The planning sheet should look like an outline, not a draft.
- Ask students who have difficulty maintaining focus to write a working first sentence for each paragraph.
- If time permits, ask students to fill out more than one persuasive organizer and then discuss which one is a better plan and why.

■ Allow students who process information slowly or who get bogged down to submit unfinished planning sheets, especially if these pages are collected before drafting. Don't grade the persuasive writing organizer.

■ Show students how to refer to their plans as they write their draft.

Writing the Draft

Observe students as they write their drafts and take notes. How are students using processes to help write their persuasive drafts? You may discover the following types of minilessons to be helpful: rereading, precise wording, reordering, and using conventions.

Many teachers find it extremely helpful to watch students begin to draft for the first ten minutes of writing. They don't confer during this time because students need time to think and write and they don't want to interrupt them. They take notes on what they see students doing and they make sure that the tone of the room is calm and focused.

Writing a draft is difficult but it is also one of the exciting parts of the writing process. Finally, all the work students have done to find a topic, create a thesis statement, think through how to present the idea, find supporting evidence, and so on comes together in one place.

Drafting is best done during the longest writing period you can provide. Try not to draft on a day when you only have fifteen minutes to let students work. On draft day, some teachers present a minilesson on how to write strong beginnings (see the minilesson on leads, page 123), while other teachers allow time for students to reread their planning sheets and just let them plunge in.

Students should keep their writer's notebook closed when they write a draft. It may feel strange to tell students to write without the benefit of the words in their notebook. On the other hand, when students draft with their notebook open, they tend to copy their words directly from their notebook onto their draft paper. This defeats the purpose.

Closed-notebook drafts are often more organized, focused, and well developed than drafts written with the notebook open. However, some students, especially third graders, seem to lose the excitement and passion they had for the topic when they first wrote about it in their notebook. To combat this problem, give students the option of recopying a few of their greatest sentences or words onto a separate sheet of paper. They can then incorporate these sentences into their draft.

When you have students write their persuasive drafts with their notebooks closed, the focus is less on recopying and more on writing and creating. Still, students aren't starting from scratch because they've have had a long time to think about their topic, positions, and support. (All of this thought work will make for a stronger draft than if students had started to draft on the first day you introduced persuasive writing.)

Make sure that students have their working plan beside them as they write. Some students will refer to this plan often as a blueprint for structure and content. Remember, though, that this is their working plan and not a contract. Students are still free to create and rethink.

Usually, a draft should be finished in one writing period. Middle school students or really strong writers who can sustain a persuasive topic over several pages may sometimes need to finish their draft on a subsequent day. But when drafting goes on for longer than two days it is often riddled with problems. Long persuasive drafts are usually redundant or unfocused. So stick to the one-day limit: tell students to write, write, write, and get it done.

* * *

Whew! Persuasive drafts are finished. What's the next step? Nope, not revision. The next step is time away. Encourage students to take a writing break for a few days. You, unfortunately, don't have that luxury, although I recommend that you don't read the drafts that evening. You've worked hard too, and a day away will help you come back to your students' work with fresh eyes.

Predictable Problems and Possible Solutions While Drafting

Problem	Solution
Students are "done" drafting after only a few minutes.	Read the draft aloud and ask students where (not if!) they can write more. Have them rehearse what they could say.
	Have students work on counterargument.
Great words, phrases, and ideas students collected never made it into their draft!	Ask students to go back into their notebooks and find the writing that has the most voice or that they are most proud of. Show them how to put these sentences into their drafts.
Drafts start out persuasive but you see them turn into informational writing right before your eyes.	Stop students and say something like, *Over here the writing is persuasive, but at a certain point it starts sounding more like informational writing. Can you locate that part?*
	Have students cut out the informational part of the draft. (They can glue these words into their notebook and use them for another writing project.) Help students begin the next paragraph persuasively.
Arguments are not well developed. Each argument is only a sentence or two.	Use the minilesson on elaboration, page 137, to guide your writing conferences.

Planning Persuasive Writing

In this lesson, students reread their writing and plan their drafts. Planning usually helps students write a better-organized first draft. **Time:** Fifty minutes

Preparation

Copy Resources 5–1 through 5–4, Persuasive Writing Planning Sheets. (Choose the one you think will work best for your grade level.)

Minilesson

Today you're going to spend time planning your drafts. The work you do today will help you immeasurably when you write your draft. With your thesis statement nearby, reread what you wrote in your notebook and think about how to organize your ideas.

Let's begin by focusing on rereading. Rereading is not skimming. Skimming is when we read just a sentence or two from each paragraph, usually looking for specific information. When we revise, we'll talk more about skimming. For now, as we plan, we'll reread. [Model rereading aloud. Read slowly and show students that you are saying every word.]

As you reread, you'll jot down important notes. You won't copy what you've written in your notebook onto the planning sheet. That seems like a waste of time. You'll jot down notes to remind yourself what you want to say when you write your draft.

When you write in your notebook you usually don't think much about organizing your writing. Today you're going to ask yourself what thoughts go together, what thoughts will make your persuasive writing strong, and what thoughts you may leave out because they don't help you make your point. Remember, too, that just because two ideas are next to each other in your notebook entry doesn't mean that these thoughts will be together on your planning sheet.

Watch me as I reread, think, and then write. [Demonstrate rereading and filling out the planning sheet. As you reread, think aloud, saying things like: *This part probably won't go into my draft. This part is good; I think it might make a good beginning. Let's see, over here I have a good example, but I know I need to explain it a little more. I'm not sure where this part goes, but it's good.*]

Did you see what I did? I am beginning to set up my planning sheet. I may not stick to this sheet exactly when I write a draft tomorrow, but I will have a tentative plan. Okay, let's begin rereading. [Confer with table groups while students work.]

Share

Ask one or two students to talk about how they planned.

Possible Problem and Suggested Solution

Students write too much on their planning sheet. There is nothing you can do about this if they are already finished! But if students are still writing as you are conferring, reteach them how to use bullets and phrases rather than complete sentences.

Follow-Up

Allow more time for students to plan.

Persuasive Writing Planning Sheet A

Thesis Statement

Point 1

[Repeat for Point 2 and Point 3]

Prove it!

(support what you just said)

First sentence

_____

_____

_____

_____

Persuasive Writing Planning Sheet B

Stance/Thesis	Reasons Why	Example
	Reasons Why	Example
	Reasons Why	Example

Persuasive Writing Planning Sheet C

My thesis is:

I am going to say or show:

I am going to say or show:

I am going to say or show:

I am going to say or show:

Persuasive Writing Planning Sheet D

Purpose   What do you wish to convince or persuade the reader to think or do?

Audience   Who is my audience? How will my audience affect my writing?

Lead   I might begin by saying . . .

Body   My first point is:

I will make this point by:

My second point is:

I will make this point by:

My third point is:

I will make this point by:

Ending

I might end by . . .

Some questions I have about my persuasive draft:

How and where will I consider counterargument?

What persuasive writing techniques would I like to try?

Leads That Capture the Reader's Interest

This lesson focuses on five common kinds of leads in persuasive writing. **Time:** Fifty minutes

Preparation

Copy Resource 5–5, Some Leads for Persuasive Writing.

Minilesson

The lead or beginning of a piece of persuasive writing is probably the most important part. If readers like what they read in the first few sentences or paragraph, they'll read on. If they don't like it, they may lose interest and stop reading. You probably have just a minute or two to grab their attention.

Sometimes students think that grabbing readers' attention means you have to say something dramatic (or exaggerated) like, "The water you're drinking could kill you!" This is a common misconception. When we think back to the leads that grabbed us as we read persuasive writing, they weren't necessarily dramatic but there was something about them—in some cases we didn't even know what it was—that made us want to read on.

In almost all persuasive leads, we know by the first sentence or two what the writing is going to be about. Keep that in mind as you experiment with your beginning. Readers should know what you're writing about before they get to the middle of your writing.

Let's look at some persuasive writing leads. You may recognize some of these beginnings from pieces we've read. Others will be new to you. Let's talk about the tone of these beginnings—whether they're formal or informal—and what we like about each one.

[Hand out copies of Some Leads for Persuasive Writing, read the examples aloud, and talk through what students like about each one.]

Think about two or three kinds of beginnings you'd like to experiment with. The kind of beginning you try should match the tone of your piece. You probably won't want to begin with a statistic if you are writing to your mom. (But I could be wrong about that!)

Share

Have several students share their leads.

If there is time, give students a few minutes to combine several leads into one. (Sometimes this works great, and students are well on their way to writing their first paragraph. Other times, this exercise doesn't work at all.)

Possible Problem and Suggested Solution

Students write different beginnings that are very similar. For example: (1) Recycling is good for the earth. (2) Is recycling good for the earth? (3) Recycling means a clean earth without garbage—a good thing. If this happens, let students select one of the leads and move on!

Follow-Up

Have students try leads different from those they've tried so far.

Have students select a lead they like from persuasive writing they've encountered and use it as a model for one of their own.

Some Leads for Persuasive Writing

State a Statistic or Fact

The National Center for Education Statistics, a branch of the U.S. Department of Education, reports that in 1998, 38 percent of the nation's fourth graders were below basic, the lowest of reading ability.

—Leonard Pitts Jr., "Illiteracy Really Scares Me"

Ask a Thought-Provoking Question

Is your school providing the best educational experience possible? If your school does not have a mandatory recess policy, the answer is no. Recess improves achievement, and without it students may not be getting a strong education.

Present a Hypothetical Situation (*picture this, imagine*)

It's Monday morning and it's time to pick out my boys' clothing for school. I select a blue shirt and khaki pants for both of them. I don't hear a whine or a cry from either boy. Why? The magic words—school uniform.

The house is silent. I sit on my couch heated up by my SpongeBob pajamas. With a pencil in my hand, I begin to write down my feelings in a beautiful blue book. I know it sounds like a diary, but you know what I'm doing, I'm writing in my reading response notebook.

State the Thesis Topic Directly

I used to love reading, but required weekly reading responses have changed that. I have never disliked reading more.

After spending most of the day in school, students are given additional assignments to be completed at home. This is a rather curious fact when you stop to think about it, but not as curious as the fact that few of us ever stop to think about it. It's worth asking, not only whether there are good reasons to support the nearly universal practice of assigning homework, but why it's so often taken for granted—even by vast numbers of teachers and parents who are troubled by its impact on children.

Use a Short Declarative Sentence

Science doesn't lie. [Advertisement for a skin care product.]

Ready, Set . . . Draft!

This lesson works best if you use your own writing to demonstrate the process of drafting. This is a less scary proposition if you think about your own persuasive draft before the lesson. Then when you demonstrate draft writing it's not as spur of the moment as it might seem. (Sneaky, but very helpful.)

Second best is to ask a strong student writer to draft a few days before this lesson and then help this student talk about his or her own drafting process. **Time:** Fifty minutes

Preparation
Look at Resource 5–6, Things You Might Demonstrate While Drafting.

Minilesson

Today we're going to write a first draft. There is no one right way to do this. Each of you will have your own unique process.

For just a few minutes before you begin, I'll show you what I do when I draft. As you draft today, try out some of the things you see me do; they may help you, too. Later on today or tomorrow, I might refer to this lesson and say something like, Remember when you saw me trying to think of a particular word? *So, watch and listen closely.*

Using Resource 5–6, as a guide, demonstrate drafting a paragraph or two of a persuasive text. Keep your demonstration to no more than fifteen minutes. If you haven't finished, stop anyway! Students need a lengthy chunk of time in which to draft. Less is more here. Select one or two things you would like to demonstrate. Demonstrate. Let the students write.

Okay. It's time to begin our drafts. We'll write for thirty minutes today. [Indicate a specific amount of time so students know how long they will be expected to write.] *Let's get settled particularly quietly today. Craft literature!*

Share
Have students talk about aspects of their drafting process: slowing down, rereading, writing quickly, etc. Ask, *What was difficult about writing this draft?*

Possible Problem and Suggested Solution
You take a quick look at students' drafts and see that the writing is not as strong as you had hoped. Don't have students begin revising their drafts until you've taken a few days to read them over very carefully and decide what needs to be taught most.

Follow-Up
Ask students questions about their draft, like:

- *Is it convincing? How do you know?*
- *Where is it most convincing?*
- *Does it sound like you want it to?*
- *Which part of the text needs work and why?*

Have them underline the section of their draft that they like the best.

Losing your train of thought:

Wait, what was I writing? Let me reread the last sentence.

Finishing a thought and not knowing what to say next:

What do I want to say next? I know, I'll say thus-and-so. No, I don't want to say it that way, it sounds too bossy. Hmmm. Okay I'll write. . . .

Not being able to think of the word you want:

I will just skip the word for now and move on.
I'll substitute this word for the time being.

Not having a good example:

I can't think of a good example right now, so I'll just write the word example *in parenthesis here and fill it in later.*

Needing to add more to a paragraph:

I need to bulk this paragraph up and add more. Oh, I know, I could write about thus-and-so. I'm not sure if that will work, but let me try.

Resource 5–6 *Things You Might Demonstrate While Drafting*

CHAPTER 6

Minilessons for Revising Persuasive Writing: Making the Argument Even More Convincing

When Revising . . .

. . . students reread their writing aloud so they can listen to their own words. Teachers show students how to experiment with changing their draft. Revision in persuasive writing most often means elaborating to make a point stronger and more convincing and changing words and phrases to make them more persuasive.

Assessing Drafts to Determine Revision Minilessons

It is tempting to jump in and begin to teach revision minilessons. Don't! Before you begin to work on revision, take time to read students' drafts and determine what revision lessons are most important. Use the chart in the Appendix titled Looking at First-Draft Writing (page 206), to help you read and determine strengths and weaknesses of your students' drafts.

Suggestions for Reading Drafts   Read only one-third to half of the drafts at once. Breaking up this reading time makes the reading more manageable. Read (or skim) each draft twice. You don't have to read every word of every draft in order to get an overall sense of strengths and weaknesses. Skimming is not only acceptable—it's advisable.

Create a systematic way of reading. Some teachers skim each piece of writing and pay particular attention to the beginning and the end. Then they do a second skim this time focusing attention on the middle paragraphs of the text.

After reading a few drafts, take notes and you will begin to see patterns of strengths and weaknesses; begin to jot down ideas for revision lessons. Use the first-draft chart in the Appendix on page 206 to help you keep track of the information you glean. When you're finished reading make a list of the specific revision minilessons you want to present in class or use in writing conferences.

How to Teach Revision

Now that students have had a few days away from their persuasive drafts, they're ready to come back to their writing with renewed energy. Use minilessons, individual writing conferences, and small-group conferences to teach revision. Be careful not to fall into the trap of telling. Rather than telling students to write a new beginning, suggest how to experiment with writing new leads and show examples of different ways to begin persuasive writing. Rather than telling a student that she has repeated the same point several times, show her where the writing seems redundant and ask her if there is another reason she can offer her audience. We want to do more than make quick fixes to the writing. We want to teach students about revision so that they are able to transfer their learning to the next piece of writing.

The hardest thing about teaching revision is knowing when to stop teaching it. The drafts are still not quite good enough, so you revise for a few more days and then a few more. And suddenly the persuasive writing unit you started on February 1 is still in progress on March 16. By March 31, students are completely uninterested in their writing and have usually come to hate revision (and dare I say, persuasive writing, too). The key to teaching revision? Teach a few minilessons, hold writing conferences, and then move on to editing!

What to Teach

The most common revision needed in persuasive writing is elaboration. If students have skimpy paragraphs or seem to repeat themselves, it's because they need practice taking one idea, one reason, or one example and writing more about it. If you have time for just one revision minilesson, it should be on elaboration. (See page 134 or 137.)

The second most common type of revision concerns content that is incorrect. Sometimes authors present gaps in their logic. Other times they give faulty reasoning like this: *We should not let people jog around the reservoir because then people will have better drinking water.* In truth, the fact that runners are throwing garbage into the reservoir and polluting it does not have anything to do with the fact that the drinking water is impure. In this case, the cause and effect are not related to one another. It is important to politely show the author that these two problems are not related and to then help her think about another argument for limiting the jogger traffic on the reservoir track.

Sometimes, gaps in logic exist simply because the author has not explained the connection between two ideas or concepts. (Not so different from presenting a new character in narrative writing without introducing or explaining who he or she is. In narrative it sounds something like this: *. . . and then Aunt Harriet saved the day.* As readers we wonder, who is Aunt Harriet, why haven't we heard about her before, and exactly how did she save the day?) If something doesn't make sense, tell students politely but directly that there are places in the writing that confuse you. Ask them to locate these places in the text. If they can find them, tell them what is missing and see if they can find ways to make that part of the writing more clear. If students cannot find places where gaps exist, show them directly and explain why that section of the writing is a bit confusing.

Vague words and ideas are another common problem in persuasive drafts. Showing students how to make overused or vague words and ideas more specific will improve their persuasive writing immeasurably. Let's look at an example. Here's the first draft:

Dear superintendent of schools,

The conduct system in your county does not work. Taking away recess is not good for kids. I understand that there are times when students don't behave well and that they need to be reprimanded, but the system that Clark County has does not work to make things better. This system is not useful.

Here's the draft after a revision conference on specificity.

Dear superintendent of schools,

The system of discipline in Clark County does not make students behave better and needs to be changed. Taking away recess makes students very antsy and not better behaved. I would like you to think about changing the system . . .

If students' drafts are vague, try the minilesson on precise words (page 92). (Many other minilessons on developing persuasive writing also apply to revision so for more ideas for revision minilessons, refer to Chapter 4.)

Transitions between sentences and from one paragraph to the next are very difficult for some student writers. Students either don't know that transitions are necessary or don't know *how* to pave the way from one thought to the next. Presenting the Smooth Transitions minilesson (page 131) in class or in writing conferences will help students understand and create transitions.

Lucy Calkins says that if our revision writing conferences and minilessons teach students how to create better writing, students will be less resistant to revising. So true!

Predictable Problems and Possible Solutions While Revising

Problem	*Solution*
The draft moves away from the original idea and goes off in a new direction.	If the new direction *works* (it's clear and fairly well developed), do nothing. If the draft is unfocused or skimpy, show students how to reread their notebook writing and their planning pages and get back on track.
The draft is all telling: *I think because, I think because, and finally I think because . . .*	Show students other ways to begin their paragraphs. Also use the ideas from Elaboration 1 in a writing conference with that student.
The draft is disorganized.	Isolate the disorganized sections. Ask students to read what they wrote, turn the paper over so they cannot see it, and then talk through what they want to say. Then have them rewrite the part that is disorganized on a separate sheet of paper.
Students make small changes to their drafts when in actuality larger changes are needed. For example, students substitute words (*harmful* for *bad*) when they have an entire draft that is unclear.	Read the draft aloud to the student and tell her where you think the draft needs improvement.
Certain drafts aren't panning out. They're hard to develop and don't seem to be going anywhere.	Give these students the option of choosing a new persuasive topic and writing a new draft. (Starting again with a new topic can be a relief for any writer!)

Smooth Transitions

A transition is like a bridge that gets us from one place to another. In this lesson, students work on transitions that take the reader from one paragraph to the next. Transitions can be one of the hardest parts of persuasive writing, but with work they can be smooth and logical. **Time:** Fifty minutes

    Warning: If the student's persuasive writing is particularly disorganized, transitions may not help the writing! First, work with these students to organize their writing. Working on transitions before organization is putting the cart before the horse.

Preparation

Copy Resource 6–1, Common Transitional Words and Phrases.

Look at your students' drafts. What do they already know about transitions?

Minilesson

I used to have a friend who'd say, "Here is one thing I want to tell you," before she said what she wanted to say. Then she'd say, "Here is something else I want to tell you," and talk some more. No joke! She felt she needed to introduce what she wanted to say before saying it.

    When you write persuasively, you don't have to announce what you're going to say before you say it. You don't have to say, I am going to tell you—*you can just say it! Buuuut (that's a transition word!) some words, phrases, and sentences in your writing can show the reader how your ideas are connected. I'm going to read you something. See if you can figure out from the transitional words—*on the other hand—*what the rest of the sentence might be. Here goes:* I believe that students should have some homework each night. Studies show that students who do fifteen or twenty minutes of homework each night learn more in school. On the other hand. . . . *Okay, what do you think will come next?*

    The words on the other hand *let you know that I was going to present another idea that was different from, maybe even the opposite of, the first idea. I could also say this:* Studies show that students who do fifteen or twenty minutes of homework each night learn more in school, but. . . . *But is a transitional word, too. What if I said,* Children learn from example; therefore. . . . *Hmm, in this instance* therefore *is a transitional word. I could also substitute the word* so *for* therefore. Therefore *sounds very formal, and* so *sounds a bit more informal, don't you think?*

    Transitional words and phrases can be found in lots of different places in persuasive writing: between sentences in a paragraph or between one paragraph and the next. Sometimes entire paragraphs are a transition from one idea to another. Does every persuasive text have transitions that we can point to and say, Hey, that's a transition? *No. And sometimes the transitions you've used in your piece are just fine and don't need to be fiddled with.*

Hand out Resource 6–1, Common Transitional Words and Phrases. Read it aloud and discuss it if there is time.

For the first few minutes today, look over your writing and find two places where you could experiment by putting in some transition words or replacing the transitions you have with other transitions. Then, read your writing aloud to your partner with your new transitions and see how they sound. Let's get to work.

Share

Ask students to talk about their work with transitions and read some of their writing where they have experimented with transitions.

Possible Problem and Suggested Solution

Students use too many transitions. You could (a) throw this book away and never discuss transitions again or (b) recognize that when students learn something new they have a tendency to overuse it. (c) Be honest with students and suggest that they take a few of their transitional words out. Show them places in the text that may sound better without these transitional words.

Follow-Up

Reread some persuasive writing and talk about the transitions the author used. If you cannot find any transitions, have the class discuss why not.

Find transitional words in persuasive writing and discuss:

1. Why the transitional words are important in this sentence—what work do they do?
2. What other transitional words mean the same thing and could also be used?
3. How would the sentence/paragraph sound with the transitional words left out?

Common Transitional Words and Phrases

Words and phrases that indicate similarity: *also, in the same way, the same is true with, that's like*

Try this: Read your writing and find a place where you show how something is similar to something else. Is there a place where you might compare one thing to another? Would that make your writing stronger? What transitions would you use?

Words and phrases that introduce examples: *for example, for instance, specifically*

Try this: Read your writing aloud omitting the phrases *for example* or *for instance* and listen to how it sounds. Sometimes it sounds better. Other times examples need transitional words. What about your writing?

Words and phrases that call attention to your point: *again, indeed, in fact, on the negative [positive] side, let's not forget, surprisingly, let's remember*

Try this: Find your strongest point and emphasize it by using words that call attention to your point.

Words and phrases that introduce additional information: *and, also, furthermore, likewise, in addition, let's not forget, besides, again, together with, on top of that*

Try this: Count how many times you have used the word *and* in your writing. Can any of the them be replaced by other words? Would the sentence sound better as two separate sentences without the word *and*?

Elaboration 1:
Expanding Someone Else's Writing

A big part of revising persuasive writing is elaboration. If your students are consistently writing three-sentence paragraphs, try this lesson. **Time:** Fifty minutes

Preparation
Copy Resource 6–2, Andrew Hennessey's letter, or enlarge it so everyone can see.

Minilesson

Begin today's lesson by complimenting the class on something they did well in their drafts.

Recently, one of my sons got a new science teacher. When I asked him about her, he told me how he felt about the new teacher but he told me too quickly. He said, "Mrs. Marks is so cool and makes science fun and easy to learn."

When I asked him to elaborate, he just said, "She makes science really, really great." I knew he thought his teacher made science fun to learn, but I didn't know what she said or did to make science such a great class.

At dinner, I tried again to ask him about his science teacher and this is where he really elaborated and I got the picture! This time he said:

Mrs. Marks draws pictures on the chalkboard to show us what she is talking about. Today, she drew a picture of the solar system and it really helped me understand it. Then she lets us talk in groups for a few minutes about what we just learned. She tries to save time for questions at the end of the period so if we don't understand something she will explain it again.

That's elaboration! My son gave examples and showed me what is fun about science class. Now I understand why he likes science class so much.

Let's try speaking and elaborating. We'll say as much as we can by adding information and imagery (words that help us see) to this statement. Okay, here we go: Yesterday recess was so much fun. Can you give examples that support this statement? [Have students talk in partnerships and then call on a few students to elaborate on the statement. Help them say more. For example, if they say recess was fun because they played tag, say, *Yes, and we can also elaborate on playing tag. We could say, We played tag for more than twenty minutes. Everybody was "it" at one time or another and George and Charlie were "it" many times, because they kept going too far away from the base.*]

Today, we'll work on elaboration with our writing partner. We are taking a break from our own writing today and working on someone else's writing. I'm about to show you a letter that could use elaboration.

Let's read the letter together. I will then ask you to work with a partner and add to this letter by giving examples and by using words that show *the reader.*

Hand out or project Resource 6–2 and read it aloud. Lead a short discussion about what kinds of elaboration could be done with the letter.

Work hard!

Share
Students should share in partnerships today. Ask, *Does elaboration make the writing more persuasive? Is this true with all elaboration? When is it not true?*

Possible Problem and Suggested Solution
Students elaborate by adding only one sentence to each paragraph. Prompt students to say more: *What did it look like? What did it sound like?*

Follow-Up
Have students write undeveloped pieces of persuasive writing that need elaboration. Then ask them to exchange papers and elaborate on the piece they receive.

Ask students to use a recent class experience like a field trip, something funny that happened in school, or a school assembly program and write or talk about it. *First ask the students to make a general statement about the topic and then give specific examples that elaborate on what they have said.*

Dear Principal Houston,

I am a second grade student. I have gotten a great education here at Parsons Road school. I have enjoyed my teachers because they have been kind and good at teaching me.

Even good things can be made better, though, and that is why I'm writing this letter to you. One of the things that would make this school even better is if the students and the teachers had more of a break during the day.

Recess is a time when students really get to relax and not worry about the pressures of school. Students need to have down time, it's important for us.

Games are played at recess, but we never get to finish the games we start.

Lunch is also down time, but it's not the same. We get time to talk, but we don't get to exercise and just run around.

I hope that you will consider making recess a little bit longer.

Your Student,
Andrew Hennessey

Elaboration 2: Expanding Your Own Writing

137
*Minilessons for
Revising Persuasive
Writing: Making the
Argument Even More
Convincing*

In this lesson, students elaborate on their writing.* Resource 6–3 show students six phrases they can use in order to expand on their writing. Select one or two phrases to review with your students. If students are in middle school and have extensive writing experience, you may want to introduce three or more phrases. **Time:** Fifty minutes

Goal

To help students elaborate by using examples and imagery

Preparation

Copy Resource 6–3, Phases That Add More to Your Writing.
Copy or enlarge a copy of your own persuasive writing or a strong student draft.

Minilesson

Add more. Add more. Add more.

Sometimes I know that you wonder why I keep asking you to add more to your writing. My high school English teacher used to say, a good idea needs more words. And that is exactly why I often ask you to add more to your writing. Good ideas need more words.

Today you'll take time to go back to your own draft and find places where you can elaborate. But it's hard to figure out how to add more words without saying the same thing over and over again. How should you go about adding more words? [Read the appropriate phrases from Resource 6–3.]

Think about the phrases and see if they can help you figure out what else you might want to say. You may want to use these words in your writing or just think about them as you reread your writing. [Use one or two of these phrases with a student draft or your own writing and demonstrate how you would use the phrase to help you add more to the writing. Ask student partners to try using these questions to elaborate on something in their drafts. Tell them that some phrases may help and others won't be appropriate.]

As you write today, find a place where you can experiment with elaboration. When we share our work at the end of the workshop, I would like some of you to read one of your original paragraphs and then the paragraph after your elaboration.

Share

Ask volunteers to share examples of elaboraton.

Possible Problem and Suggested Solution

The elaboration isn't that elaborate. Students only added a few words, like very *and* a lot!
  Present the lesson again a bit later in the unit.

Follow-Up

Find examples of excellent elaboration in persuasive texts.
Create a bulletin board on which students can display their before-elaboration and after-elaboration paragraphs.

---

*The idea for this lesson comes from Lucy Calkins.

Phrases That Add More to Your Writing

The reason I say this is . . .

For example *or* for instance . . .

This would look like . . .

One thing I know is . . .

In fact . . .

If . . . then

Using Bulleted Lists

Students rarely use bullets in their writing. In this lesson, students discover when and how bulleted lists can be used in persuasive writing and experiment with adding them to their own pieces. (During the writing time students are asked to work on revision, not to specifically put bullets in their writing. During writing conferences you may want to discuss with students where they could try adding bullets. Do this only if bullets make sense with what they have written.) **Time:** Forty minutes

Preparation
Copy Resource 6–4, Example of Using Bulleted Lists.
Find and copy other examples of bulleted lists in persuasive writing.

Minilesson
[Read the resource page aloud. Call attention to the bullets on the resource page.]

How many of you have come across these marks in your reading? [Notice how many hands are raised.] *These dots are called bullets. Bullets are used to call attention to several facts or reasons. Because bullets are easier to read than paragraphs and because the words after the bullets stand out, bullets are used to call attention to certain words—mostly facts or reasons.*

In this piece of writing the author says, the Cattington Inn is the perfect getaway. *Further down, he lists some important facts about Cattington in bullet form. He chose facts that will help support the statement that Cattington is the perfect getaway. He didn't say that the walls of the rooms are blue because even though wall color is a fact it isn't that important and it doesn't support his sentence before the bullet.* [Read each bullet and tell why you think the author made each statement a bullet point.]

Bullets are used with more than two items in a group. [If time allows, look at Chris Wondra's letter in the Appendix, and discuss why he used bullets.]

Some authors use bullets in their persuasive writing. Bullets are commonly used in advertising and travel brochures. You may or may not have an occasion to try out bulleted writing during this study. [Ask students to do more revision work today.]

Share
Students read some of their work to the class. If a student did try using bullets, ask her to share her writing.

Possible Problems
None.

Follow-Up
Show students more examples of bullets in writing.
Discuss when an author might choose to make a numbered list and when an author might choose to use bullets instead.

Example of Using Bulleted Lists

Visit us in Cattington, New Hampshire

Nestled in the heart of the White Mountains, a stay at Cattington Inn is the perfect getaway. You'll encounter gracious hospitality, homestyle cooking, walking trails right on our property, a country porch with rocking chairs, and charming bedrooms filled with contemporary luxuries.

The Inn is located close to the main square with restaurants and shops. If you are looking for a quiet, relaxing vacation, you have found the right place. If you want a more active vacation, you have also found the right place. We are centrally located to all the White Mountains have to offer:

- Nestled between Mosaic Montage Art Gallery and Mitties Tea House

- Home to the award-winning Cattington Institute

- Steps from unique shopping on the square

- Walking distance from the famous Eckhard House Cinema

- 20 minutes from Cattington International Airport (CIA)

- Within 20 to 30 minutes of four world-class ski resorts

Cut It Out! Deleting Unnecessary Words

It is interesting to note that at times students use too very many unneeded and unnecessary words, and that this word usage sometimes can clutter up what would have been really good writing. Or should I say, *Student writing usually benefits from deleting unneeded words.* Let me say it succinctly: *Some words are unnecessary and should be deleted.*

If you see that the drafts are generally too wordy, do this lesson. If only a few drafts are excessively wordy, consider teaching students about concise language in writing conferences. **Time:** Forty-five minutes

Preparation
Copy Resource 6–5, Pulling Out the Weeds: Cutting Unneeded Words.

Goal

To prompt students to reread their writing aloud looking for unnecessary words

Minilesson

What is the worst part of taking care of a garden? Weeds! They grow all over the place and they grow so quickly. I can weed the garden on Tuesday and by Thursday more weeds have sprung up. The worst part about weeds is that if they are left to grow, they take away some of the beauty of the garden. It's much harder to see the flowers and focus on their beauty when they are being crowded out by weeds. That's why gardens should be weeded regularly.

Yes, in case you're wondering, there is a point here about persuasive writing. Today, we're going to talk about unnecessary words in your writing. In lots of ways, these words are like weeds. They seem to come out of nowhere. And just as weeds distract from a garden's beauty, unnecessary words stand in the way of a great piece of writing.

In a few minutes you will look at your writing and see if any words can be weeded out. It is likely that some words or even whole sentences can be cut. Sometimes this is true because you already said what you wanted to say and you said it again a few sentences later. In this case, one of the sentences can be cut. Sometimes part of a phrase can be cut, like in this case: Getting up early is difficult for me. Getting up early is so difficult that I usually just can't do it. *Ask yourself, how can these sentences be put together in another way that is not overly wordy but still has a rhythm that feels right?*

Other times, you can remove common extra words that don't do any work in the sentence. These are words like: often, really, very, a lot, for example. *Let me be clear here, not all of these words can be removed all of the time. Sometimes though some of these words clutter up the sentence and can easily be taken out.*

Let's take a look at the Resource page for this lesson. [Read and review Resource 6–5.]

Before you go write today, let's do a sixty-second find and see if we can find a place or two where we can cut words. This is difficult so you may not find a place yet, but let's try . . .

Allow sixty seconds and then have a few students share what words they think they can cut. They may have to read some of the words around the sentence so the other students can understand why those words can in fact be cut. If students select words that shouldn't be cut because the sentence will not make sense, let them know that you think these words are needed.

As you reread your writing today read it aloud. When you hear yourself talking you can more easily find the weeds. If you're not sure if a sentence or thought is needed, read the writing with and without the words and see what sounds better. Let's do it.

Share

Ask, *Were you surprised by the amount of word clutter?*

Possible Problem and Suggested Solution

Students take out nothing. They are really attached to their words and like the length of their writing. This is a predictable problem and as long as they have learned from the experience, you're still in good shape.

Follow-Up

Find examples of word clutter or possible word clutter in other writing and use them in a homework assignment. Common culprits: *really, totally, that, very, often, one thing I would like to tell you is . . . , In this paper I will talk about . . . , It is important to remember that . . .*

Pulling Out the Weeds: Cutting Unneeded Words

This wordy sentence: Students often write required writings that help them fulfill a graduation requirement so they graduate.

Could become: For many students, writing is a requirement for graduation.

This wordy sentence: When you write persuasively, you should consider making your argument very compelling by considering all of the reasons that are possible and then selecting your best one.

Could become: When writing persuasively, think of many different arguments and chose the strongest one.

This wordy sentence: The sun was so hot it made us all too overheated and we were really unhappy because we were just too hot and cranky.

Could become: We were overheated from the hot sun. This made us cranky.

Sentence or word I removed because . . .	I did not need this sentence or word word because . . . (*Examples might include:* I already said this earlier in the same piece of writing, I had other words that meant the same thing, the sentence has too many words and was hard to read, etc.)

Goal *To help students write short direct sentences*	**I came. I saw. I conquered.** **Short Declarative Sentences Persuade**

Short declarative sentences can strengthen a persuasive text. It's true. Short sentences are easy to read. (Some authors think that the more emotion associated with a topic, the shorter the sentences should be.) Ernest Hemingway loved the short sentence. He despised sentences sprinkled with flowery adjectives. He got straight to the point. **Time:** Forty minutes

Preparation
If desired, copy Resource 6–6, Examples of Short Declarative Writing

Minilesson

Ernest Hemingway was once challenged to tell a story in six words. Here's what he came up with: For sale: baby shoes, never used.

Persuasive writing lends itself to short direct sentences. Of course, all your sentences do not need to be short. We don't need to go overboard. But a short sentence at the start of a paragraph gives readers a bit of a break. And here's a secret: Short declarative sentences work at the end of a paragraph, too! They can be a great transition to the next paragraph.

Let's look at some declarative sentences in persuasive writing. [Refer to the sentences on the first half of the Resource. The second half of the Resource for this lesson can be used if you want to quickly review and talk through the different kinds of sentences.]

Find places in your writing where you can experiment with the length of your sentences. Often, you can take a long sentence and work with it so that it becomes two sentences. Try some short sentences today but don't overdo it or your writing will sound choppy. Try experimenting with short sentences and let's see how it goes.

Share
Have students share their short sentences.

Possible Problem and Suggested Solution
Short sentences are overdone. Ask students to reread their writing and find just a few places where the short sentences sound best.

Follow-Up
Look for interesting short declarative sentences in examples of persuasive writing. Where are they located within the paragraph? How do they sound?

Ask students to try speaking in short declarative sentences.

Show students the opposite of short sentences, often called *cascading or long windy sentences.* (A good place to find them is in "The New York Times Book Review." Book reviewers excel at the long, windy sentence.)

Examples of Short Declarative Writing

Examples

Science doesn't lie. (Advertisement for a skin-care product)

Imagine yourself a million miles away.

It's summer and it's hot. (Advertisement for lemonade)

Motor vehicle crashes are the number one cause of death for teens. *It's time for a change.*

Summer vacation is a time for fun. We get more exercise, read, sleep late, swim, hang out with friends, and just enjoy our down time. You remember down time? That unstructured time you had when you were our age. The truth is not just that we want this time, we need this time. We are only human, something I think our parents may forget sometimes. *We need a break from school.* (Student editorial)

Just tell her the truth. Needing some time alone is nothing to be ashamed of. (Advice column)

Kinds of Sentences

A *declarative sentence* makes a statement. It ends with a period. Example: *Rice is a popular food.*

An *interrogative sentence* asks a question. It ends with a question mark. Example: *Where did you find the card?*

An *exclamatory sentence* shows strong feeling. It ends with an exclamation point. Example: *The monster is attacking!*

An *imperative sentence* addresses someone directly. It can end with either a period or an exclamation point. The subject of an imperative sentence—you—is understood. Examples: *Cheryl, [you] try the other door. [You] Leave me alone!*

Goal

To prompt students to read their writing, note what they did well as a writer, and then use what they like about their writing to help them write more

Copy Cat! Finding Great Writing and Doing It Again

The lesson has three steps:

1. Students reread their writing and identify the parts they like the best. They think about why particular parts of their writing stand out.
2. Students decide what they specifically like about these best parts. (Is it precise word choice, sentences length, great persuasive imagery, an excellent use of questions?)
3. Students experiment with doing the same thing again in their writing. This may mean that they use the same technique in the same piece of writing or try the technique out in a new piece of writing.

If students are unaccustomed to rereading and evaluating their writing, do this lesson as two separate lessons. Steps one and two are the first lesson and step three is the second lesson. (You may also want to try this lesson as a writing conference first and then have the student you conferred with help you teach the lesson on the following day.) **Time:** Fifty minutes

Preparation

Choose a student's writing to use as an example: Copy or project that student's work. Copy Resource 6–7, Working from Areas of Strenghts.

Minilesson

Today, we are going to look at a mentor author. We will find something the author did really well and we'll try it. You all know this mentor author quite well and I don't just mean that you know the author's writing. You actually know the author. Any guesses?

It's you!

Today you are going to be your own teacher. You will study your own persuasive writing, figure out what you did really well, and do it again!

Perhaps, more explanation is needed here. Sometimes when we revise our writing, we look at what we don't like and make it better. Other times, like today, we can work from an area of strength. [Give an example.]

Today, you'll take the time to reread your writing and find a few places where the writing really stands out. You will try to figure out what you did as a writer that made this part one of your favorites. Once you have an idea what you did, then you will try it again.

You might, for example find a place where you particularly like the length of the sentence. You might find a place where you like the imagery you've created. You might find a place where you wrote a very specific example and feel that there is a place you could do that again. [For more ideas on techniques students might find in their own writing see the Persuasive Writing Techniques Linked with Examples chart on page 202.]

Let's take a few minutes to look at [student's name] *writing. She did this work yesterday. Let's see what she found.*

Guide the student as she discusses what she likes about her writing and specifically where in the text she would like to try to copy cat.

Spend just a few minutes finding something you really like or think we did particularly well in your writing. When you think you might have something, share this information with your writing partner. Okay, let's get to work.

Share
Have students share in pairs.

Possible Problem and Suggested Solution
Some students have trouble locating places where they particularly like the writing. This will get easier as they see other students finding their favorite parts of their writing.

Follow-Up
Repeat lesson task.

Working from Areas of Strength

Part I Like	What I Did as a Writer

Call to Action

Most persuasive writing involves a call to action—it asks the reader to do something or think or believe in a particular way. Sometimes this call to action is stated directly and forcefully, as in the case of a petition or some advertisements. But it can also be more indirect and subtle.

In this lesson, students look at excerpts from persuasive texts and study the call to action in these texts. Then they write (or experiment with rewriting) their own calls to action. This lesson refers to "Sis! Boom! Bah! Humbug!" and to the A-1 Limousine Advertisement (both in the Appendix). It is helpful if students have read this writing. **Time:** Fifty minutes

Preparation

Copy Resource 6–8, Examples of Calls to Action, or gather examples of calls to action from your students' own writing.

Minilesson

When your reader reads your writing, you want them to be affected by it. In some cases, we may want the reader to smile and think—yeah, that is true. That may be what Rick Reilly wanted when he wrote "Sis! Boom! Bah! Humbug!" When the advertising agency for A-1 Limousine wrote their advertisement, they were hoping that as readers put down the ad they thought about the advantages of a limousine for a special occasion. They were hoping that the reader would run to the phone and call A-1 and book a limo.

Many of you want your reader to do something as a result of your writing. [Quickly refer to students' pieces and the action they want from their readers: _____ *wants us to* _____ *and* _____ *wants us to* _____.] *Some of you want us to think differently about a topic. For example* _____ *wants us to think* _____.

Here's the question that gets at the heart of what you'll do today in your writing: If you—the author—want me—the reader—to do something, or believe something, how will you tell me that? Today you are going to look at how to write a call to action. *For those of you who have already written a call to action, you will spend some time experimenting with writing it in a different way. You may end up liking what you wrote first even better, but in revision it's important to experiment and work on more than one way to say something.*

Let's spend a few minutes looking at the Resource page for this lesson and noticing all of the different ways to call to action. [Read and review the Resource.]

As you write today, experiment with different ways to call your audience to action. You may also think about where in the text the call to action should go. Sometimes, like in the case of the movies on the airplane petition, it went at the beginning. Most often though, calls to action go at the end of the writing. (And in just a few persuasive pieces, the call to action is in the middle of the article.)

And now let me call you to action. Please get to your writing seats and begin your work immediately. (Wow, that sounds like a very bossy call to action. I need a different call to action voice.) Let me try again: Since this is the time when you work on your writing, please consider going back to your seats and writing. (Nah, that doesn't work either.)

Share

Have students read some of their calls to action, then discuss the difference in word choice and tone.

Possible Problems

None.

Follow-Up

Write a call to action that would never generate a response and talk about why it wouldn't.

Notice calls to action in print advertisements and radio and television advertisements. In what part of the advertisement do they appear—the beginning, the middle, or the end? What words are used?

Examples of Calls to Action

The following are different calls to action. Some are more subtle and others seem almost to be yelling at the reader. Some calls to action have a formal tone, while others sound more informal and friendly.

I would like you to consider . . .

So please, rethink your punishment . . .

Be a role model.

Our concern is loud and needs to be heard. Congress must act immediately to protect our children.

Order before midnight tonight and . . .

If we pull together, can we change the culture of news delivery on TV?

We demand that the United States Congress act immediately to put an end to unrated and violent films being shown to children on commercial flights operating in the United States airspace.

Here is a challenge to you my readers: If you are a teacher or work in a school, make an effort to notice the boys . . .

Stand together now to help support the continuation of the "Pledge of Allegiance" in schools!

Don't send me to educational camp!

7

Minilessons for Editing Persuasive Writing: Not the Same Old Thing

When Editing Persuasive Writing . . .

. . . students work on punctuation, capitalization, spelling, and anything else that makes their writing easier and more enjoyable to read.

I love to edit what I write! Editing is a time to read my writing and think about what I can do to make it easier for an audience to read. This is an opportunity for me to experiment with what I have already learned and to learn great new ways to rework my writing so that it has even greater meaning and impact on the reader.

—Kenneth Hucklebee, fifth grader

Okay, the truth. There is no Kenneth Hucklebee. I made him up. I wish that he did exist, that there were many Kenneth Hucklebees in our classrooms. There aren't.

As we help students edit their persuasive writing, let's strive to teach them to love (or at least not hate) editing. I know some of you are thinking that a student doesn't have to like [math, spelling, studying for a test, cleaning his room] to learn how to do it. And in some respects, it's true. Life certainly isn't just doing what we love. On the other hand, it's much easier to get students to put more time and energy into something when they like it. Desire to learn makes our job—the job of instruction—so much easier.

There are two predictable traps teachers sometimes fall into when teaching editing. Trap one is the hurry-up-we-need-to-finish-this-unit approach. This usually happens when we feel behind and quickly want to move on to the next unit. When this happens we assign editing but do not teach editing. In other words, we ask students to edit, but don't teach them how to be better editors. This leads to frustration on their part and ours.

The second and more common editing trap teachers fall into is the beat-it-to-death trap. We teach editing. And teach it. And teach it. When this happens the study loses stamina and unfortunately some students tune out. Before beginning to edit with your students, ask yourself these questions.

What is a reasonable amount of time to teach editing to this grade and this group of children? (Usually somewhere between one and four lessons work best for most students in elementary school through middle school.)

What will I review with students? How will I do this review? (If most students can successfully place end marks at the ends of their sentences, do not teach this skill as a minilesson to the whole class. Instead, gather a small group of students who are still having trouble and teach these students the skill.)

How much brand-new editing information will I present? (Usually presenting one or two new editing marks and then reviewing previously taught skills works well.)

What can I teach in editing conferences to students who are already proficient editors? Very proficient editors can work on varying their sentence lengths by experimenting with word choice and end punctuation. They can also work on placing punctuation in the middle of their sentences in order to slow the reader down or have the writing sound more informal. (Dashes help make writing sound and look informal.) There are many things to teach proficient editors.

When Teaching Editing

When we teach editing, sometimes we do things a particular way because, to be honest, we've always done them that way. Editing worksheets is one way to teach editing but is it really the best way? We do want students to practice the editing skills they have learned and frankly, we want to assess how well students know how to use a particular editing skill. But if we only have three days to teach editing, we probably don't want those days spent on worksheets and only one day spent on editing an actual paper. In some ways editing is a time game. We have to decide what is most important to teach and the absolute most effective way to teach it. So, consider this:

- Teach minilessons on punctuation and editing. Using fewer editing worksheets and more actual writing will help students learn how to apply what they know.
- Use mentor texts to teach editing. Reread some of your students' favorite persuasive writing and use this writing to teach punctuation.
- Teach editing skills that are particularly relevant for persuasive writing, for example, dashes, headings, exclamation points, italics, alliteration, quotation marks, ellipses, and so on.
- Ask students to edit in a different-color pen or pencil so that they can see their edit marks more easily and so can you. Use a second color when you do an editing conference with that student (so you can see what marks you taught).
- Show students when they can make decisions about the way they can edit a sentence or a group of sentences. There is often not only one right way to edit.

Coaching the Reader by Using Punctuation

This lesson will be "out there" for some of you—and if your students are generally punctuating well (congratulations!), they may not benefit from it. But if, like most teachers, you are frustrated by incorrect or missing punctuation in your students' writing, try it. This lesson has been used successfully at many different grade levels. **Time:** Forty-five minutes

Preparation

Before this lesson, copy and hand out Resource 7–1, Punctuation: What's the Point? Have students fill in the answers on the page. (Students will use their answers to review the punctuation rules.)

Minilesson

When we edit our writing, we do everything in our power to help our readers read and understand our writing. When we punctuate our writing, we give the reader an idea of how our writing should be read. Let's think about that. It's as if with punctuation we are saying, slow down, speed up, pause after that thought, read that loudly, ask that as a question. *When we edit today, we'll make decisions about punctuation based on three questions:*

1. *Regarding rules we'll ask ourselves: What punctuation rules do I know?*
2. *Regarding breathing we'll ask: Where do I think my readers will need to take a breath and what can I do to help them take this breath?*
3. *Regarding desire, you'll ask: How do I want our writing to sound when it's read— what thoughts do I want separated, read quickly, and so on?*

In the past we've talked about the rules of punctuation. Let's quickly review some of these rules before we move on. [Quickly review students' answers to Resource 7–1, Punctuation: What's the Point?]

Today as you edit your persuasive writing, you're also going to focus on new strategies for punctuating.

First, let's talk about breathing. [Exaggerate your breathing throughout the following.] *When I speak, there are places in my sentences where I have to breathe. Sometimes I need to take a breath in the middle of a sentence because the sentence is too long. Where I breathe naturally is an excellent spot to consider placing punctuation. You know? So today we'll use breathing to help us punctuate.*

Next, we'll think about desire. I have lots of ideas about how I want my writing to be read, and I can consider this as I punctuate my writing.

Today you will reread and punctuate your writing. There will be places in your writing where you have a decision to make about punctuation. For example:

■ *If you know the reader will need to stop in the middle of a long sentence, you may want to try to make two sentences instead.*

■ *If you know the reader has to stop at the end of the sentence, but are not sure if the end mark should be an exclamation point or a period, try it both ways and see what works better.*

Okay, let's work on punctuation!!

Share

Have students read a sentence and tell how they punctuated it.

Possible Problem and Suggested Solution

Students put in too much punctuation. They have gone punctuation crazy. Tell them that too much punctuation may be confusing to the reader and ask them to find places where the mark they put in may not be necessary.

Follow-Up

Reread excerpts from a favorite piece of persuasive writing and discuss how and why the author punctuated the writing that way.

Punctuation: What's the Point?

When I want my reader to stop at the end of a sentence, I . . .

When I want the reader to read with excitement, I . . .

When I want the reader to ask a question, I . . .

When I want the reader to pause, I . . .

or I . . .

or I . . .

Optional

When I want to show that someone is talking, I . . .

When I want the reader to put emphasis on a particular word in a sentence, I . . .

Capital Letters:
Know the Rules, BREAK THE RULES!

Doesn't it drive you crazy when students put capital letters in the wrong place? In this lesson, students review the "standard" rules for capitalization and then BREAK THEM.
Time: Forty-five minutes

Preparation
Copy Resource 7–2, Common Rules for Capitalization.
Get Dave Barry's article, "Science: It's Just Not Fair!" (search the title in Google or another search engine), and/or copy Tim Furnish's article, "Should We Take Away the Voting Rights of 18-Year-Olds?" in the Appendix.

Minilesson
As students are gathering their materials for writing workshop, write this sentence on the blackboard in capital letters: STOP RIGHT NOW. After most students stop, tell them that they can continue getting ready for writing workshop. Then officially begin the lesson.

When I wrote the words stop right now *on the board, many of you read the directions and followed them immediately. I wonder if I had written these words in lowercase letters if you would have done the same thing.*

As we already know, there are rules in English about when to use capital letters. Today, we're going to review these rules and then BREAK THEM. Yes, you heard correctly. Let's begin by reviewing. [Read and review Resource 7–2, Common Rules for Capitalization.]

Now that we have reviewed these rules, let's look at how *and think about* why *some professional writers break them.* [Hand out copies of Dave Barry's and/or Tim Furnish's articles and discuss where and why they've broken capitalization rules. Often entire words are capitalized in these articles for emphasis or for humor.]

Today, look back at your own writing and find one or two places where you can experiment with making a few words all capitals. Work hard!

Share
Have students share with their writing partners.

Possible Problem and Suggested Solution
Capital letters are everywhere. Set a maximum number of capital letters allowed per page.

Follow-Up
Divide students up into groups of four and give each group a copy of a persuasive text. Ask them to determine which words they would capitalize and why.
Ask students to collect persuasive writing, especially advertisements with capital letters that break the rules. Discuss why the writer might have chosen to break the rules.

Goals

To prompt students to review the rules for using capital letters and apply these rules

To help students determine where capital letters would be useful in their writing

Common Rules for Capitalization

1. Capitalize words at the beginning of a sentence:

   Hey, good job.

   Why did she do that?

   Yes!

2. Capitalize the pronoun *I*:

   I just love strawberry ice cream.

   Tell me what I have to do.

   Am I going to go to school?

3. Capitalize the names of specific people, places, or things:

   John Smith

   Leonardo Di Vinci

   North Dakota

   Duke University

   South Africa

   Statue of Liberty

   Toyota Sienna

   Memorial Day

   Atlantic Ocean

   Grand Canyon

4. Capitalize the first letter of the first word in a direct quote:

   "Who's been sleeping in my bed?" Papa Bear cried.

   John F. Kennedy said, "Ask not what your country can do for you . . ."

   The teacher asked, "Can you answer this question?"

Reading Lead Sentences to Determine Balance and Clarity

Balance and clarity are important in all nonfiction writing. This lesson helps students see how well their writing is balanced. This is an ideal lesson for students who are able to write in paragraphs. **Time:** Fifty minutes

Preparation

Copy Resource 7–3, Organization and Balance: Questions to Ask About Your Writing, and Resource 7–4, Living on Long Island.

Minilesson

Hand out copies of the Resources for this lesson.

We will begin today by reading an essay about Long Island. This essay was writen to convince the reader that Long Island is a great place to live. (The essay was actually written by a teacher who was trying to show students the kinds of problems that essays can have.) [Quickly read the essay aloud. Then ask students to talk to their partner about the weaknesses of this writing and how they might fix these problems.]

Okay, so I hear that you think that this essay has some problems and indeed it does. [Repeat back some of the most astute comments you heard while partners were talking.]

In order to see how well balanced an essay is and how clear it is to the reader, writers sometimes read the first sentence of each paragraph aloud and see how these first sentences work together. This gives the reader some idea if too much of the essay is about idea or if the essay jumps around too much. This is an extremely advanced editing and revision skill. Let's try it.

Read the lead sentences for each paragraph in succession. Point out to students that some of the lead sentences seem to go off track. Then check the lead sentences with the rest of the paragraph and talk about where the essay seems balanced and where it doesn't.

Quickly review the Organization and Balance Resource sheet. You will have already answered some of these questions with regard to the Long Island essay.

Today you will use this same strategy to read your own persuasive writing. This will help you determine what revision work you will do today. Read your writng aloud to a partner and then make a plan to make some changes—usually these changes involve rewriting a paragraph or changing the order of what was said. This is difficult work, but will pay off in the end. I know because I use this reading lead sentence strategy all of the time. Good luck!

Share

It has been a long lesson—so just do a *feel for how the lesson went* share by asking: Who thought this work was really hard today? Who found places that you would like to revise because of this strategy? Who has already revised those places?

Goal

To have students read the first sentence of each paragraph aloud in order to determine if their writing is balanced and clear

Possible Problem and Suggested Solution

Students become frustrated because they are suddenly aware of too many places in their writing that need revision. Speak with these students and help them find one place that would most benefit from revision.

Follow-Up

Have middle school students make a "reverse outline" of a persuasive text. A reverse outline is simply outlining a piece of writing that has already been written. This will help them see how the piece is organized and whether it is balanced. Use the reverse outline to talk through how the writing might be organized and balanced differently. (For more information on reverse outlines online, type in the words *teaching reverse outlines* into a search engine.)

Organization and Balance:
Questions to Ask About Your Writing

Does it make sense? Is it coherent?

Is there too much repetition?

Did I spend too long talking about one thing?

Did I say something too quickly?

Do the first sentences of my paragraphs make sense?

Do I get off track at any point?

Living on Long Island

Long Island is a great place to live. There are so many things to see and do here. Most people think that Long Island is a good summer spot, but they think that it's boring in the winter. They also think it's not exciting and they are wrong. I have had a really good life here, and it has been exciting too.

Long Island has lots of good restaurants. In the summer these places are crowded, but in the winter there is no line to eat dinner. Since Long Island is on the ocean, there is always good seafood to eat.

Shrimp is healthy and so are different kinds of fish. My whole family stays healthy because we now live on Long Island. When we lived in Tennessee we weren't as healthy because we didn't eat fish. When we went to visit Long Island, I thought it would be boring. It wasn't.

The beach is a great place and you can get a permit for your car so you only have to pay $40 for the whole summer. We go to the beach on Saturday afternoons and we really get our money's worth. We play in the sand and in the water. The water is nice and cold so you don't get that overheated feeling.

The beach is the best thing about living here on Long Island. The beach is good for kids and for adults. Everyone loves the beach—the water and the sand and the hot dogs from the concession stand. Who doesn't like that?

Headings

Students may already be familiar with headings from reading nonfiction. In this lesson, they will get the opportunity to write headings.

If you have talked about white space, you may also want to discuss headings as a way the author creates a bit of white space where the reader's eye can pause before moving on to the next section. This lesson is particularly useful when studying advertisements or travel brochures. **Time:** Forty-five minutes

Preparation

Prior to this lesson students should have read Chris Wondra's persuasive letter (in the Appendix). Copy or enlarge this letter for this lesson.

Copy Resource 7–5, How Headings Are Used.

Minilesson

What is a heading? Well, the word heading *can mean more than one thing. Sometimes it refers to what teachers want you to write at the top of each of your papers. Usually, this kind of heading gives the student's name, the date, the assignment, and sometimes the grade level or class number. But a heading can also be a word or a few words that tell the reader what the next section of writing is about. Let me show you an example.* [Show a heading from a nonfiction book or article students have already read. Read the heading aloud and think aloud about what you, as the reader, would expect to find out in the section of text that follows.]

Some types of persuasive writing also include headings. [Name the kinds of persuasive writing that you have looked at as a class that had headings.] *An author uses headings to help the reader. Talk to your partner about how these headings might help the reader.* [Call on a few students to share their thoughts/ideas.] *Here is a list of ways headings are used. Let's see what they are.* [Read Resource 7–5, How Headings Are Used, and then hand out copies of Chris Wondra's letter.] *Now let's look at Chris Wondra's headings and figure out why he used each one.* [Look at the headings in Chris' letter and talk about why Chris put each heading where he did.]

Today we will experiment with headings. Our goal is to add headings to your list of writing techniques, not necessarily to use headings for this piece of writing. You may find after experimenting that you like the way your persuasive writing looked and sounded without headings. It will be interesting to hear what you think. You may end up publishing your persuasive piece with or without the headings you write today. Today though, I want you to create some possible headings.

When you go off to write today, start by rereading your draft. Reread the whole draft. Then figure out where you think a heading might be helpful and write one. Good luck!

Share

Have students share their headings. Ask, *Why did you think a heading would be helpful at this part of the text? What does your heading say? What information comes after the heading?*

Possible Problems and Suggested Solutions

Students confuse headings *with* titles. The two have a lot in common. Let students know that they are both meant to help the reader know what is coming.

Students write a summary of the paragraph instead of a heading (*Recycling is good because it helps the environment,* for example). If this is a common problem, present a lesson that shows students what short, two- or three-word headings look like.

Follow-Up

Study headings while reading nonfiction.

We can use headings in persuasive writing to:
    Let the reader know what is coming.
    Help the reader organize the ideas being presented.
    Help the reader move from one section to another.

Headings phrased as questions usually anticipate (guess) readers' questions.

Resource 7–5 *How Headings Are Used*

Please Excuse Me for Interrupting

Dashes and persuasive writing go together like peanut butter and jelly. Dashes do so much for persuasive writing. Perhaps most important, they make the writing resemble thinking on the page—less formal. In this lesson, students experiment with dashes—and therefore voice—in their persuasive drafts or any other writing in their writer's notebook.

This lesson mentions in passing that dashes can take the place of parenthesis. If students use parentheses correctly in their writing, you may want to show students examples of dashes as a replacement for parentheses. **Time:** Forty-five minutes

Goal

To *help students
understand when
and why dashes are
used in writing*

Preparation

Copy Resource 7–6, Using the Dash.

Minilesson

Show students examples of sentences that include dashes. Here's one: *We should ask Samantha—the new girl in our class—to the party on Thursday.*

All of these sentences have something in common—a punctuation mark we don't see that often. It's this mark right here [circle the dashes], *and it's called a dash. Its full name is the em dash, because it's as wide as the letter M—see? Okay, so what is this dash all about and when do we use it?*

The dash is probably the trickiest punctuation mark but maybe the most interesting too. A dash can be used to take the place of commas, parentheses, or semicolons. [Draw these marks on chart paper as you say them so students are reminded of what they look like.] *The dash slows the reader down. In persuasive writing, dashes usually make the writing sound more informal—like talking or thinking aloud—or like an interruption—a sudden change of thought. Let me show you what I mean.* [Show an example of persuasive text with and without dashes.]

Today we will spend the first few minutes of writing workshop experimenting with dashes. This may be easier for some of you than others because some of you are writing to an audience that allows and encourages you to be informal. One of the things a dash can do is to make your writing sound like thinking on the page—so the truth is that dashes are used more in informal writing than in formal writing. (If you're writing to your sister, for example, you can be more informal than if you are writing to the governor of the state.)

Let's try this: Look for a place in your writing where you might be able to change a few words and put in a dash or use the examples on the Resource sheet as a guide to create your own sentence using a dash. You can work with a partner to do this work. [Allow five to ten minutes for this work. If students cannot find or think of a sentence, suggest that they start with the same words as the example sentences on the Resource.]

As you write today, think about using dashes in your writing. Don't worry if using a dash seems impossible in the piece you are writing right now. If it doesn't work there, you can try experimenting with the dash in some of the entries in your writer's notebook.

Share

Have students share examples of where they added dashes to their writing.

Possible Problem and Suggested Solution

Dashes are everywhere! Ask students to experiment with using other punctuation marks.

Follow-Up

Ask students to find examples of sentences that contain dashes in material they are reading in school or at home. Have them copy these sentences on index cards and place them on a bulletin board. Study these sentences: *What punctuation mark could go in place of the dash? What work does the dash do? Why do we think the author used a dash?*

Resource 7–6

Using the Dash

A dash is used:

To emphasize a point or to offset a comment that explains.

Example: For some students, the writing was sad—even difficult to get through.

To show a sudden change of thought.

Example: What he told me about persuasive writing was accurate—or so I thought.

In place of parenthesis.

Example: All of the students agreed to give up their spring break in order to work on their writing—even agreeing to work on the weekends—but if anyone tried to take away their reading time, they would have been upset.

Examples of other sentences I have found or written with dashes:

Proofread Carefully

In this lesson, students poofread (I mean proofread) their writing one last time. **Time:** Forty minutes

Preparation

Copy Resource 7–7, Proofreading Strategies.
Enlarge your own writing to use to model proofreading strategies.

Minilesson

Yahoo! We are almost there. You've written and rewritten and read and reread, and you're very close to finishing this piece of writing. It's time to proofread your writing one last time before you publish it.

Today, I will show you some strategies to use when you proofread your writing. You may already be familiar with some of these strategies, but others will be new to you. [Hand out copies of the Resource, Proofreading Strategies.]

Watch as I show you how to use some of these strategies. [Using the Resource as a guide, demonstrate how to use two or three strategies you think will most benefit your students. Ask students to place a star next to the strategies that you've demonstrated to remind them of what to work on when they are proofreading.] *All right, start proofing!*

As you confer while the students work, skim their writer's notebooks or old drafts and point out recurring errors. Show students how to avoid these errors.

Share

Ask, *What changes did you make?*

Possible Problem and Suggested Solution

Weak editors become frustrated. Suggest to these students that they do separate read throughs for spelling and punctuation. Compliment these students on what they are doing well!

Follow-Up

On another day, demonstrate some other proofreading strategies from Resource 7–7.

Proofreading Strategies

The Standard Stuff

Make sure that each sentence has ending punctuation and correct capitalization.

Read Backward to Check Spelling

This technique is a good one for catching spelling errors. If you read backward (word by word, not letter by letter), you are more likely to read what is actually on the page. Your brain will more easily spot spelling errors.

Check for Common Errors

1. Omitting little words, like *and, the,* and *a.*
2. Selecting the wrong pronoun: using *they* instead of *he* or *she,* or vice versa.
3. Going comma crazy! Putting commas everywhere, even where they don't belong.

Look for and Remove Unnecessary Sentences or Words

As you or your partner read aloud, you are likely to notice words and phrases that don't help the writing (*very, really, that is why, the reason is, again, I think,* are some examples). Take them out.

Ask Questions and Locate Answers

Place a question mark next to places in your writing that you are unsure how to edit. Use available resources to figure out the answer to your questions. Examples are an actual or online dictionary or thesaurus, your computer's spell-check program, or an editing expert in your class or home.

Check for Errors You Are Prone to Make

Everyone has things that consistently trip them up: misspelling certain words, capitalization, comma usage, and so on. Identify *your* common errors and watch for them.

CHAPTER 8

Minilesson for Publishing, Celebrating, and Assessing Persuasive Writing

When Persuasive Writing Is Published and Celebrated . . .

. . . the pieces students have written are read or heard by an audience. Sometimes the text reaches a very specific reader, like the recipient of a persuasive letter. In other cases, the audience is a group of people—the readers of a school newspaper or the class, for example. Regardless of the audience, writers should receive comments about and praise for their work.

When Persuasive Writing Is Assessed . . .

. . . students are evaluated on their process (how they went about the work, made decisions about what to do, and worked in partnerships, and so on) as well as the quality of the final product (its ranking on a predetermined scale).

Putting Persuasive Writing into Final Form

There are as many philosophies about helping students put their writing into final form as there are writers themselves. Should we ask students to recopy their writing and then check to make sure it is letter perfect? Many teachers want to do this but then feel guilty that the process takes so long. (We teachers are all too familiar with guilt!) Or should we let students edit their writing to the best of their ability and then read it to the class without copying it over? But then we worry that students will think that the final form is unimportant.

How do we resolve this dilemma? If the audience consists solely of other class members, I feel it's acceptable for students to self- and peer edit and then read from this polished-but-not-perfect draft. This type of publishing is particularly useful for younger students (grade 3 and below), since it takes a long time for these students to recopy their work. It's also useful if you want students to write more than one piece in a unit, since they can go on to the next one without getting bogged down in typing and formatting.

If you decide to let students read from their rough drafts, let the audience know that the students know their writing has not been perfectly edited. If you know reading from a rough draft will be frowned upon at your school, or if teaching writing as a process is new to your school, you'll probably want your students to publish their writing in perfect final form—and give students the extra time this requires.

Secretly (well, maybe not so secretly), I hope that your students have a larger audience than their classmates for their persuasive writing. If this is the case, then I'm convinced that a letter-perfect final product is the only option.

If your students are in the lower elementary grades, don't know how to keyboard, are second language learners, or have trouble putting their writing into final form for some other reason, call in the reserves. Get help!

Suggestions for Speeding Up the Process of Putting Writing into Final Form

1. Ask parents or other adult volunteers (older students who are particularly good editors are an acceptable alternative) to come to class and type students' persuasive writing. They should do this in the classroom, if at all possible, so that any questions they have while typing can be answered immediately.
2. Schedule extra time in the computer lab, if your school has one.
3. Set aside as much time as possible for students to put their writing into final form. A solid hour and a half in one morning is much less frustrating than three, thirty-minute writing periods.
4. If students do not have access to a computer and are expected to rewrite their writing, give them time to start this recopying work as homework.
5. Let students recopy the fastest way they know how. Often students who have trouble tracking will have trouble recopying because they lose their place as they recopy. Show these students how to: cover the rest of the page with another sheet of paper so their eyes are naturally drawn to the right part of the page or speak the sentence aloud and then say it again as they write it. Also, you might try asking one student to read the paper aloud to the student who is recopying.

Making Sure Persuasive Writing Is Read and Celebrated

Persuasive writing, more than any other kind, is meant to be read by an audience. How can the writer convince the reader if in fact there is no reader?

There are many ways that students can publish their persuasive writing, often to multiple audiences. If a student writes a letter to a local elected official, for example, he should of course send the letter to that person, but the letter can also be printed in the local newspaper.

The wider the audience, the more debate and dialogue there will be on the topic. There is no greater thrill for writers than knowing that readers are reading and discussing their ideas. Will the piece persuade readers to do or think as the writer had hoped? Writers certainly hope so. But just getting their words into readers' hands gives students great pride. Students are thrilled to know that people will read their words, understand their thoughts, and give time and attention to their ideas.

Publishing also gives students a sense of closure. As teachers we know this, but in the rush to move on, we sometimes forget to give students the time they deserve to put their writing out into the world and bask in the glory of work that has gone through a long thinking, planning, and composing process and is finally finished. Unlike earlier in the writing process, we now welcome the words, *I'm done*.

There are many ways student writing can be read by others. The following is a brief list of ideas. If this is your first time publishing persuasive writing, keep it simple.

In Class and School

- Have students read their writing (or excerpts) to the class. Set aside an hour or more and let all students read on the same day. Or, allot ten or fifteen minutes a day and assign two or three student readers each day.
- Have one student each day read his or her persuasive writing (or an excerpt) during schoolwide morning announcements. Suggest that students from other classes respond to what they heard.
- Keep a three-ring binder filled with examples of students' great lines or great punctuation. Ask students to read each other's best lines before they go into the binder.
- Have students read their writing to an older or younger student in the school. This works best when the students already have an established relationship with the other student. (They are reading buddies, for example.)
- If there is an existing weekly or monthly newspaper or literacy arts magazine, encourage students to publish their persuasive writing in the next issue. If the school does not have an existing publication, ask a parent to put together a persuasive writing magazine that can be handed out to students or made available electronically. This is a big undertaking so be sure you have enough volunteers who are willing and able to put in lots of extra hours.
- Get volunteers to type your students' persuasive writing on the school's website.
- Set up and maintain an interactive school bulletin board of persuasive writing.

In the Community

- Have students read their work to a respected (and willing) adult.
- Have students submit their work to the local newspaper.
- Have students read their work at a local bookstore. Even the big bookstores are often willing to entertain a night of student readers. Also ask the manager if he or she is willing to display samples of student writing in the store window.

- Have students read their work to residents of a nursing home or an assisted living facility.
- Have students read their writing at a local and appropriate venue—a school board meeting, faculty meeting, or city council meeting.
- Post student work on a community bulletin board. (I am referring here to the old-fashioned kind that you can buy at office supply stores, not a website.)

In the Wider World

- Have students submit their work to newspapers, magazines, radio commentary programs, and contests.
- Suggest that students include their persuasive writing on personal websites and blogs (with adult permission and supervision).

Celebration

Students, like adults, crave celebration for a job well done. Students, like adults, want to take a few minutes to breath and to think, *Wow, I finished and wow, I did well.* In another era, when there was less pressure on teachers to raise test scores, and a reasonable amount of curriculum to cover, teachers often had writing celebrations that they called publishing parties. Some of these parties were elaborate celebrations that involved special lunches and desserts and juice, while other celebrations were smaller and more low key. It didn't matter how students celebrated, it was just that they celebrated.

You certainly don't have to plan a festival or a gala or even a party. Just a small bit of merriment, a little ceremony (and maybe some juice) is perfect. Writing is hard work and finishing that work, even if only for a few days, deserves recognition. That's my plug for celebration. Know that it's heartfelt.

Making the Most of Assessment

Both teacher assessment and student self-assessment are important for student writers. This feedback helps provide students with valuable insight into the strengths and challenges of their writing and their writing process.

It's difficult to figure out which should come first: student self-assessment or teacher assessment. If teachers assess first, students just echo what we say. After all, we are the teachers, we must know the right answers. (Unless you are teaching middle school students, in which case you know close to nothing. Maybe a little more than the students' parents, but just a little.) And if self-assessment comes first, students will not have a chance to consider our feedback and take it seriously. Right? No, not exactly.

My suggestion is to let students assess themselves *before* we assess their work. Believe me, your feedback is still important. But I believe that if the ultimate goal is to have students set some of their own writing goals, and to be critical readers of their writing, that work starts with their own evaluation of their writing.

Let me be clear. You are the expert. You know more about writing than your students do, that's why they're your students. So you teach minilessons, and teach in writing conferences, and teach during the share time. But in the end, when they are not with you anymore, when they are writing for work or for pleasure in their lives, the most useful skill they can have is to be critical readers of their own words. That skill, the ability to find greatness and weakness in their writing, is one of the most difficult and most important things we can teach students. Self-awareness and self-evaluation are urgent. And it doesn't happen overnight. It takes practice.

We don't just expect students to know how to assess themselves. We teach them how to do it and do it well. So that in the end, they don't just say or write what they think we want to hear, but they write what they actually see and feel. Remember students are not born knowing how to do this work, we have to teach them how to do it.

If you haven't asked students to assess their own writing work, try it. You will be surprised with the results.

Predictable Problems and Possible Solutions When Students Assess Their Own Writing

Problem	Solution
Students' self-assessments are filled with generalities like, *My writing is good here*, or, *I like what I wrote here because I say it in a good way.*	Direct students' attention to what their writing did for the reader. Why did the student use those particular words, or particular punctuation, or organize their writing in that particular way?
Students are too critical of their own work. They can't find the strengths of the writing.	Ask students to point out their favorite part and talk with them about why that part is their favorite. (You may also want to begin this work by showing students your favorite part of their writing.)
It is difficult for you to grade students' work because their writing is far below grade level but their effort deserves an "A."	Write a separate note to these students or have a longer assessment conference and focus on what they did well and evidence of their learning during your persuasive writing unit. If you are required to give a grade do so and be honest about the grade. If you are not required to give a grade (but have always done so), focus on self-assessment and ask students as part of their self-evaluation to determine the grade they deserve. Grades that are given by a student to himself within the context of other assessments are the most meaningful kind of grades.

Self-Assessment: How to Say More Than "I Think My Writing Is Good"*

In this lesson, students assess their own writing. It may take more than one lesson for students to answer all of the questions on the assessment sheet, but don't cut out the part of the lesson when students talk to one another. Talking about their answers before writing them improves their answers tremendously. So does your conferring as they talk with one another. **Time:** Fifty minutes

Preparation

Copy Resource 8–1, Self-Assessment Form for Persuasive Writing.

Minilesson

Begin today's lesson by commenting on the writing celebration, if you had one.

Today, you'll do some of the most important writing work you have done all year. You will reread your writing and assess your writing. You will reflect on your own writing and what you've learned during this persuasive writing unit.

When you do this work, think about each self-assessment question and give a thoughtful answer. Don't just write down a quick, I-want-to-be-done answer. When I read each assessment I should be able to say, before I even look at the name on the paper, Oh, that must have been written by [name a student].

Let me give you some idea of the kinds of things that other students have written. This will help you think about what you can say and what I mean by a thorough and specific answer. One of the hardest questions for students to answer is, Where in the text did I do my best writing? *This is the question we'll consider.*

One student wrote this: "I like it when I wrote: *Brring Brring Brring goes the alarm clock on life.* I found a different way of saying that life is passing you by. I could have just said, *Hurry up* but instead I put sound to my description of time passing by. It is a more interesting way to say the same thing."

Another student wrote: "I like it when I wrote: *I am always in last place in the race.* I really wanted my readers to know what it is like to feel behind in school. I tried to make the sentence visual so that the reader could see what it is like to feel behind. I thought about races because I figured that many people have had that experience at one time or another—even if they don't race, they probably have had races in P.E. and stuff."

A third student wrote: "I actually think my title is my best writing. 'It's a Game Coach' was my second title. My first title was, 'Don't Take It Too Seriously' but that title sounded kind of boring. The final title is actually talking to the coach and makes a bigger impact on the reader."

You see how these answers were very clear and told the reason why the writer considered this writing to be strong writing? Now you're going to talk about the the first three questions with your writing partner. You'll talk before writing your answers because talk-

---

*The idea for this lesson comes from Isoke Nia.

ing will help you figure out what you want to say. When it's your turn to listen, gently prompt your partner to give examples or say more or say something more clearly. Here are questions you can use to get your partner to be more specific:

What is an example of that?
Could you say more?
When you say the word_____ do you mean _____ or _____?

All right, get to work. Remember to begin by rereading your writing and reading the assessment questions.

Give students time to talk through the first three questions with their partners. As they talk, gently prompt their listening partners to ask questions. Make sure both students in the partnership get a chance to answer and prompt. Then give students time to write their answers to the first three questions. If possible, give students more time to talk and then write the answers to the other two self-assessment questions.

Share

There may not be enough time to share today. If there is time, ask a few students who feel comfortable doing so to read (not paraphrase, but actually read) their answers to the class.

Possible Problem and Suggested Solution

Some students did not find examples of their best work. Ask the question another way. Try this: If you had to read only a few sentences for share time, what sentences would you select? Why?

Follow-Up

Have students share some of what they wrote on their self-assessments. Students can share their answers with partners, in small groups, or with the whole class.

Self-Assessment Form for Persuasive Writing

1. What have I learned about writing a persuasive text?

2. Where in the text did I do my best writing? What did I do that makes this good writing?

3. What would I do differently next time?

4. What is one goal I have for my next piece of writing?

5. What other comments would I like to make?

Here are some possibilities:

- Persuasive writing was different than I first imagined because . . .

- One of the things I learned from other writers during this unit was . . .

- Something I learned about persuasive writing that I may be able to try in other kinds of writing is . . .

- One mistake I think writers make when they try to persuade their audience is. . . .

Self-Assessment: Assessing the Process of Writing

In this lesson, students assess their own writing process. If you think that two assessments are too many for your students, try to do this assessment as a class discussion. You will not be able to hear from all of the students, but you will get a general idea of what worked for most students and what didn't. **Time:** Fifty minutes

Preparation

Copy Resource 8–2, Assessing My Process of Writing.

Minilesson

In today's lesson, I will learn from you. I would like to know a little bit about your persuasive writing process—what worked well for you and what didn't. [Review the questions on the Resource page for this lesson. Briefly show students what kinds of things they might say.] *All right, go to it. Remember to begin by rereading your writing and reading the assessment questions.*

Give students time to talk through the first three questions with their partners. As they talk, gently prompt their listening partners to ask questions. Make sure both students in the partnership get a chance to answer questions. Then give students time to write their answers to the first three questions. If time allows, give students more time to talk and then write the answers to the other two assessment questions.

Share

End the lesson by thanking students for their feedback.

Possible Problems

None.

Follow-Up

None—it's definitely time to be done!

Assessing My Process of Writing

Talk about and then write your answers to questions below. (Feel free to also say what didn't work well too.)

What really worked for me when I collected persuasive ideas was . . . I think this is because . . .

What really worked for me when I developed my ideas was . . . I think this is because . . .

Was drafting hard, easy, medium hard, etc.? Why?

What really worked for me when I revised was . . . I think this is because . . .

What really worked for me when I edited was . . . I think this is because . . .

CHAPTER 9

Minilessons for Persuasive Writing on Standardized Writing Tests

I don't hate standardized writing tests. True, these tests are given too much weight in planning curriculum and instruction throughout the year, and it's crazy to think that they're often considered to be the one true measure of learning. But despite the many issues surrounding standardized writing tests, the tests are here to stay (at least for awhile) and hating them zaps my energy and makes it more difficult to teach.

Of course, as educators, we're leery of the term *teaching to the test*. We're afraid teaching to the test will compromise our curriculum. If we teach to the test, we won't teach what matters most in teaching writing, like the love of writing, techniques for getting our thoughts and ideas on paper, rereading and revising strategies, and so many other things. We know there is so much more to writing than being able to respond quickly to a timed prompt.

But if we look at what we should do to prepare students for standardized writing tests, we find that much of this preparation is not only *not* a waste of time but is actually useful. So let's forget for a moment the circumstances surrounding standardized writing tests and focus on the tests themselves.

We do want students to be able to do certain things in writing, and many standardized writing tests provide practice in doing these things. Here are just a few:

1. Writing under timed conditions.
2. Developing a position on an issue.
3. Using evidence to support an argument.
4. Writing with voice, or style.
5. Writing an organized and cohesive text.
6. Selecting words that are specific and precise.

General Information on Standardized Writing Tests

Each state requires different standardized tests at different times in students' educational progress. A common schedule includes one or two standardized writing assessments in elementary school, at least one in middle school, and at least one in high school. (This does not include the SAT or ACT that college-bound students are required to take.)

In some states, students take a standardized writing test each year. Some of these tests may be practice tests that don't appear on students' transcripts. Parents—and even the students themselves—may not see these scores.

Some states give timed writing tests; other states give untimed ones. The tests may be administered in one session, in two sessions on the same day, or in sessions on two different days. Some states require students to use a planning sheet.

In some states, portfolio assessments have replaced standardized writing tests especially in the elementary grades. In my opinion, these assessments are also riddled with problems and are in some cases much worse than the original timed writing tests. This is because when assessment changes quickly and abruptly teachers are often given no support in helping students prepare for these assessments. When assessment changes teachers often feel as though they have to guess at instruction. What now? Also, with portfolio assessment, teachers are asked to collect many samples of student writing throughout the year. In effect then teachers feel as if they have to teach to push students to produce writing quickly. The result is that children hardly ever get to think through the process of writing. They are asked to "hurry up and draft" for most of the year. Maybe the concept of portfolio assessment is a good one, but the execution has been poor.

No matter what kind of writing tests each state gives, one constant throughout the country is that the majority of writing assessments require students to write persuasively.

When to Begin Test Preparation

Ideally, students should begin preparing for a standardized writing test three or four weeks before the date of the text. If the test will include persuasive writing, it's best if students have studied this kind of writing earlier in the year; that way you can simply revisit some of the techniques they've already learned. This second-time-around approach makes presenting a test-preparation unit easier and will likely result in better test scores.

If you begin test preparation two or three months before the test, students will almost certainly become bored. Their enthusiasm for learning and the energy they expend doing so fade. You don't want this! You want students to want to learn, because when they do, your job is that much easier.

We know this to be true, but sometimes we panic. The more panic we feel, the earlier we begin test instruction. I know; I've done it. The teacher next door to me began preparing students for the standardized writing tests early in the year, so I did too. It was not my best year of teaching, and my students did no better than others had done in previous years. (They may have even done worse.) So here's my challenge to you: Start your test-prep sessions a little later this year.

Helpful Hints

During your test-prep unit, limit the amount of writing students do in other subject areas. Writing is physically and mentally tiring. This is not a good time to schedule a big social studies paper or a science essay test. It's also not a good time to ask students to write reading responses, book reports, or one-act plays. Assign as much creative, hands-on work as you can in all other subjects.

Limit the amount of homework you assign. More homework means kids will be less fresh and more tired in class the next day. When this happens, you will have to work harder to keep their attention on the lesson and students will actually learn more slowly.

Help students feel less nervous and more confident. Be careful what you say (or communicate nonverbally) to students about standardized tests. Putting too much pressure on students will increase the chances that they will become anxious and begin (or continue) to doubt themselves. Suggest that parents remain calm (even if they have to pretend!).

A Plan of Action

Instruction and practice are the keys to helping students do their best writing on persuasive writing tests. Since time in the classroom is always limited, start by assessing what students do and don't know how to do. Otherwise, you're likely to waste time teaching something students already know. Or, even more likely, you may build a lesson on knowledge students do not yet have. For example, you may present a minilesson on how to plan writing when students first need a refresher on how to correctly read the prompt.

Spending a little time watching students begin to answer a prompt will go a long way in helping you decide what to teach. This doesn't require an entire writing period—just long enough for you to observe their writing and take notes on what they are doing well and what challenges they face. This informal assessment can save you oodles of teaching time.

Although there is no *formula* for teaching students how to do well on standardized tests, there *are* many ways to help students with these tests and to teach them about persuasive writing in the process. The following is a plan for a unit on persuasive writing test preparation. As always, this is not the only way, merely one possible way.

1. **Give a quick assessment.** Give students time in class to answer a prompt similar to the one they are likely to encounter on the standardized writing test. This quick assessment should take no more than one writing period. (Make sure students understand that this assessment will not be graded.) Skim these assessments. Jot down what students still need to learn. What do students know how to do? What are the students' challenges?

2. **Introduce sample work.** Give students samples of test essays written by other students that received high scores. Let students get a feel for how these essays should sound and how they look.

3. **Study the rubric.** Give students copies of the rubric that will be used to score their writing. Explain how the test will be graded. Talk about each category and what the categories mean (for example, elaboration, voice, grammar, punctuation, and so on).

4. **Read student sample work and identify strong writing.** Look at high scoring papers and specifically note why the paper got a high score. Look at each category on the rubric and find examples of where the students did that work well. Briefly review low scoring sample papers and discuss why they receive low scores.

5. **Teach a few minilessons.** Select three or four. Ask yourself, *What is most important for my students to know how to do?* Or, read through the minilessons in this chapter and ask yourself, *Would my students benefit from this lesson?* As you teach these lessons, draw on what students have already learned (for example, *Remember when we read the letter by Michael Matthews and added to each of his paragraphs to bulk up his writing? We're going to do the same thing here*).

6. **Ask students to write a persuasive prompt.** If you have last year's prompt, use it. If you don't, select one of the prompts provided in the next section. Give students ten or fifteen more minutes than they will have on the actual test. This is their first try, and you don't want to impose too much stress. Students need to feel as successful as possible and see themselves as people who can handle this kind of test. Note the students who finish much too early; it's usually the result of not having done enough preplanning and then running out of things to say.

7. **Teach students how to score the test writing, and then have them grade one another's essays.** Blacken out student names, then have two students separately score each paper. Score each paper yourself as well. Average these three scores to create a final score. Write two comments on each paper, one highlighting what the student did well, the other identifying a challenging area. Give students time to look at their grades and their comments.

8. **Teach two or three more minilessons.** Repeat or extend lessons or teach something new. Ask yourself, *What are the most important lessons I can teach at this point?*

9. **Give a practice test or two and simulate test conditions.** Five or six days before the actual test, give students a practice test. Simulate actual test conditions as closely as possible:

   - Administer the practice test at the same time of day the real one will be given.
   - Arrange the room—chairs, desks, clocks, and so forth—as it will be during the actual test.
   - Write the time remaining on the board every few minutes.
   - Give oral or written directions that exactly or closely match the real ones.
   - Time this test and collect test papers when time is up.

10. **Give students last-minute advice or reminders.** Look over the student responses on the practice tests and think about one or two things you can say to the class that will help them the most right now. Should students be more cognizant of time? Should they recheck their spelling? Should they work on stronger endings for their essays?

Persuasive Writing Prompts for Younger Elementary Students

Some people do kind things to help one another. Write a letter to someone convincing them to give a medal to a person who has helped other people in a major way.

One way to stay healthy is to exercise. Write a letter to a friend convincing her or him to exercise.

Your teacher is considering getting a class pet. Write a letter to your teacher convincing her to get a class pet.

Pretend that you are running for president of your grade. Give your views about why you would be a good class president.

Should students have more or less homework?

Persuasive Writing Prompts for Older Elementary Students

The local newspaper is having a "Good Friend" contest. To enter your friend, you must think of a time in your life when your friend did something with you or for you that showed what a terrific friend he or she is. Choose an event that shows how your friend is a good friend to you. Write a letter to the newspaper that tells about that event so that people will know why your friend deserves to win.

Your teacher will not be in school tomorrow. He or she is looking for one student to be the teacher for the day. Write a letter to convince your teacher that you should be chosen.

Some people like to live in small towns where people know each other. Others prefer to live in a city where there are more people. Where would you like to live and why? Convince your reader to move to a small town or a big city.

In order to save money, your principal is thinking about canceling all field trips for the remainder of the year! Write a letter to your principal persuading him or her to allow students to continue going on field trips. Give at least three reasons to support your position.

Write a persuasive essay stating whether children under the age of sixteen should be required to wear helmets while biking, skateboarding, rollerblading, and skiing. Remember, you must argue in such a convincing manner that others will agree with you. The outcome of the state legislature's vote on helmets could be decided by your essay.

Persuasive Writing Prompts for Middle School Students

"All Americans are free." Write a persuasive essay that agrees or disagrees with this statement.

Because of potential problems, many middle schools have banned cell phones. Do you agree or disagree with the cell phone banning? Write an essay in which you agree or disagree with the cell phone banning. Convince the reader of your opinion and support your opinion with reasons and examples.

Research suggests that because teenagers have different sleep patterns they should begin middle school at a later time in the morning. The school board is considering adopting a plan where these schools would start school ninety minutes earlier and end school ninety minutes later. Please prepare a speech for or against this plan. Remember to use reasons and examples.

Some of the parents at your school have started a campaign to limit the amount of homework that teachers can assign. Teachers at your school have argued that the homework is necessary. What is your position? Write a letter to the editor of your local newspaper stating your position and supporting it with three convincing arguments.

Some people believe that boys and girls should go to separate schools. Decide whether you think it is a good idea and persuade your readers to agree with your decision.

Words That Mean *Persuade*

There are many reasons why some students have difficulty understanding language. In this lesson, students learn the words that will signal them to write persuasively. This lesson is particularly good for students who have word retrieval difficulties, have weak vocabularies, are not fluent in English, or may encounter difficulty understanding the directions on a persuasive writing test. **Time:** Fifteen minutes

Preparation

Copy Resource 9–1, Words and Phrases That Signal Persuasive Writing.

Minilesson

As you know, we are preparing for the writing test that you will all take soon. There are some words that you might see in the questions that you may not know. The writing test is a persuasive writing test. When you write, you will try to convince the reader that what you are saying is true.

Some words are what we will call signal words, *and when you see these words, your brain should say,* Oh, I know what they are asking for: persuasive writing.

Hand out Resource 9–1 and review and discuss the words.

Share

None.

Possible Problems

None.

Follow-Up

Help students understand other words they may not be familiar with (for example, *prewrite, rehearse,* and *conventions*).

Words and Phrases That Signal Persuasive Writing

Persuade

Convince

Suggest

Request

Give your opinion

Recommend

Sell

List pros *or* cons

Give your view

Tell what you think

Analyzing the Writing Prompt

It is not uncommon for students to misunderstand the prompt on a persuasive writing test. This usually happens because students either skim the prompt instead of reading it or do not understand the language in the prompt. In this lesson, students examine prompts, read them slowly, and concentrate on understanding them. **Time:** Thirty minutes

Preparation

Copy Resource 9–2, Strategies for Reading the Prompt.

Copy the pages with the writing test prompts for your grade level (see pages 182–183) or use some old prompts from your state writing test. (To get the lastest prompts from around the country, go online and search the words *state department persuasive prompt* and put in the name of the state you are interested in.)

Minilesson

Do you know who Charlie Brown is? [Show a picture of Charlie Brown and the entire Peanuts gang.] *Charlie Brown used to get really nervous in school sometimes. Once he was taking a test and this word was written on the top of the test:*

NAME_____

He was rushing because he wanted to do well on the test. He read this word and instead of writing his own name, he began to panic: Name. Name what? Name who? I don't know how to answer this question! *Sometimes in an effort to get started right away, we act just like Charlie Brown.*

Today, we're going to talk about reading the prompt on the test and then rereading it in order to figure out what it is asking. I'm not saying we should take all day and slowly kick back and relax. But I am saying that spending just a minute or two or three on reading the prompt will help you figure out what exactly *is being asked and then what you should write.*

I'm going to teach you three strategies for reading the prompt and then we will practice using these strategies. [Hand out and review Resource 9–2, Strategies for Reading the Prompt.] Key words *are the words you think are most important in understanding the prompt. It is difficult to figure out which words are key words. Key words are words that are most important in helping students understand what the prompt is asking.* [Read the prompt aloud and then show students how to circle the key words. Discuss why these words are key words.]

The next step is to find a place where we can quickly write examples or reasons. [Show students how to do this work. For example, if the prompt says we are looking for a student to be teacher for the day, near the words *teacher for the day*, you might write the words: *responsible, controls the class,* and *knows the work.*]

Before beginning to write, underline what the question is asking you to do. [Show students how to underline words like write a letter to convince your teacher that you should be chosen.]

Now, watch me as I go back and quietly reread the prompt. I'll read slowly, and I may even mouth the words as I read. Today, I have given you a few different prompts to look at. These prompts have been given to students about your age on actual standardized writing tests. Using your Resource, try to write around the prompt like we did together. Remember to circle key words, write examples or reasons, and underline what the question is asking. Then, remember to reread the prompt one or two more times. Go to it.

Share

Students share how they figured out what the prompt asked them to do.

Possible Problem and Suggested Solution

Students still have difficulty analyzing the prompt. Practice analyzing more prompts.

Follow-Up

Try this lesson again with another prompt. Practice makes prompt reading easier.

Many students benefit from "trying to see" what the prompt is asking. Ask students to picture (visualize) the words in the prompt; for example, *Picture yourself teaching the class when your teacher is out,* or *Picture yourself in a big city instead of a small town. What do you see. . . ?* This picture taking helps some students think of reasons and examples.

Strategies for Reading the Prompt

Circle key words.

Write examples for some of the key words.

Underline the words that tell you what to do.

Go with What You Know

In this lesson, students draw on personal experiences to answer the prompt. **Time:** Forty minutes

Preparation

Copy Resource 9–3, Using What You Know, or have students do the writing for this lesson in their writer's notebooks. (They can do this by folding the page in half and creating a crease down the middle.)

Minilesson

Sometimes after we read a prompt, our first reaction is, I don't know what to write because I don't know about this topic. *But often we do know about the topic, we just don't realize we do. Some personal experience, something that happened to us, can help us answer the prompt. Today's lesson is called* Go with What You Know. *It's about searching the files in your brain to find a personal experience that can help you answer a prompt.*

A third grader named Marc encountered this prompt on his writing test:

Write why your class should or should not get a class pet.

At first he thought, Oh, no, I haven't been in a class that has had a class pet. I really don't know much about this subject. *Then he reread the prompt and thought about what experiences he'd had that could help him:*

Umm, I've never owned a pet, but I guess having a class pet would be fun. No, that's not a good reason. Oh, but wait, there was that time when the next door neighbors went away and asked us to watch their dog. That was the worst! I had to walk that dog four times a day. Mom said it was my responsibility. Hey, that's it—that could be one of my reasons—class pets teach students responsibility!

Let's try this together. Here's a writing prompt:

Schools should/should not give students iPods for perfect attendance.

Think aloud with your writing partner. Start by telling each other your first reaction (this might become your thesis statement). Then, and this is the most important part, see if you can find a personal experience or story that would be helpful in supporting your opinion.

Give partners two or three minutes to talk. Listen to the students' conversations. Then share with the class a few effective experiences or stories students have come up with. Add additional ideas: *Because students really want to get iPods, they might go to school when they are really sick and should stay home. You could be sitting next to someone who is sick and you could get sick yourself. And what about students who have to miss school because of religious holidays not on the school calendar?*

Today, you'll be given a list of three prompts. For each prompt, try to write what you already know about the topic based on your own experiences and stories. As you work today, you can talk quietly with a partner and share stories with each other.

Share

Ask, *What personal stories were you able to find to support your argument?*

Possible Problem and Suggested Solution

Students' experiences need to be tweaked in order to support the point. For example, someone sitting next to someone who is sick might not have gotten sick but just been afraid of getting sick. Remind students that this is not a lie detector test, it is a writing test. A little tweaking here and there is acceptable, even expected. If students are uncomfortable stretching the truth this way, suggest that they write a what-if or a this-could-lead-to statement.

Follow-Up

Present the lesson again!

Using What You Know

Prompt Schools should/should not give students iPods for perfect attendance. *What you believe:*	*Personal Stories*
Prompt Your teacher will not be in school tomorrow and is looking for one student to be the teacher for the day. Write a letter to convince your teacher that you should be chosen. *What you believe:*	*Personal Stories*
Prompt Teachers should/should not accept late homework from a student. *What you believe:*	*Personal Stories*

Goal

To help students learn how to change a skimpy idea into a paragraph full of writing

In this lesson, students work on turning a list of ideas into paragraphs. One of the biggest difficulties that students have on standardized tests is that they give too little information and end up with poorly developed paragraphs and essays. **Time:** Forty minutes

Preparation

Copy Resource 9–4, A Test Prompt Answered with a Sketchy List.

Minilesson

Listen to this paragraph I wrote last Saturday night:

> I read a great book this morning. Then I made a tuna fish sandwich for lunch and sat outside in my backyard as I ate it. And then before bed, I went for a walk and saw a beautiful butterfly.

This writing sounds like a list. First I say that I read a great book. Then I sat outside and had lunch, and then I went for a walk and saw a butterfly. This all happens very quickly. In just a few sentences, the reader knows everything that happened to me but nothing about the details or how I felt about what I did.

Today we are going to talk about slowing down our writing and taking quick lists and turning them into paragraphs. Let's see if we can try to say more about each part of the list.

First I read a book. *How can I say more about that without including anything else I did? Hmmm, first I read a book. What kind of information might be related to reading the book? Maybe I could say what the book was about, or where I was sitting when I read it, or how what I was reading made me feel.*

Then I had lunch. *What more could I say about that?* [Elicit student responses.]

Now help me elaborate on the last event, going for a walk and seeing a butterfly. But let's change how I start the sentence. Instead of beginning, And then, *I'll say,* After dinner I. . . . *Okay, help me—remember to stick to the walk and the butterfly and don't jump to later that evening or the next day.* [Elicit student responses.]

Do you see the way we stuck to one part of the story for a long time? We provided more information about each of these events and made the writing longer and better.

Now we'll look at a standardized writing test answer that is also just a brief list of things. Let's figure out where this writing could be developed—where we can write more so it sounds less like a list and more like longer and more interesting writing. When we come back together to share, we will look at what you did to improve this writing.

Read Resource 9–4 and discuss it. Ask students to work with partners and talk about the answer so it is not just a brief list. Students may not actually agree with what the writer wrote but they should try to support the argument anyway.

Share

Have students display their writing in a central location so they can read everyone's work. (Taping it to a blackboard works well.) Have students compare two papers. What is the same and what is different about how these students lengthened the answer to the prompt?

Possible Problem and Suggested Solution

Students lengthen the answer but jump to another topic. Point this out politely and help them reconsider what else they could say.

Follow-Up

Present this same lesson again or just have students practice writing paragraphs from lists. Ask students to reread some of their writing and find a place where they wrote a list.

A Test Prompt Answered with a Sketchy List

Prompt: Would you rather live 100 years ago or today?

Student Response: I would rather live today because there are more things to do. One hundred years ago there were no fun toys. There was also no way to talk on the telephone and talk to your relatives far away. School is better now too because there is more to learn.

How might you elaborate on this response?

Don't Forget Voice!

Students' test writing is often flat and lacks voice. When this happens, students receive low scores in the style categories (and comments such as, *The writer's words do not convey enthusiasm or emotion*). In this lesson, students are reminded to write with voice by experimenting with sentence length and word choice. **Time:** Forty minutes

Preparation

Copy Resource 9–5, A Fish Story!
Copy a test prompt or some writing that students are involved in writing.

Minilesson

Today we are going to talk about writing your persuasive test answer so it sounds unique. If I opened your writer's notebooks, how could I tell whose notebook was whose if your names weren't in them and I didn't know your handwriting? I might know the people that you refer to or the places you wrote about. But imagine that I don't know where you went or the names of your relatives. How could I tell who wrote what? I might be able to do it by looking at your writing voice.

Voice in writing is the way a writer chooses to say things. When we write for a writing test, just like when we write for ourselves or for school, we think not only about what we want to say, but about the way we want to say things. A writer's voice is unique. No two voices sound alike.

Let's take a few minutes to read over a persuasive writing test answer. I'll read it aloud first, and then I want you to read it to yourself. [Hand out copies of Resource 9–5, A Fish Story! and read the piece aloud.]

Two things that contribute to a writer's voice are:

1. *interesting word choice*
2. *sentences with different lengths*

Let's try this: Go back and skim the story and find three places that you think are written with a particularly strong voice. [Discuss.] *Today as you do your writing, think about voice.*

Share

Have students share excerpts of their writing they think have the most voice.

Possible Problem and Suggested Solution

Some students misunderstand the term voice *and think you mean* dialogue. As you confer with these students, make sure they understand that *voice* does not only refer to dialogue.

Follow-Up

Ask students to reread some of their favorite persuasive pieces and underline words, sentences, and paragraphs that have a unique voice.
Present the lesson again!

A Fish Story!

The best pet for our class is a fish. Fish are beautiful pets and very little trouble to take care of. You may think that fish are too common, but think about it, when was the last time you saw a fish tank in a classroom?

Some people think that fish are boring. They're wrong! Have you ever watched a fish looking at his reflection in the tank? He thinks it's another fish and tries to play with it. He will do that for hours at a time, never realizing that his friend is actually himself. Many fish also scurry around on the bottom of the tank and like to hide inside big shells. They can stay in place in the water and for some reason love to be alone in dark places. It's fascinating.

Talk about easy to take care of—fish are known to be the easiest pets to have. They don't require large amounts of food. Just a drop of fish food every other day will do. There will be no big cost involved with feeding fish like there is with a dog or a cat.

Fish are harmless. There is no biting or mean behavior. Once I had a hamster, but it bit my sister, so my mom said we had to get rid of him. She still has a scar from that bite. Fish don't bite, at least not the kind of fish we would have in our classroom. Fish get a bad rap, but they are interesting creatures who make great class pets.

—By Eric

Additional Resources

Sample Writing Resources
Editorial, Op-Eds, Persuasive Essay

Advice

Speeches

Petitions

How These Minilessons Align with Persuasive Writing Standards

General Topic	Standards Might Say Something Like	Minilessons That Align with These Standards	Page Number of the Lesson
Selecting Topics of Interest	Considers audience when determining a persuasive topic	Finding Persuasive Ideas: Rereading Written Responses	42
		Things That Bother Me In the World	44
		Hunting for Persuasive Topics: Wandering and Wondering	47
		Finding an Audience: Whom Would You Like to Persuade?	50
		Uncovering Persuasive Topics	55
		Selecting a Topic	84
Counterargument	Addresses the reader's concerns	Some Might Think: How to Write Counterarguments	96
Leads	Attracts the reader's interest	Leads That Capture the Reader's Interest	123
Length/Development	Addresses the topic adequately Develops ideas fully	Writing Quickly and Continuously to Find First Thoughts	74
		Elaboration 1: Expanding Someone Else's Writing	134
		Elaboration 2: Expanding Your Own Writing	137
Main Idea/Thesis Statement	States a main idea and supports it with details and examples States a clear position in support of a proposal Establishes and develops a controlling idea	Writing a Thesis Statement	86

(continues)

How These Minilessons Align with Persuasive Writing Standards (Cont.)

General Topic	Standards Might Say Something Like	Minilessons That Align with These Standards	Page Number of the Lesson
Opinion/Position	Uses information from personal experience to form and express ideas States and supports an opinion Recognizes and defends a point of view	All Reasons Are Not Created Equal Call to Action	90 149
Voice	The reader writes with a unique sense of voice and style	Using Precise Words and Phrases Loaded Language: Using Positive, Neutral, and Negative Words	92 94
Research Skills	Uses research and technology to support writing in a variety of ways	Learning More About Your Topic 1: What Kinds of Research Can You Do? Learning More About Your Topic 2: Internet Research Learning More About Your Topic 3: Writing Strong Survey and Interview Questions	60 63 67
Organization	Uses strategies that organize writing Uses strategies that helps the writer plan the writing Adopts an organizational format that is appropriate for the writing	Examining the Structure of Your Persuasive Writing Repetition, Repetition Planning Persuasive Writing Smooth Transitions Reading Lead Sentences to Determine Balance and Clarity Headings	108 110 118 131 159 163
Techniques	Uses persuasive elements and techniques	Using Humor to Entertain and Persuade	71

How These Minilessons Align with Persuasive Writing Standards (Cont.)

General Topic	Standards Might Say Something Like	Minilessons That Align with These Standards	Page Number of the Lesson
Techniques		When Deception Meets Persuasion	76
		Storytelling in Persuasive Writing	104
		Rhetorical Questions: Statements in Disguise	99
		May I Ask You a Question?	102
		Using Bulleted Lists	139
		Copy Cat! Finding Great Writing and Doing It Again	146
Supporting Evidence	Supports argument with detailed evidence	Ready, Set . . . Draft!	125
Voice	Uses voice appropriate for the intended audience Uses voice to develop the reader's interest	*I came. I saw. I conquered.* Short Declarative Sentences Persuade	144
Word Choice	Uses precise vocabulary	Using Precise Words and Phrases	92
		Loaded Language: Positive, Neutral, and Negative Words	94
		The Idea Is a Good One or *I'm Hip to That*: Formal Versus Informal Language	106
		Cut It Out! Deleting Unnecessary Words	141
Conventions	Varies sentence structure according to purpose Edits to correct errors in spelling and punctuation	Coaching the Reader by Using Punctuation	154
		Capital Letters: Know the Rules, BREAK THE RULES!	157
		Please Excuse Me for Interrupting	165
		Proofread Carefully	167

Persuasive Writing Techniques Linked with Examples

Technique	Why This Technique Might Be Used	Examples
Anecdote	To give us an example that feels real	Chris Wondra's Letter to His Students
Imagery	To prove a point or create a mood by "showing" the reader	Animal Cruelty in Circuses Movies on Airplanes
Comparisons	To show us how unlike things can be the same To prove a point	Chris Wondra's Letter to His Students
Rhetorical questions	As if to say, "It's just common sense." Humor device	Sis! Boom! Bah! Humbug! Watching *American Idol*
Questions (other types besides rhetorical)	Humor device Interest device Getting us to question deeply held beliefs	Sis! Boom! Bah! Humbug! Tonight At . . . Kids in Training
Voice or tone (formal, informal, expert)	Formal—helps us hear how urgent or important something is Informal—gets the reader to feel as if their speaking to a friend	Kids in Training Zahra's Letter to Her Parents About Educational Camp (informal voice)
Exaggeration	Humor device To prove a point	Kids in Training Schools Go Too Far to Play It Safe Should Trans Fats Be Banned?
Sarcasm/irony	To make a point strongly To create a feeling of guilt	Al Gore Cartoon Don't Sugarcoat Cupcake Menace
Elite/distinct (*far above the rest, only for the special people, because I'm worth it . . .*)	To tell the reader that if . . . then they are special	A-1 Limousine Advertisement
Strong language/precise word choice	To make a point more forcefully	All public service announcements Zahra's Letter to Her Parents About Educational Camp Watching *American Idol*
Hypothetical words and situations (*imagine if, imagine this, have you ever*)	To help the reader envision	Calendar Direct Mail Advertisement

Persuasive Writing Techniques Linked with Examples (Cont.)

Technique	Why This Technique Might Be Used	Examples
Bullets	To list information quickly	Chris Wondra's Letter to His Students
Actual images (not imagery but real pictures)	To create emotion	All public service announcements and political cartoons
Dialogue	To make a point forcefully	Don't Sugarcoat Cupcake Menace (ends with dialogue!) Kids in Training Is This Really a Discount? Animal Cruelty in Circuses Boys Are Invisible in School
Dashes	To sound informal or to make writing sound like thinking or thinking aloud Interruption	Is This Really a Discount?
Short declarative sentences	To make a direct statement or give information	Chris Wondra's Letter to His Students Boys Are Invisible in School I Am Not a Nerd Letter
Headings/subheadings	To help organize writing	Chris Wondra's Letter to His Students
Storytelling	To illustrate a point To allow readers to persuade themselves	Chris Wondra's Letter to His Students
ALL CAPS (some word with all capital letters)	To emphasize important words	Should We Take Away the Voting Rights of 18-Year-Olds?
Call to action	Gets audience to do something	Almost all examples of persuasive writing
Repetition	To seem outraged or determined To build on a point	Home Depot Gets It: Consumers Rule Winston Churchill Speech

Possible Topics for Persuasive Writing

Education
School uniforms
Policy and procedures
Grades and competition
Special education
Extra credit/service credit
Required courses/electives
Disciplinary action (detention, loss of recess, etc.)
School choice
A moment of silence/prayer in schools
Gifted programs
Bilingual education
Locker searches
Homework
Pledge of Allegiance
The teaching of evolution
School fundraisers
Single-sex education

History and Social Issues
Women's rights
Civil rights
Vietnam War
9/11
The war in Iraq
The death penalty
Cruelty to animals
Gun control
Cloning
Peer pressure
Adolescents
Bullying
Bias in the news
Violent video games
Song lyrics and freedom of speech
Smoking in the movies and on TV

Political Issues
Health care
The economy
Tax plans
The president's agenda and policies
Democrats and Republicans

Sports
Dangerous sports
Competition in sports
Coaching

Religion
Houses of worship
Attending services
Spiritual leaders
Prayer

Family Issues
Things that must happen in a family
Taking care of pets
Brothers and sisters
Parents' rules
Divorce
Getting an allowance
Harry Potter books
Blogging and Internet safety

During an Election Year You May Want to Study
Local politics and political leaders and:

Persuasive techniques in political speeches
Persuasive techniques in political television commercials
Persuasive techniques in political debates
Persuasive techniques in a State of the Union address

May be photocopied for classroom use. From *Writing to Persuade* by Karen Caine. 2008. (Heinemann: Portsmouth, NH).

Evaluation Form for Published Persuasive Writing

Name: _____

Title of Article: _____

Author of Article: _____

What works well?

_____

_____

_____

_____

What does not work well?

_____

_____

_____

The bottom line is . . . (How persuasive? How well written?)

_____

_____

_____

Looking at First-Draft Writing

STUDENT NAME	BEGINNING Thesis/Stance	END Restatement (and More)	MIDDLE Clear Sentence, Clear Paragraphs, Order of Paragraphs	MIDDLE Supporting Evidence	OVERALL Elaboration	OVERALL Persuasive Techniques (Word Choice, Structure)	COMMENTS

May be photocopied for classroom use. From *Writing to Persuade* by Karen Caine. 2008. (Heinemann: Portsmouth, NH).

A Persuasive Writing Rubric

Always done: 5
Sometimes done: 3
Never done: 1

The writing is persuasive not just informational.

Thesis statement or stance is clear to the reader.

The beginning starts the text off. . . . The ending makes sense and draws the piece to a natural close.

The author gives more than [number] reason(s) for believing as he or she does.

The writing has clear (and compelling) reasons.

The writing provides effective transitions between ideas (sentence to sentence and paragraph to paragraph).

The writing is organized in a way that makes sense to the reader.

The tone and voice of the text is well suited to the audience.

Two crafting techniques learned are used.

The piece is edited to the best of the student's ability.

Strengths of This Piece/Something to Keep in Mind

Where to Find More Persuasive Writing

Editorials/Op-Eds/Persuasive Essays

To find more sources online, enter these words into a search engine: *editorials for kids* or *persuasive writing websites*
Junior Scholastic
Scholastic News
Scholastic Choices
New York Times Upfront
Time for Kids
Freep.com (opinion)
Miamiherald.com (columnists Leonard Pitts, Dave Barry)
Teenink.com

Advice

Boys' Life magazine (Ask Us Anything)
www.kansascity.com (columnist Steve Rosen)

Petitions

Gopetition.com
Petitiononline.com

Public Service Announcements

To find more sources online, enter these words into a search engine: *public service announcement print* or *public service announcement award winning*
www.redcross.org/press/psa/psa.html

Political Cartoons

Scholastic News
New York Times Upfront
Time for Kids
http://cagle.msnbc.com/politicalcartoons/

Persuasive Letters

oregonstate.edu/dept/eli/buswrite/persuasive_letters.html

Advertisements

Chinaberry catalog
Hammacher Schlemmer catalog
Skymall (in-flight magazine)

Books with Persuasion

Dr. Seuss Goes to War: The World War II Editorial Cartoons of Theodor Seuss Geisel
Earrings! by Judith Voirst
Emily's Runaway Imagination by Beverly Cleary
Hey, Little Ant by Phillip M. and Hannah Hoose
I Wanna Iguana by Karen Kaufman Orloff
I Want a Dog by Daydl Kaur Khalsa
Judy Moody Predicts the Future by Megan McDonald
Lucy Rose: Here's the Thing About Me by Katy Kelly
The Butter Battle Book by Dr. Seuss
The Cat in the Hat by Dr. Seuss
The Landry News by Andrew Clements (chapter book)
The True Story of the Three Little Pigs by John Scieszka

This is an editorial written by Maureen Downey for the *Atlanta Journal Constitution*. What does the author do in her writing to make this editorial persuasive? Where do you stand on the issue?

Don't Sugarcoat Cupcake Menace

The concern is not that children will gather in a circle and throw the cupcakes at a hapless victim, although some overcooked versions of the childhood classic could double as paperweights. Instead, schools fear a homemade pastry could trigger food allergies or taint the class with bacteria from an unsanitary kitchen.

So, rather than classes celebrating Valentine's Day with cupcakes from little Debbie's mom, kids would have to make do with Little Debbies. The mass-produced Little Debbie treats have the advantage of emerging from commercial kitchens that undergo health inspections. (Of course, anyone who believes that health inspections indemnify commercial kitchens from contaminants has obviously never worked in a restaurant.)

Here in Georgia, Forsyth County was contemplating a ban on homemade cupcakes as part of its overall wellness policy, but backed off last week. However, many other districts around the country have gone ahead and adopted bans, understandably upsetting homebaking dads and moms.

Schools can safeguard kids without forcing parents to hang up their oven mitts. If the problem is a student's peanut allergies, a note to home stating that treats should not contain peanut oil should be sufficient. If the allergic child's parents want to be 100 percent safe, they can provide the teacher with a stash of Hostess cupcakes for their child.

It's contradictory for schools to forbid foods made from fresh ingredients as a health measure, in favor of processed muffins, cookies, and cupcakes that contain enough preservatives to outlast an ice age.

These days, freshly made foods are a rarity for some children. One first-grader, enthusing over a tray of homemade brownies, asked for a description of the box containing the brownies, so he could tell his mother which brand to buy. Not all foods come out of a box, the child was told.

"I know—most food comes out of cans," the bright little fellow responded.

—Maureen Downey, for the editorial board (*mdowney@ajc.com*) Wednesday, 6/21/2006

Is America's Food Supply Safe?
E. coli in spinach, salmonella in peanut butter—a string of recent contaminations has prompted questions about food safety

YES

Americans have one of the safest food supplies in the world. The Food and Drug Administration (FDA) works closely with federal, state, and local agencies, private companies, and consumers to make it even safer.

The FDA is always working to protect food from bacterial, viral, and chemical contamination. We use the most modern scientific methods available to learn how contamination occurs and how to prevent it.

We have 625 investigators working out of 20 different offices all across the country who are dedicated to inspecting our food supply and working with food companies to make sure they do everything they can to keep food safe. If we suspect any food is unsafe, we work to catch problems early. We try to find out how the problem started, fix it, and prevent it from happening again.

Our food comes from all over the world. The FDA has inspectors at our borders to prevent unsafe food from entering our country, as well as experts in foreign countries who help ensure that food exported to the U.S. meets our standards.

Besides working with the food industry to prevent contamination of food, the FDA educates consumers to do their part to ensure that the food they eat is safe. This includes cooking food to appropriate temperatures, keeping it refrigerated, and properly handling raw meat, seafood, and poultry.

The FDA works hard every day to ensure the safety of America's food.

—**Dr. David Acheson**, Assistant Commissioner for Food Protection Food and Drug Administration

(continues)

continued

NO

Ashley Armstrong of Indiana was just 2 years old when she became critically ill from eating contaminated spinach last year. She survived, but she will need a kidney transplant and intensive lifelong medical attention to counter the devastating effects of being infected with *E. coli* bacteria.

Ashley is just one of thousands of Americans who get sick or die from something they ate each year. The Centers for Disease Control and Prevention estimate that 76 million Americans get sick, 325,000 are hospitalized, and 5,000 die from food-borne illness each year.

Part of the problem is that U.S. food-safety laws are quite old. Most were drafted a century ago, after Upton Sinclair's novel *The Jungle* exposed filthy conditions in meat-processing plants.

The job of monitoring our food supply is divided—often haphazardly— between the Food and Drug Administration and the Department of Agriculture (USDA), and that allows things to fall through the cracks.

Americans get 13 percent of their diets (260 pounds per person each year) from imported food, and this creates another hazard. Ninety-nine percent of FDA-regulated imported food reaches grocery-store shelves without ever being checked for faulty labels or the contaminants that cause food-borne illness.

In the 21st century, the U.S. food supply faces many threats, ranging from accidental contamination to bioterrorism. We must work harder to ensure that Americans can trust the food they put on their plates.

—**Caroline Smith Dewaal,** Food Safety Director Center for Science in the Public Interest

This is an article written by Maureen Downey for the *Atlanta Journal Constitution*. What persuasive writing techniques does the author use?

Schools Go Too Far to Play It Safe

Staff

Childhood ought to include scraped knees, flushed cheeks and maybe even the occasional bloody nose, the "battle scars" of growing up an active, outdoor, tree-climbing kid.

Unfortunately, too many schools are trying to eliminate those scars by banning tag, touch football and other chase games from gym classes and recess. A school system in Willett, Mass., a suburb of Boston, is the latest to turn the schoolyard into a no-contact zone, joining systems in Wyoming, Virginia, Florida, Washington and South Carolina.

Yes, children might be safer, cleaner and bruise-free in Plexiglas bubbles, but that doesn't mean they would be healthier or happier.

A chief concern is that litigious parents will sue if their child slips during a vigorous game of freeze tag or ends up with scars from a wild round of dodgeball. Schools worry about psychological scars as well. In Florida, Broward County schools banished dodgeball following the advice of the National Association for Sport & Physical Education. In its position paper on PE practices, the association states:

> Activities such as relay races, dodgeball, and elimination tag provide limited opportunities for everyone in the class, especially the slower, less agile students who need the activity the most.

Now, instead of dodgeball, Broward children enjoy far tamer activities, including balancing bean bags on their heads. If someday balancing beanbags comes to seem too wild, risky or foolhardy, the children could play tiddlywinks. But only after signing releases that indemnify the school against broken nails.

—**Maureen Downey,** for the editorial board (*mdowney@ajc.com*) October 20, 2006

This excerpt of a persuasive text was written by Timothy Furnish, Ph.D., an assistant professor of history at Georgia Perimeter College. As the title implies, Mr. Furnish argues that the voting age in United States should be raised.

Should We Take Away the Voting Rights of 18-Year-Olds?

Lowering the voting age such that all college freshmen, and even many high school seniors, could help choose the Republic's leaders was undoubtedly one of the dumbest things ever done in this country's history. We can't totally blame Nixon, since this misguided movement had been supported earlier by Presidents Eisenhower and Johnson and, of course, practically the entire Congress in Nixon's time. May they all fry in one of Dante's lowest circles of Hell for this transgression against political sense.

What is wrong with such young folks voting? Doesn't democracy work better when the franchise is extended to as many Americans as feasibly possible? And isn't it true that "old enough to die, old enough to vote?"—as the amendment's supporters argued during the Vietnam War?

To answer these questions in reverse order: no, no and ARE YOU KIDDING?! Democracy works when KNOWLEDGEABLE citizens vote, as was recognized as long ago as Plato's and Aristotle's time. Can any rational member of the human species watch Jay Leno's "Jaywalking"— in which he roams the streets of Southern California, interviewing folks who don't know the vice president's name, which hemisphere they live in—and possibly think it's a good idea for these people to be left alone with a voting machine of any kind?

My point is not to score cheap points at my students' expense. The point is that we allow such uninformed people to vote! Indeed, we encourage it: MTV's "Rock the Vote," P. Diddy's "Vote or Die." There's even an organization, Youthrights.org, that demands we lower the voting age to 16! (Just what we need: presidential candidates taking stands on their preferred anti-acne medication.)

Now there is no guarantee that a 30-something voter will be more informed than one just out of high school—but it's a good bet. As Michael Barone points out in his book *Hard America, Soft America*, this nation's 18-year olds are, on average, coddled, spoiled and ignorant; but by the time they hit their third decade, most of them are extremely competent and productive (thanks to good colleges, the business world or the military). I'll settle for raising the voting age to 20—with a major caveat, addressing the "old enough to die, old enough to vote" argument.

We dodged a bullet in this election, when the ignorant youth masses turned out in record numbers (51 percent of the 18–29 year olds voted; figures for subslice of that pie that includes only 18–20 years olds is unavailable), which broke for Kerry by about 10 points. Only the fact that most other age groups voted in even larger numbers drowned out the callow masses' otherwise influential cluelessness.

So I say: dock the 18-year-olds' vote!

Repeal the 26th Amendment before President P. Diddy is sworn in.

—Timothy Funish

Originally appeared in *History News Network,* November 15, 2004. Reprinted with permission.

Home Depot Gets It: Consumers Rule

If only we knew it was so easy. . . .

An MSN.com columnist complains about indifferent Home Depot customer service, inspiring a flood of "amens" from readers, prompting new CEO Frank Blake to pledge big changes at the home improvement chain, from more attractive stores to more knowledgeable clerks. Maybe we're onto something here. Maybe we need to complain about buying coffee in the morning in the drive-through, asking for two sugars and getting a pepper package instead. Maybe someone needs to complain about the cable company charging $5 for a channel guide you never ordered, or about waiting on hold for 25 minutes only to be disconnected.

Then there's that cashier at the grocery store, the one suffering from either narcolepsy or a rough night, who moves so slowly that your milk turns to butter before you reach the car.

To all the CEOs of fast-food restaurants, cable companies and grocery stores, you're on notice. Next time, we name names.

—Maureen Downey, for the editorial board (*mdowney@ajc.com*) March 15, 2007

May be photocopied for classroom use. From *Writing to Persuade* by Karen Caine. 2008. (Heinemann: Portsmouth, NH).

214

This article written by Rick Reilly caused quite a stir when it was published. Mr. Reilly said he received more letters about this piece than any other pieces he has written to date.

Sis! Boom! Bah! Humbug!

Every Friday night on America's high school football fields, it's the same old story. Broken bones. Senseless violence. Clashing egos.

Not the players. The cheerleaders.

According to a report by The Physician and Sports [M]edicine, cheerleaders lose more time from their activity because of injury—28.8 days per injury—than any other group of athletes at the high school level. The University of North Carolina found that cheerleading is responsible for nearly half the high school and college injuries that lead to paralysis or death.

It's crazy, isn't it? We have girls building three-story human pyramids, flipping one another 30 feet in the air, and we give the boys helmets.

A buddy of mine has twin daughters, both cheerleaders. At the end of last school year one needed plastic surgery on her cheek after another girl's teeth went through it during a pyramid collapse; the other broke her hand and finger. They're not cheering anymore.

I don't hate cheerleading just because it's about as safe as porcupine juggling. I also hate it because it's dumb. The Velcroed-on smiles. The bizarre arm movements stolen from the Navy signalmen's handbook. The same cheers done by every troupe in every state.

What's even dumber is that cheerleaders have no more impact on the game than the night janitorial staff. They don't even face the game. They face the crowd, lost in their bizarre MuffyWorld. They cheer, they rah, they smile, they kiss, they hug. Meanwhile, Milford High just scored three touchdowns against their guys. A UFO could land at the 30-yard line, disgorging a chorus line of tiny, purple Ethel Mermans, and most cheerleaders would still be facing the other way yelling, "We got the fever!"

Exactly what does a girl get out of cheerleading, anyway, besides a circle skirt and a tight sweater? Why do we encourage girls to cheer the boys, to idolize the boys? Why do we want them on the sideline when most of them could be between the sidelines?

Studies show that by the time otherwise smart girls hit high school, they start to raise their hands less in class, let the boys take the lead. Isn't cheerleading the same thing, only outdoors?

(continues)

Reprinted with permission from *Sports Illustrated*.

Look, I married a cheerleader. My sisters were cheerleaders. I could see it then: Cheerleading was just about the only way a girl could be a part of sports. Not now. Not in the age of Mia Hamm and Marion Jones and the Williams sisters. Not when most high schools offer as many girls' sports as boys'.

Oh, right, nowadays cheerleading is classified as a sport. There are now "cheer gyms," where kids go to learn to throw each other around like Frisbees. You can even watch the National High School Cheerleading Championships on ESPN, just after the Harley-Davidson Olympics. This is the event in which 408 girls named Amber attempt to create a human Eiffel Tower, screaming, "Two! Four! Six! Eight!" while displaying all their gums at once. I'm not saying it's not hard. I'm just saying it's pointless.

Do you realize colleges are even giving cheerleading scholarships? Can you believe that? Sorry, Mrs. Roosevelt, we just gave away your daughter's chemistry scholarship. But you should have seen Amber here do "We've got spirit!"

If cheerleading is a sport, Richard Simmons is a ballerina. It's athletic, but it's not a sport. In fact, what's sad is that most cheerleaders would make fine athletes. Watch for five minutes and you'll see. But these girls won't be on anybody's gymnastics or diving or basketball team because every season is cheerleading season.

Cheerleaders don't just shake their pom-poms at football games; they're also at baseball games and wrestling matches and girls' soccer games and most everything else short of chess-club tournaments. No matter how many hours they've already put in, no matter how freezing it is, no matter how few fans are at the jayvee badminton match, the cheerleaders are out there in their short skirts.

What's that spell? Frostbite!

If they're lucky, they might grow up to become Dallas Cowboys Cheerleaders. In the book *Deep in the Heart of Texas*, three former Cowboys Cheerleaders wrote that they snorted coke, gobbled diet pills and vomited to lose weight.

Rah!

I guess this is like coming out against fudge and kittens and Abe Lincoln, but it needs to be said. In four years my little girl hits high school. It's up to her, of course, but if my wife and I could choose her after-school activities, cheerleading would be next to last.

Just ahead of Piercing Club.

—Rick Reilly

Reprinted with permission from *Sports Illustrated*.

This persuasive essay is written by Karen Caine, author of *Writing to Persuade*, and mother of three boys, who do in fact play sports.

Kids in Training

In elementary school we were introduced to games like basketball, baseball, soccer, and volleyball. We learned the basics of these games in P.E. class—although back then it was just called gym.

In middle and high school there were team sports and whether you were in the game or on the sidelines screaming, *Go Brian go, get around him*! You were a part of something bigger than just the sport. You were part of school spirit. Ice cream after the game was a must. If your team won, you would shout *We're the best*. If you lost you ate more quietly and talked about how this call and that call by the ref was so cheap. Yeah, I remember a lot about those days.

What I don't recall about team sports back then was the cutthroat, get ahead, obsessively competitive edge I see today. I don't remember it simply because it didn't exist . . . not in the same way it does today.

I don't remember kids taking pitching lesson at age six. Pitching was what you learned how to do during the once a week practice you went to. Practice was what you did in the yard on Saturday with Dad. Not for two hours. Not because you were "In Training" but because it was something fun to do with your father.

I don't remember private tumbling lessons at age seven. Or eight. Or even ten. You practiced gymnastics in gymnastics class and if you were *really* serious you took gymnastics twice a week.

James can't play baseball, I overheard his mom admit at a school picnic. *He hasn't played for two years and now he's too far behind.*

You can't start *playing baseball at age nine*, the other mother responded, *that's why I made sure that Owen didn't quit.*

James' mom made a cardinal mistake by removing him from sports to focus on his piano lessons. Two seasons ago he was on par, maybe even a little bit ahead. But now . . . now he would never be able to catch up. Rookie mistake. He was cut. Permanently.

Travel teams begin earlier than they used to and separate the men from the boys. The preparation for travel team try outs is grueling. There are extra pitching lessons at $70 an hour and, of course, daily practice. When you find a good pitching coach for your little one—the rules are clear. Stick with him and for goodness sake don't tell anyone else on the team.

(continues)

The actual traveling for the travel team is tough—up to an hour and a half each way. Dad leaves work early or Mom gets a babysitter for the other kids. But it's worth it. I mean these kids are no spring chickens anymore. They're ten already.

What? Football practice is canceled? That's ridiculous. The other coach didn't cancel practice just because it's 98 degrees with a heat index of 104. Drink some Gatorade and toughen up. If we don't show up and the other team does, we'll have to forfeit. In effect, we'll lose and we all know that we can't have that happen.

Practice is important but the actual games are what count. Last Thursday, the War Eagles Central lost to the War Eagles South, but that's just because Brett, their star player, had pneumonia. He wasn't still sick in bed but the doctor said he had to rest for a few more days. It's ridiculous. Sometimes you have to push yourself a little.

I can hear the critics now. Sports are more serious than they used to be. Life is more serious. What's the big deal? Exercise and a little healthy competition never hurt anyone. We want our kids to do well at their chosen passion and if that happens to be sports, all the better. Who is it hurting?

It's hurting the competitors, I mean the kids. The pressure to perform, the constant intense competition, and the win-at-all-costs attitude is downright unhealthy.

The other day a little league baseball player from Chattanooga, Tennessee, was interviewed on TV and was asked if he gets sad when the season is over. *No*, he commented, *because I am happy when the pressure is off and I can just hang out with my friends.*

Out of the mouths of babes. Well in this case, a nine-year-old boy.

—Karen Caine

This persuasive piece was written by a Carol Herson, a student at Oglethorpe University who is getting her Master's Degree in Education. By the time this piece is printed, Carol will be a teacher and may even use her writing with her students. Look at how she uses dialogue to prove her point and how she varies the length of her sentences. What other persuasive writing techniques did she use?

Tonight At . . .

"Will the weather ruin your morning commute? We'll let you know tonight at 6:00."

"Find out what these neighbors are angry about tonight at 10:00."

"A missing woman's family speaks out tonight at 11:00."

Do any of these teasers make you want to set your watch so you won't miss the exciting revelations? Do you change your schedule so you'll be in front of the TV at 6:00 or 10:00 or 11:00? Are you breathless with anticipation? Riveted to the couch?

Apparently, our local news stations think so. Throughout the day and evening, we are bombarded with enticing tidbits of news stories yet to come; each one designed to capture the attention of the viewing public and create "must see TV." Certainly, television stations are in business to make money and high viewership is one way they do so. But when did it become okay for the local evening news to assume the persona of a soap opera or tabloid tell-all? When did it become a requirement to fill an hour with what could be reported in twenty minutes?

According to Webster's *New College Dictionary*, news is defined as "1. Recent events and happenings, especially those that are notable or unusual 2. Information about recent events of general interest and 3. Newsworthy material." You may notice that there is nary a mention of entertainment or amusement. But perhaps I'm splitting hairs here, after all, those news stories are recent events and they are information and they MAY be newsworthy, at least to some. Perhaps I'm letting a personal pet peeve taint my perception. So let's move past my irritation with news "teasers" and take a look at the content of the local news programs. Usually, the local news anchor will provide a brief background for a breaking story and then go to a reporter on the scene:

"What was your first reaction when you saw the turnip in the shape of Santa Claus?"

"Well, I was sure surprised."

"How did you feel when the tree fell on your garage?"

"Well, I was sure surprised."

Is this really news? The event—maybe. The reaction of the victim—definitely not.

Teaser leads and in-your-face reactions trivialize the news and turn it into infotainment. A long time ago, news used to be news; you know, facts and information in a clear concise manner. If we all pull together, can we change the culture of news delivery on TV? "We'll let you know tonight at . . . "

—Carol Herson

Is This Really a Discount?

10% off. That's 50¢ on a $5.00 purchase. You call this a discount?

Drugstores, supermarkets, restaurants, even your local pet groomer all offer rebate, discount, double-the-face-value of your coupon programs. Somebody! Please, please, please make me stop buying two-for-one toilet tissue.

Are you feeling me yet? Who are the most susceptible to this free money game? Newly wed brides, pregnant women, new moms, people saving for a new house . . . okay just about everyone. We are all lured by the idea of free! Why not? But, I digress.

Think about this. Attached to the bottom of the receipt from my favorite national chain drugstore was a $3.50 coupon.

"Congratulations. You have received a coupon valued at $3.50."

"Great! Please apply it to these purchases."

"Oh, I can't do that. I've already completed this transaction. But, please, plan to use it on your next visit to any one of our gazillion stores."

The next time I return? By then the coupon is lost, forgotten, eaten by the dog. Are you kidding me? Who needs the $3.50 more—me or the gazillion drug stores?

And, how about those computer company rebates? You need a playbook to follow those rules. Please mail the original receipt, original UPC number from the box, rebate application from the store and a SASE (for the newly initiated that's a self-addressed stamped envelope) to the following address within 10 days of purchase or all bets are off. How many people really bother? Half the people can't figure it out so they don't even bother to apply for the rebate. A lot of others file the rebate, but don't make a carbon copy of the documents. Twelve weeks later, you remember and ask the company about your refund check. "Sorry. Please send me that copy of your documents that you forgot to make." Gotcha.

You have a cart full of products. You have a coupon for every item in your cart. The cashier cocks her head to the side, sorts the coupons like a Vegas blackjack dealer and says, "I'm sorry. These coupons expired last week." Enough said on that.

(continues)

continued

Just last weekend, a lady plunked down three chocolate bars and a bright red coupon, "Buy Two—Get One Free."

"Please don't forget to ring my coupon," she said.

"I'm sorry Ma'am, I can't ring this. You need to read it."

She reads aloud, "Mail coupon and original receipt. You're kidding! That's false advertising. Keep the chocolate!"

Sound familiar? Chocolate, computers? But, I digress.

We've all been there. Trying to be thrifty and using coupons to save money. Years ago, our grandparents collected books for company stamps and redeemed them for appliances, furniture and cigarettes. The scheme was a little different; the payout is the same.

I suppose coupons serve a valuable service in our society. Their prevalence makes that statement true. I just wish I understood why. I'm convinced that we should give up using coupons. We're not *really* saving money. There's not really a discount. Discount coupons aren't worth the trouble. I say we make them go away . . . right after I find that coupon for toilet tissue.

—Lisa Mullins

Should Trans Fats Be Banned?

Commentary	Rebuttal
The U.S. Food and Drug Administration (FDA) exists to protect the American public from harm. This function serves the American public and it isn't a violation of individual rights.	When a lawyer files a lawsuit to ban Nabisco Oreo cookies, we've gone off the deep end. Stephen Joseph wants the removal of Oreos from shelves across California because they contain trans fats. The California legislature is actually considering a state-wide ban on all trans-fats cooking in restaurants—and a similar ban went into effect against New York City eateries a few weeks ago.

The U.S. Food and Drug Administration (FDA) exists to protect the American public from harm. This function serves the American public and it isn't a violation of individual rights.

Just recently the FDA banned the import of some types of farm-raised fish and shrimp from China, because they found a link to cancer-causing drugs. In the past, the FDA has banned the non-water-soluble form of a red food dye because it produced tumors in male rats.

Last year, the FDA began mandating that food labeling in this country include information about the amount of trans fats in processed food. That began a chain of events in which several cities, led by New York, have either banned the use of trans fats in restaurants, or they are talking about it.

The backlash has a lot of folks suddenly anxious about their Happy Meals.

Trans fat is made when hydrogen is added to vegetable oil. It contributes to increasing the production of "Frankenfat" or LDL, the bad kind of cholesterol.

The Harvard Law and Policy Review says the "oils (are) attractive to food manufacturers because they have a longer shelf life and longer fry life than other oils. That makes them useful for fried foods like French fries, donuts, and taco shells. And they give baked goods like cookies, crackers, and pies the texture that previously came from lard."

Now, food distributors are basically more concerned with profits than public health. They are in business to make money, not play fitness coach.

Chefs resent the FDA tinkering with their recipes and affecting the unique taste that attracts customers. And customers resent the idea of government food police. I mean, it isn't like anyone

(continues)

I'm not arguing that trans fats are a beneficial part of the American diet, but there's a reason the FDA hasn't banned them thus far: they're merely . . . unhealthy. Not unsafe. And the problem is, there simply isn't a trans-fat alternative out there that tastes the same. At least not yet.

A whole lot of foodstuffs aren't good for you. But should the government ban them for everyone just because a sizeable chunk of the population (pun intended) refuses to consume them in moderation? After all, a few Oreos won't make kids fat. But lots of junk food, sedentary lifestyles, sugary drinks, and lack of parental oversight might. A 2004 Gallup poll included two separate studies isolating sugary sodas as a huge contributor to teen obesity problems.

A ban on trans fats sounds great on paper, but so did Prohibition a century ago—and look how that turned out. Unlike with tobacco, which appears unsafe even in small amounts, people rebel against someone controlling their guilty pleasures when they are just fine in moderation. Someone can drink a glass of wine with dinner a few times a week—or indulge in a luscious dessert at a restaurant—and still stay healthy. It's got to be up to the individual to have enough sense not to inhale a package of cookies at one sitting.

The real break-through on trans fats actually came a few years ago, when the FDA began requiring trans fat amounts to be disclosed on food labels. And almost

(continues)

continued

Commentary	Rebuttal
thinks that french fries are really good for them. They just taste good. But to state the obvious, the public doesn't know what it doesn't know. The FDA's objective is not out to make meals taste like hospital food, but to research and make sure what we consume every day is healthy. Clinical Dietitian Erin C. McAllister of Atlanta's Emory University Hospital offers this bit of trans fat-free wisdom: "When people start claiming it is a violation of their rights to ban trans fats," says Clinical Dietician Erin C. McAllister, "the key to remember is it is a man-made fat that we have added to the food supply and then discovered is harmful and contributes to the development of heart disease. "To me, it is like recalling a harmful food product off the market. Why would we want to contribute to all the diseases we already have with trans fats when they can be removed and replaced with something 'natural?' " —Diane Glass	instantly, customers began pressuring restaurant chains and food manufacturers to find a healthier alternative. As long as consumers are being given the real information, the market will generate a solution to this that is less nannying, less burdensome, and still allows us to enjoy—from time to time an Oreo dunked in a glass of milk. —Shaunti Feldhahn

Reprinted with permission from *The Atlantic Journal-Constitution*.

This persuasive essay was written by Blake, a fourth-grade boy in Norcross, Georgia.

Boys Are Invisible in School

Yahoo! I made it into the honor society. Despite my I-am-too-cool-for-this attitude, I was really happy to be a part of the awards banquet.

At this year's awards ceremony there were also citizenship awards. I thought I was a shoo-in for this one! After all when Emily was sick with the flu, who called her every night and gave her the homework? I did. When Rick needed help with division, who came in early every day for a month to help him? I did. Would I get one of the ribbons or the big award on the table?

I listened carefully as names were called. Lindsey, Maddie, Emma . . . Denise, Jo Ann, Gabby . . . Maia, Danielle . . . Wait! They forgot to call my name.

What? Was it over? Yes, all of the citizenship awards were gone.

But how could that be? What about me? For that matter what about Mathew and Nate? Nate is the kindest kid in the school. Nate is the guy who everyone goes to for help in school. Nate is the guy that lets anyone play basketball at recess, even if they aren't good at the game. Nate is the guy who always lets anyone use his pencil sharpener whenever they want to.

Not one boy in the fourth or fifth grade received awards for citizenship! Not one. How could it be that not one boy qualified for a citizenship award?

I have always felt that girls get called on more in school. Girls get in trouble less often and teachers compliment girls more than they do boys. *Oh Sara, what neat work. Good Job. Maia would you help Brad with his Language Arts?*

Boys get in trouble more than girls do. *Sloppy work Jonathan, please work harder! Andrew, please stop talking when I am talking.*

I have always noticed that girls get treated better than boys do. Were these citizenship awards proof of that? It seems obvious that the answer is yes.

Look for it and you'll see it's true—girls really do get treated better.

Here is my challenge to you my readers: If you are a teacher or work in a school, make an effort to notice the boys.

There are some really great ones.

—Blake, fourth grader

Emily's Five-Paragraph Essay

Picture, if you can, a classroom full of children who are unable to express their patriotism for their country. By terminating the "Pledge of Allegiance" in schools, Congress would be taking away children's right to respect those who have sacrificed their lives for the greater good of their country. Congress would also be taking away a tradition that children throughout America have been participating in since the early 1920s. The more disturbing issue, however, is that if Congress takes God out of schools now, would they be willing to take God out of students' lives later?

One of the reasons the United States should continue the pledge in schools is that it is the student's right as an American citizen to recite the pledge. More importantly, it is their civic duty, just as taking off your cap is when the National Anthem is being played. If the government abolishes children's rights to pledge allegiance to their country during school hours, and with children disregarding their civic duty, it will have a major impact on the future generation's patriotism.

Another reason the "Pledge of Allegiance" should continue in schools is that it is a tradition recited on a regular basis, about 10 million times a day, and has been since 1924. The pledge should be a daily tradition that unites the millions of people in America. Instead, it's dividing this great nation.

The last reason to keep the pledge in schools is to help maintain a source of God in children's lives. It is depressing to know that people want to take freedom of religion, one of the main reasons immigrants come to this country, out of students' lives. It's peculiar how people object to "under God" in the pledge, but when it comes to "In God We Trust" on the dollar bill, it's not an issue.

It's up to Congress. Are they willing to allow the "Pledge of Allegiance" in schools, or are they willing to sacrifice children's rights to respect veterans, years of tradition and God in order to please a select few? If there was ever a time to stand united in America, that time is now. Stand together now to help support the continuation of the "Pledge of Allegiance" in schools!

—Emily Nabong

May be photocopied for classroom use. From *Writing to Persuade* by Karen Caine. 2008. (Heinemann: Portsmouth, NH).

This article was written by Steve Rosen who writes a column called Kids and Money for the *Kansas City Star*.

Deal with a Kid's Designer Genes by Using a Clothing Allowance

Your teenage daughter is sifting through the jeans racks at the department store when she gives you the gotta-have-it look. The object of her affection: a $200 pair of designer jeans.

Nearby, your son has zeroed in on a $125 designer-label sweater. He has no qualms asking you to shell out the money.

You react, well, like many parents: "Are you kidding? I'm not paying several hundred dollars for one pair of jeans and a sweater."

They're mad at you, you're unhappy with them, and the drive home ends with a lecture on the ravages of being label-conscious.

Is there a better way to deal with your children's designer genes?

The best way I know of is to put them on a clothing allowance. That way, their own money—and their own choices—will be on the line when shopping for clothes.

If your daughter receives an allowance of $400 for clothing, for example, she may think twice about dropping half on a pair of jeans. Or, if she opts for the designer label, she'll quickly learn she'll have to cut back on the other items on her list or find cheaper alternatives.

Shopping is more real to children when they have to look into their wallet and count out their bills instead of tapping the Bank of Mom and Dad, says Susan Beacham, who runs The Money Savvy Generation, a Chicago area company that promotes financial education.

"When children have to use their own money, not ours, labels matter less," Beacham said.

If your children are doing a good job of managing their money, this may be the time to test a clothing allowance. Never mind that their new fall wardrobe may be hanging in the closet; retailers say the cooler weather tends to bring out more student shoppers who have now had plenty of time to figure out what's trendy in school fashion this year. Besides, any parent with kids going through growth spurts knows that the school-clothes shopping season never really ends.

(continues)

Start by settling on a reasonable amount, say, what you'd typically spend on the children's clothes each season. You can also use catalogs and online research tools to come up with a budget. Or, for practice during the end-of-year sales season, hand out enough money to cover a couple of purchases and see what your shopper comes home with.

It also may help the pocketbook if your children are required to wear school uniforms (I love uniforms) or if there is a dress code.

Whatever the amount, tailor it to your own situation and family income. For example, you continue to buy the basics—socks, underwear, jackets and shoes, and your children cover the rest.

Janet Bodnar, author of *Raising Money Smart Kids*, put her three children on seasonal clothing allowances when they were teens—once in the fall and once in the spring. The clothing allowance didn't include everything, but worked well.

"We had a $50 sneaker rule," Bodnar said. "I was willing to spend that much on a pair of sneakers, and if the kids wanted a more expensive pair, they had to make up the difference. I also didn't include formalwear, like dresses for prom or homecoming. For that, we had separate rules. I had a $100 limit. If she wanted a more expensive dress, she would have to make up the difference, like the sneaker rule."

The key idea behind a clothing allowance is to give your children responsibility in managing their money. Let them make choices.

They'll also learn from their mistakes. They may have to make do with last year's winter jacket because they spent too much for the expensive logoed shirt. But when the clothing money is gone, it's gone.

It won't always be easy, and your children may complain to you repeatedly that their friends are wearing trendy designer labels, so why not me? That's where holiday and birthday gifts come into play.

Children also learn from example. So it's important for your son or daughter to see you deny yourself some fancy leather jacket or designer dress that you want because it won't fit your budget.

"It's all part of learning to function independently," said Adrian Mastracci, a financial adviser from Vancouver who writes a newsletter on children and money. And as with any experience working with children, Mastracci added, "having a dose of patience helps immensely."

—Steve Rosen

Dear Mrs. Web,

Dear Mrs. Web,

My son just went to a birthday party with fifteen of his classmates from last year's first grade class. It was an amazing production with two clowns, a magician, pony rides, and a dog act. I kid you not. They even had a lifeguard by the pool.

    We had exchanged birthday invitations with this boy and a few other classmates. We had planned a small party and sleepover out in our tent in the yard. I am feeling inadequate right now. What can we do?

People have different tastes and pocketbooks. Do not underestimate the charms of a tenting sleepover. All children from 6 to 60 love that sort of thing. Hot dogs and marshmallows roasted over the grill, birthday cake for dessert. Flashlights as gifts to each with their names printed on in marker. An interested and caring adult to supervise and games, songs and stories. Some unstructured playtime. Absolute bliss, count on it.

Source: http://www.dearmrsweb.com/Children.htm

Sir Winston Leonard Spenser Churchill lived from1874–1965. He was a British politician and prime minister (1940–1945 and 1951–1955) of Great Britain. He led Great Britain through World War II. Churchill published several works, including *The Second World War (1948–1953)*, and won the 1953 Nobel Prize for literature. This speech, which was given on June 4, 1940 (during World War II), was one of the defining speeches of the war.

We Shall Fight Them on the Beaches

I have, myself, full confidence that if all do their duty, if nothing is neglected, and if the best arrangements are made, as they are being made, we shall prove ourselves once again able to defend our Island home, to ride out the storm of war, and to outlive the menace of tyranny, if necessary for years, if necessary alone.

At any rate, that is what we are going to try to do. That is the resolve of His Majesty's Government—every man of them. That is the will of Parliament and the nation.

The British Empire and the French Republic, linked together in their cause and in their need, will defend to the death their native soil, aiding each other like good comrades to the utmost of their strength.

Even though large tracts of Europe and many old and famous States have fallen or may fall into the grip of the Gestapo and all the odious apparatus of Nazi rule, we shall not flag or fail.

We shall go on to the end, we shall fight in France,

we shall fight on the seas and oceans,

we shall fight with growing confidence and growing strength in the air, we shall defend our Island, whatever the cost may be,

we shall fight on the beaches,

we shall fight on the landing grounds,

we shall fight in the fields and in the streets,

we shall fight in the hills;

we shall never surrender, and even if, which I do not for a moment believe, this Island or a large part of it were subjugated and starving, then our Empire beyond the seas, armed and guarded by the British Fleet, would carry on the struggle, until, in God's good time, the New World, with all its power and might, steps forth to the rescue and the liberation of the old.

—Sir Winston Churchill

Safa worked for over a month on this speech and then delivered it to the entire second grade at Hampton Elementary. Do you think this speech is formal or informal? Would you be likely to vote for Safa? Well many people did. Fifty-one people liked what she had to say. Unfortunately, fifty-five people voted for the other candidate. Safa says that she will try again next year. What can you learn about persuasive writing from looking at Safa's speech?

Safa for Class President

Good afternoon, I'm Safa and I am running for president of second grade here at Hampton Elementary.

I believe that what makes me different is that I am an honest person. Very honest. It sounds simple, but it's true. I have known some of you since kindergarten. *You* know I always tell the truth. So I will tell it like it is. I will not say one thing and then do something different like many of the candidates running for president of our country.

Here is what I think:

There should not be a no-talking policy in the cafeteria! We need time to talk to each other in order to enjoy our day.

There should be more science in school. Science will help us get into better colleges. Getting into college is important for our future.

We should have school assemblies. An assembly is a time when the whole school gets together and sings songs and has a speaker talk to us. This will be fun and it will help us get to know each other better.

When you go to vote next week, ask yourself who is the best person for the job. It's me. Vote for Safa!!

Enjoy the rest of your day.

This animal rights petition was written by PETA (People for the Ethical Treatment of Animals) on October 16, 2007.

Animal Cruelty in Circuses

Behind the scenes, elephant trainer Tim Frisco instructs would-be trainers how to dominate elephants and make them perform circus tricks. "Sink that hook into 'em. When you hear that screaming, then you know you got their attention."

An elephant trumpets in agony as Frisco's bullhook, with its sharp metal hook and spiked end, tears through her sensitive skin. Frisco, a Carson & Barnes elephant trainer, learned the trade from his father, a former trainer for Ringling Bros. and Barnum & Bailey Circus.

The fact is, animals do not naturally ride bicycles, stand on their heads, balance on balls, or jump through rings of fire. To force them to perform these confusing and physically uncomfortable tricks, trainers use whips, tight collars, muzzles, electric prods, bullhooks, and other painful tools of the trade.

We applaud trapeze artists, jugglers, clowns, tightrope walkers, and acrobats, but let's leave animals in peace. Sweden, Austria, Costa Rica, India, Finland, and Singapore have all banned or restricted the use of animals in entertainment—it's time for the U.S. to do the same.

Petition

Parents, members of the community, and even students need to meet with school boards to discourage school promotions of circuses with animal acts. When they do, school boards listen!

One high school student wrote to PETA after her presentation and reported, "[The school board] thought that the presentation was very good, they enjoyed the packets that you sent, and the superintendent agreed NOT to approve any field trip that is related to any non-animal-friendly facility, including circuses."

Let's help stop animal cruelty in circuses. Sign the petition.

May be photocopied for classroom use. From *Writing to Persuade* by Karen Caine. 2008. (Heinemann: Portsmouth, NH).

231

What movies to show on airplanes is a hot topic among parents of young children. This petition was written by a man named Jesse Kalisher and was signed by many people. At this point it looks like airlines will have more restrictions on what they are allowed to show. What is your opinion?

Movies on Airplanes Petition

To: U.S. Congress

We demand that the United States Congress act immediately to put an end to un-rated and violent films being shown to children on commercial flights operating in United States airspace. Today, infants and toddlers who fly on America's commercial airlines are exposed to images of murder, torture, electrocution, people who catch fire and worse. These images, while acceptable to adults under the right circumstances, are never acceptable to children.

We all know that films are rated by the MPAA. Movie theaters then voluntarily adhere to the MPAA guidelines and thus eliminate the need for government intervention. The only films the MPAA approves without qualification for children under the age of 13 are rated "G." However, the films appearing on airlines flying through American airspace are edited by private companies who work for the individual airlines. Neither those private companies nor the airlines they serve are members of the MPAA and, as a result, the final edits of the films shown on airlines are not rated.

During the in-flight edited version of King Kong, children on a recent Delta Airline flight watched the monster of a gorilla destroy buildings, cars and elevated trains, while tossing human beings aside like tissue paper. In addition, there were gunfights, fistfights, SUV-sized insects which attacked people in the dark and a spiked club which someone used to (nearly) impale another human being in the face.

In the first five minutes of another in-flight movie on US Airways, children on board watched one beating, three boys trading guns, one lethal drive-by shooting, one car crushing a young man to death against a fence, and one armed convenience store hold-up.

To be clear, our concern is only with the screens that drop down from the overhead bin and are shown on screens at the front of a cabin. These are the images we cannot prevent our children from watching.

Our concern is loud and needs to be heard. Congress must act immediately to protect our children.

Sincerely,

The Undersigned

—Keep Our Children Safe

www.petitiononline.com/mod_perl/signed.cgi?kidsafe

Some public service announcements are more persuasive than others. In this anti-drinking and driving campaign the authors use the technique of surprise. Did you expect the last line to say, "your life?" I didn't. What other public service announcements use the element of surprise?

You Drink, You Drive, You Lose

Your license.
Your freedom.
Your life.

You Drink & Drive. YOU LOSE

The image is the most important part of this public service announcement. Why?

Peace Corps

Your daily work will be anything but a chore.

800.424.8580
www.peacecorps.gov

Life is calling. How far will you go?

Courtesy of the Peace Corps

Notice the use of statistics and the words *disaster threat*. Do you think this public service announcement is persuasive? (Or is it informational? Or is it both?)

Fire Checklist

4 Out Of 5 Americans Are Unaware That Home Fires Are The Most Common Disaster Threat.

Preparedness is your best defense against deadly fires.
Use these checklists to make your home safe and prepare your family.

To prevent fires before they start:
☐ Never leave burning candles unattended
☐ Keep fuel (paper, clothing, bedding) at least three feet
  away from heat sources

To stay safe from fires:
☐ Create a home fire escape plan
☐ Practice your plan at least twice a year
☐ Install smoke alarms and escape ladders
☐ Replace smoke alarm batteries at least once a year
☐ Purchase and learn how to use fire extinguishers safely

Visit www.redcross.org or contact your local American Red Cross chapter
today to learn more.

American
Red Cross

Litter Bugs Me

There aren't many things that truly irritate me, but one thing that sends me into a tizzy is the sight of a litterbug in action. I've seen litterbugs of all kinds—young, old, rich, poor—apparently the role of litterbug is open to anyone with a complete disregard for a clean environment. Why is it that some people think the earth is their trash can? What's the sudden urge to discard trash anyway?

According to the Georgia Department of Transportation, 75% of motorists say they've seen trash thrown out of a car, yet only 10% admit to littering from their vehicles. Interesting.

Recently, I witnessed an SUV pull over on a residential downtown street apparently to ask a pedestrian for directions. As the car proceeded on its newly directed course, the back windows descended and simultaneously two arms loaded with an arsenal of fast food containers protruded from the vehicle. The arms engaged the street as their target, dropped their ammunition and returned to their now trash-free interior. Perhaps the SUV was out of cargo room. [Yeah, right!] Maybe the passengers were taunting the "Keep Atlanta Clean" campaigners to see if they were serious about the $200 fines. [Does anyone ever get fined for littering?]

Litter is not your problem. Right? Think again. Cigarette butts contain poisonous chemicals harmful to wildlife, water quality and the environment. And that gum wrapper that was casually tossed from a car window could take 30 years to degrade. 30 years! Beyond the environmental consequences, litter affects *our wallets*. Litter leads to crime and lower property values. Litter costs you, the Georgia taxpayer, $11 million a year. Nearly $3 million of that spending goes to metro Atlanta pick-up programs alone. That's millions of dollars a year.

The next time you see someone flick a cigarette butt or toss a soda can because *everyone else does*, ask them to pick it up and throw it away. You're not like everyone else. You take a stand against litter.

—Robin Hollis

Notice the use of symbolism in this political cartoon. What is the cartoon saying about immigration?

Reprinted with permission of Copley News Service.

In this political cartoon we learn how Ricky Yoder, a middle school student, feels about Al Gore's stance on the environment. Ricky shows the reader and tells the reader what he believes.

Al Gore Cartoon

This is a short excerpt of a sales letter from a company that sells calendars and organizers. This is less than 10 percent of the letter; the actual letter is much longer than this. In fact it is more than 800 words! Who do you think the audience is for this letter? What techniques does it use to persuade the reader to purchase the organizer? If you were going to finish the letter, what would you write?

Calendar Direct Mail Advertisement

Dear Productivity-Minded Friend,

What would it mean to you to gain an extra hour of productive time a day . . . 5 days a week . . . 250 hours (equal to more than 30 eight hour days—a whole extra month!) each year?

    Well, you're about to find out.

    Imagine. More time to spend with your family. More time to catch up on your reading, play golf, or do what's important to you. When your life is more organized, you can relax. Stress disappears.

This advertisement has been extremely effective for A-1 Limousine. Why do you think this is true?

A-1 Limousine Advertisement

A departure from the ordinary

For 40 years, A-1 Limousine has provided special distinction and style to every special occasion. Wherever your bound - an evening out on the town, sports events, or celebrating a special moment - A-1 is bound to please with the elegance, convenience and luxury you deserve.

- 24/7 door-to-door service
- Online reservations
- Over 250 late-model Sedans, Limousines, Vans and Motor Coaches to serve you

A-1 Limousine *For People Going Places...*
Over 250 vehicles to serve you

1-800-367-0070
www.a1limo.com
Offices in Princeton, Piscataway and Lehigh Valley, PA

For People Going Places and A-1 Limousine are registered trademarks of A-1 Limousine
Licensed by NJ D.O.T.I.C.C. & A.B.C., MC77751, PA PUC A-00110212

Courtesy of A-1 Limousine.

May be photocopied for classroom use. From *Writing to Persuade* by Karen Caine. 2008. (Heinemann: Portsmouth, NH).

Letter to His Students

Dear Student:

You know that feeling you get on the last day of school? That mix of freedom and excitement—that feeling of pride—knowing you've worked hard and are ready for the next grade? About 3 years ago two of my 8th graders were each filled with just those feelings, excited about what the summer (and the future) held.

These two were alike in many ways. Both had gotten A's and B's. Both were nice kids, and both were looking forward to the future.

Recently, these two students returned to visit me.

Although a little older, they are still very much alike. Both are now in 9th grade. Both have many friends. And both, it turns out, have joined the same clubs and play the same sports.

But there is a difference. While one is still getting A's and B's, is a member of the student council, a starting forward on the junior varsity basketball team and a reporter for the school newspaper; the other is now a straight A student, student council president, captain of the varsity basketball team and editor-in-chief of the school paper.

What Made The Difference

Have you ever wondered what makes this kind of difference? Have you ever wondered why some kids seem to get all the breaks and have all the fun? It just doesn't seem fair. After visiting with those two students, I started to ask myself this same question.

I wanted to find out what was making the difference for these two students. Why was one still doing well while the other was a raging success? I thought I'd start my research by looking back at the work they did in 8th grade.

What I found was amazing.

One of them paid very close attention during our unit on persuasion. He studied many persuasive texts, wrote often in school and at home, and revised his writing. He got an A.

(continues)

continued

The other didn't write that often, didn't pay close attention during lessons and didn't try that hard. He only got a C. That was the only difference. I guess the secrets I teach about persuasion are even more powerful than I imagined because the student who got the A is the student with all the success.

A Unit Unlike Any Other

You see, if you work hard this next unit can teach you some very unique and powerful skills, like:

- how to organize information so that people pay attention to you
- what types of evidence are the most convincing
- three types of persuasive statements
- and much, much more

These are secrets that you can use right away to help you become more successful at *anything* you want to accomplish. For example, just by using a couple of the simple skills from this unit, you'll immediately double your chances the next time you ask for a raise in your allowance!

Knowledge Is Power

Wouldn't you like to know how to . . .

- make a great first (or last) impression?
- write a letter that gets results?
- get people to cooperate with you?
- win people over to your way of thinking?

If you said "yes" to any of those questions, then this might be the most important unit you've ever had.

I can't guarantee that you will be as successful as the student I mentioned above. But I can promise you this: If you pay attention and work very hard during the next few weeks, you will become a much more persuasive person. And a persuasive person is a powerful person.

What you do with that power is up to you.

Sincerely,

Mr. Wondra

Zahra's Letter to Her Parents About Educational Camp

Dear Mom and Dad,

It's summer! That means no more school, no more education for 2 months. What's with all the educational camps you're trying to send me to though?

Come on guys, I've been learning for 10 months straight. Don't you think I deserve a break? I mean a kid's gotta do what a kid's gotta do. I want to play and have fun without having to worry about homework and stuff. It'd make sense if I was failing and I was going to go to summer school. Guess what though? I'm not. I'm an A grade student. I don't need camp!

Ya'll are already pushing me enough during the school year. Can't you let me do what I want to do for at least 2 months? Listen. You want me to learn. right? Well, take this in. Fun summer + boring camp = A BUMMER SUMMER! Please mom, please dad: Don't send me to camp!

Love,

Zahra

Michy's Letter to the Dollar Store General Manager

Dear Mr. Bob Kesing (Dollar General Manager),

I am addicted to your store. My sister and I shop there at least once a week. We always get cool things. One time, we got the colored puzzle and it took us a really long time to figure out how to put it together. Yup, that was a tough one!

Recently my dad and I bought the purple top from your store and liked it so much I decided to make it my birthday party giveaway. I had six kids at my party so I had to buy two packs since five come in a pack. You can't have one kid with no giveaway.

The next day three of the kids at school told me that their tops already broke. One girl even said, well you know how those dollar store toys never work! She is kind of bratty and always wants more and more expensive toys.

I am writing to you because I know that most of the things you sell really do work. Also, I know that you don't want to have people thinking that your toys are just junk.

Mr. Kesing, can I have my money back to purchase another giveaway from you? We can't find the receipt but I can bring in some of the broken tops if you want me to.

I would be happy if you answered this letter or called my mom to work this out with her. (I have written my phone number on the yellow information sheet that is also in this envelope.)

Thank you for listening to a nine year old. I appreciate your time and attention to this very important matter.

Michy

In these letters, a third grade student named Max tries to persuade his mom to plant a vegetable garden. The first letter on the page was Max's first draft. The second letter is after Max did some revision. Why is the second letter more effective?

Vegetable Garden Letter (Draft)

Original Vegetable Garden Letter

Dear Mom,

I think a vegtable garden would be good for our family. It would save you money on vegtables and they would be fresh from the garden. How cenvennent! Plus it only takes a month or two to grow them. So we should grow a vegtable garden in our back yard.

Vegetable Garden Letter (Final Draft)

Futher Developed/Expanded Letter

Dear Mom,

I think a vegtable garden would be good for our family. Who really wants to buy them? They are so expensive and are not fresh!

It would save you money on vegtables and they would be fresh from the garden. How cenvennent! With this you will never have trouble with unffreshenes for example, have you ever tasted half [?] dry[?] squash? Well let's just say you don't want to. With your own vegetable garden it will be the freshest thing you have ever tasted!!!

Plus it only takes a month or two to grow them. So we should grow a vegtable garden in our back yard. I know as you kid that you're thinking it will be a lot of work but the only work you have to do is decide which ones you want to eat! I will water them. Now you're thinking it will cost a lot to buy seeds but you have three kids and you want them to be healthy. (We can eat a lot). So why spend money buying six servings of green beans.

I Am Not a Nerd Letter

Dear Josh,

Hey, how are you doing? I hope you are doing well. I just wanted to write to you about something that kind of upsets me. I want you not to call me a nerd anymore because I am not a nerd. I'm a regular boy. Now, I am going to tell you the reasons I am not a nerd.

The first one is that I'm not a nerd just because I read comic books. I'm a regular kid who likes to read about Spiderman. I even asked Papa and he said that he liked to read comic books when he was my age and I don't think Papa is a nerd. Do you?

My second reason is that I don't ACT like a nerd. I don't go around playing Dungeons and Dragons and I don't play any silly card games. I like to play basketball and make three pointers.

My third reason, is that I don't DRESS like a nerd. I don't run around in capes and costumes and act like a superhero. I have a most decent wardrobe. I don't own a pair of pocket protectors and I don't look weird . . . usually. I do own a pair of glasses. But they are only to help me see. Just because I own a pair of glasses does not really make me a nerd. (Is everyone who walks into a hospital necessarily a doctor?)

Josh, I just want you to reconsider. If you still think I am a nerd, I will tell you the reasons again so that you are convinced of the truth. I'm not a nerd just because I read comic books. I don't ACT like a nerd. I don't dress like a nerd.

I hope I have convinced you fully.

From Your Cousin,

Benjamin

Watching *American Idol*

March 2007

Dear Mom,

Have you ever had that feeling when you're under stress and you need to kick back and relax with your family? Twice a week I get an opportunity to watch *American Idol* with my family. When we watch, we don't think about the stress of everyday life. We watch to have a good time while we listen to the ups and downs of the music biz. Twice a week I have a chance to let go of all of the usual stress and relax.

Tonight I was very overwhelmed by the amount of homework I had. I said some things I shouldn't have said. My punishment is not being able to watch *American Idol*. I am already overworked so won't taking *American Idol* away from me tonight make me more anxiety ridden?

You may think watching TV is bad for me but what you have to remember is that, for me, TV is not a replacement for reading or physical activity. I take karate classes three times a week and enjoy playing sports with my friends. Just last week, I read the first two books of the Eragon trilogy.

So, please rethink your punishment.

From your loving son,

Michael

Persuasive Writing Exercises

Convincing Your Parents

Find a partner. One student is parent and the other is the child. Create and practice a short skit in which the child tries to convince the parent that he or she should be able to see a movie the parents do not want him or her to see. Remember to use the persuasive techniques you have learned. (*Hint:* Persuasive language, tone of voice, and facial expressions)

While skits are performed, study what other students do to try to convince the parent.

Discuss: What words and actions were persuasive? What were we able to see in the skit that we could not see in persuasive writing?

Examples and Statistics Don't Lie

Find a partner. Take a few minutes to write down fake statistics to support this claim.

Video games help students perform better on standardized tests.

Example: The Iowa institute for elementary education found that 50 percent of third-grade students in public schools in Iowa scored 10 points higher on the same standardized math test.

If you want to make the task more challenging, tell where they facts came from (Make it up!—I did! There is no Iowa Institute for Elementary Education! Gotcha!).

Persuasion in Everyday Life

Make a list of the times in real life when you tried to persuade someone. What you will find is that persuasion is all around you! Here are just a few examples from students in fifth grade.

I tried to persuade:

My brother not to hog the computer.

My dad to do the dishes for me after I mowed the lawn for one and a half hours.

My mom to let me have outside time before I started my homework.

Christian to clean out his desk in school because his stuff was falling into my desk. (It didn't work.)

My mom to let me sleep over at a friend's house. (Mission accomplished!)

Know Where to Go

Where would you get evidence to support these claims? The first one is done for you.

Children who have no siblings do better in school than children with brothers and sisters

    Child psychologist—especially a well-known psychologist

    Interview with an only child

Students should be required to write in pen after the age of six.

Prunes are healthy.

The chemicals used to clean carpets are not harmful to humans.

Football is dangerous and should be banned from elementary and middle schools.

Convincing the Principal

Find a partner. One student is principal and the other is the student. Create and practice a short skit in which the student tries to convince the principal that he or she should be able to go out for lunch on Fridays. Say ALL OF THE WRONG THINGS that make the principal never want you to go out for lunch.

While skits are performed, study what other students do to try to convince the principal.

Know Your Audience—Use Logic

Your task? To convince your audience to take you to the museum.

Information on the museum:

It is located ten blocks away. There are three exhibits in the museum: animals, ocean plant life, and Native Americans of the Southwestern United States. The museum has admission that is $2.00 per student.

The first audience is your math teacher. The second audience is your P.E. teacher. The third audience is Aunt Matilda.

Would You Like to Buy a Bridge?

How do you think you would do if you had to sell something? Now how would you do if you had to sell a useless product that nobody needs? Your job is to create a print advertisement for one of the following products. You can draw or say anything to convince the consumer to buy the product, but you cannot lie. Here are your product choices. (Number 3 is the most difficult.)

1. Green overalls
2. A pen that writes in yellow ink
3. An empty tissue box

Become an Advertising and Marketing Executive

Today you are an advertising executive. Study this radio advertisement. Figure out who the target audience is and then write more in order to make the ad longer and stronger.

Ever have one of those days when you feel like you're forgetting something? Let's see . . . kids, cell phones, seatbelt—Oh yeah, now I remember STAR 99.1. STAR 99.1, finally a radio station that is family friendly!

The Difference Between a Fight and a Persuasive Argument

There is a big difference between a fight and a persuasive argument. In a fight, you are in it to win. In a persuasive argument, your goal is to convince the other person or group of people that your way to thinking is correct.

Option 1
Half of the class creates a comic strip that illustrates a fight. The other half of the class creates a comic strip that illustrates a persuasive scene. Compare.

Option 2
Half of the class writes a how-to piece called "How to Have a Fight." The other half of the class writes "How to Have a Persuasive Argument." Compare the writing.

Looking Closely at Junk Mail

Read and study a few different pieces of junk mail. Work in groups and make a poster that lists the persuasive techniques you see. Discuss: *What is persuasive and what holds the readers' attention?*

You Started It!

Finish these paragraphs and make them persuasive!

Could someone please explain to me what this country is coming to? The other day I turned on the TV and sat down to watch. I could not believe my eyes . . .

I am writing to request a free sample of your coffee . . .

Tell It Like It Is!

Look at the top ten persuasive writing myths on the inside front cover of this book. Take two of the myths and rewrite them so that you believe they are true! You can begin like this: *One thing to keep in mind about persuasive writing is* . . .

Everything Sounds Delicious

Have you ever opened a menu at a restaurant and thought to yourself *everything sounds so delicious* only to find out later that the description of the food was better than the real thing? Here is a description of meatloaf:

Comfort food at its best. Our sensational meatloaf is made with pure Black Angus Beef and stuffed with cheddar cheese and applewood-smoked bacon. Then it is drenched and covered with our sweet 'n spicy BBQ sauce.

Pretend that you write copy for a restaurant and your job is to make the food sound as tasty as possible. Write a description for the following items:

A tuna sandwich with lettuce and tomato with a side item of whatever you like.

A grilled cheese sandwich with a pickle.

Grilled shrimp with rice and broccoli on the side.

Tone of Voice

Sometimes the tone of our voices changes the meaning of our sentences.

Practice saying these sentences with different tones of voice. Think about how each tone changes the meaning of what you're saying. You can change one or two words in each sentence but do not change the general meaning of the sentence. Do the example as a class:

Example: Why did you do that? (Say it happily. Now say it sadly. Now say it sarcastically.)

Now, try these:

Yes, that certainly is true.

She is telling the truth.

That is not what actually happened.

Though you may have no interest in golf, one visit to the masters will change your mind.

Coupons serve a valuable service to society.

We've all done that before.

Discuss: How would this tone translate into writing? (Italics, different punctuation, slightly different word choice. The sentences that might come before or after the sentence, etc.)